HOME MADE

FARINE DE BLÉ MÉNAGÈRE
250
500
2000
1000
1500
le lait
Tout Simplement
demi écrémé

USEFUL TIPS

All recipes serve 4, unless indicated otherwise.

I bake in a convection (fan-forced) oven. Baking times may be longer or shorter in other ovens. Baking times in this book are therefore provided for information only. It is best to rely on your own experience with your own oven. I typically use extra-large free-range eggs. I always use free-range or even better, organic meat, but that seems like a no-brainer to me.

* * *

First published in 2010 by Fontaine Uitgevers, 's-Graveland, The Netherlands, www.fontaineuitgevers.nl
THIS EDITION PUBLISHED IN 2011 BY MURDOCH BOOKS PTY LIMITED

Murdoch Books Australia
Pier 8/9,
23 Hickson Road
Millers Point NSW 2000
Phone: +61 (0)2 8220 2000
Fax: +61 (0)2 8220 2558
www.murdochbooks.com.au

Murdoch Books UK Limited
Erico House, 6th Floor,
93–99 Upper Richmond Road
Putney, London SW15 2TG
Phone: +44 (0) 20 8785 5995
Fax: +44 (0) 20 8785 5985
www.murdochbooks.co.uk

TEXT, DESIGN AND ILLUSTRATIONS: Yvette Van Boven
PHOTOGRAPHY: Oof Verschuren
EDITOR (DUTCH EDITION): Hennie Franssen-Seebregts
EDITOR (ENGLISH EDITION): Carol Jacobson
TRANSLATION: Olivier De Vriese, www.dutch-translator.co.uk

National Library of Australia Cataloguing-in-Publication entry

Author:	Boven, Yvette van.
Title:	Home made / Yvette van Boven.
ISBN:	978-1-74266-399-9 (hbk.)
Notes:	Includes index.
Subjects:	Cooking
	Cooking (Natural foods)
Dewey Number:	641.5

A catalogue record for this book is available from the British Library.

Printed by 1010 Printing International Limited, China

To my mother Mariëtte, who encouraged me to cook
To her sister Emilie, who encouraged me to make a book
To their children, my sister Sophie & my cousin Joris,
who encouraged me to do both.

I am no stranger to writing cookbooks. I wrote my first one when I was four years old. From then on I started with my almost morbid passion for collecting recipes and cookbooks, preferably illustrated.

It is actually odd that I ended up doing nothing with them until later, but strangely enough the idea never occurred to me. After some wanderings I did end up in the kitchen eventually. I can most often be found in my own kitchen, but I currently also work in a professional kitchen, which is completely mine. Okay, it also belongs to my cousin Joris, since I run a restaurant and catering business with him. So it turned out all right.

I have been writing and drawing recipes for numerous periodicals, websites and newspapers for years and at some point also started doing so for our restaurant. I primarily draw inspiration from my memories, for example from my youth, which I spent in Ireland.

My mother and the women in our street made a lot of things with their own hands, out of necessity or by tradition, and my sister and I did the same. We made soda bread, scones, shortbread, jelly and stew for our toy restaurant, which we built in our room or in the garden. We made ice creams, cheeses, yoghurt, butterfly cakes and ginger ale for our dolls or friends.

Fresh memories were created during summers with the Colombet family in their orchard in Provence where Oof, my husband, has been part of the family from a young age. Each time these visits resulted in a slew of family recipes. George and Jacqueline taught me to make liqueurs, nut wine, jams and all manner of dishes from their vegetable gardens. With Norbert we built campfires each summer, and we walked along the Durance in search of fennel to grill fish over the open fire. The Colombet family took us to the 'courses camarguaises', innocent races between bulls and husky men, called 'rasateurs', and to charettes, fabulous traditional parades in the surrounding villages. Afterwards, we received recipes for bull meat, bohémien and chi chi stews and we drank cold beer, pastis and cool red wine.

Travel to Italy, our life in Paris and working with the chefs in our restaurant 'On the Amstel', in Amsterdam, resulted in so many memories that my collection eventually started to burst at the seams.

I had to start writing, sorting, photographing, drawing, editing and cataloguing the recipes. All that work resulted in this book—a book in which I aim to show you that preparing your own food is simple. I chose recipes which I am certain are easy to make; recipes that will not let you down because you do not own the right appliances. Sometimes you don't even need anything, just a little patience. I have learned to be creative and to cook with what I have available. That is what I wanted this book to be about. Do not let yourself get discouraged if there are no blueberries, just look at what is available; perhaps it is raspberry season and the fruit grows in your own backyard free of charge.

I have used things that I thought you will have in your house—an oven, a cooktop, maybe also a food processor or hand blender, but in any case a knife and a colander, etc.

I hope that this book will encourage you to collect jam jars or beautiful bottles with matching corks, as you won't need more than those for preserving. My recipes represent a starting point to help you on your way, but I hope you will make up your own versions and create fresh memories. Be sure to invite me. Who knows, I could write another book about it.

Yvette van Boven

CONTENTS

We start the morning with strong coffee. After which we dash out the door most of the time. Without breakfast.
But if we have a day off, we fill the table. Or the floor, or the bed.
Since we are off, we prepare something we have been looking forward to for a week.
Or we allow ourselves to be seduced by our Parisian baker's window, when we are out walking the dog.
Or we bake delicious bread the previous evening.

MAKING JAM

BREAKFAST STARTS WITH HOME MADE JAM, WHICH IS MADE IN A FLASH. YOU REALLY DON'T HAVE TO MAKE A GAZILLION JARS: SOME THREE JARS ARE ENOUGH. I WILL RUSH YOU THROUGH IT IN EIGHT STEPS. I MADE A NUMBER OF JARS LAST SUMMER WITH GEORGE USING FRUIT FROM HIS GARDEN.

PICK THE FRUIT YOURSELF (WHATEVER IS GROWING AT THE TIME) OR PICK UP LEFTOVER FRUIT AT THE MARKET, AT THE END OF THE DAY. IF YOU ARE UNABLE TO GET FRESH FRUIT, FROZEN FRUIT ALSO WORKS WELL.

>> >> ALWAYS USE YOUR LEFTOVER FRUIT FOR JAM, AS YOU WILL WANT TO EAT YOUR GORGEOUS FRESH FRUIT.

COLLECT A MAXIMUM OF 3-3.5 KG (6-7 LB) OF FRUIT EACH TIME.

WASH CAREFULLY UNDER COLD RUNNING WATER.
REMOVE ANY TWIGS, LEAVES AND STALKS.

WEIGH AND ADD APPROXIMATELY THE SAME QUANTITY OF JELLING SUGAR (OR USE GRANULATED SUGAR AND PECTIN - ADD PECTIN ACCORDING TO INSTRUCTIONS ON THE PACKAGE). CUT LARGER FRUIT INTO SMALLER CHUNKS OR CRUSH SMALL FRUIT COARSELY. THIS RELEASES THE ALL-IMPORTANT PECTIN, WHICH IS AN ACID THAT ENSURES THAT THE JAM SETS MORE EASILY. YOU CAN ALSO ADD IT SEPARATELY: PECTIN IS PRIMARILY FOUND IN APPLES AND LEMON.

BRING THE JAM TO A BOIL. ABOUT 15-30 MINUTES COOKING (DEPENDING ON THE TYPE OF FRUIT) IS OFTEN ENOUGH. IF YOU COOK IT FOR TOO LONG AND YOU WILL MAKE THE JAM MORE LIQUID.
DO THE REFRIGERATOR TEST
PLACE A TEASPOON OF JAM BRIEFLY IN THE REFRIGERATOR AND CHECK WHETHER IT HAS SET SUFFICIENTLY AFTER 5 MINUTES. YOU CAN ALSO PURÉE THE JAM, BUT KEEPING IT A LITTLE CHUNKY IS ALSO AN OPTION.
WHATEVER TAKES YOUR FANCY.

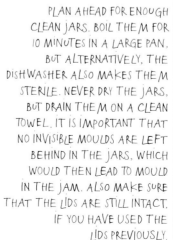

PLAN AHEAD FOR ENOUGH CLEAN JARS. BOIL THEM FOR 10 MINUTES IN A LARGE PAN, BUT ALTERNATIVELY, THE DISHWASHER ALSO MAKES THEM STERILE. NEVER DRY THE JARS, BUT DRAIN THEM ON A CLEAN TOWEL. IT IS IMPORTANT THAT NO INVISIBLE MOULDS ARE LEFT BEHIND IN THE JARS, WHICH WOULD THEN LEAD TO MOULD IN THE JAM. ALSO MAKE SURE THAT THE LIDS ARE STILL INTACT, IF YOU HAVE USED THE LIDS PREVIOUSLY.

FILL THE JARS TO THE RIM USING A LARGE SPOON: (I OFTEN USE A JUG). WARNING! THE JAM WILL BE VERY HOT, SO USE GLOVES TO BE ON THE SAFE SIDE.

SCREW ON THE LIDS AND TURN THE JARS UPSIDE DOWN, ALLOWING THE HOT AIR IN THE JARS TO CREATE A VACUUM AND THE JAM TO HAVE A SHELF LIFE OF AT LEAST ONE YEAR!

AND THEN OF COURSE, ALL THOSE STICKY UTENSILS HAVE TO BE WASHED IMMEDIATELY.

George

GOOSEBERRY JAM WITH ORANGE

1 kg (2 lb) gooseberries (green or red)
juice and zest of 2 large juice oranges
2 kg (4½ lb/9 cups) jelling sugar or use granulated sugar and pectin (add pectin according to instructions on the package)
4 clean jam jars

Wash the gooseberries, remove stems and crowns and heat in a layer of water until soft. Add orange zest and juice and return to a boil. Add all of the sugar. Stir using a wooden spoon (a metal spoon will get too hot!) until the sugar is dissolved. Test whether the jam is setting properly: put a drop of jam on a saucer and place in the refrigerator for 1 minute. If it has thickened nicely the jam is ready. Quickly fill the jars and apply the lids. Tighten the lids securely and turn the jars upside down in order for the vacuum to be created. The jam will have a shelf life of one year.
After opening, store in a cool place.

LET'S GET GOING...

NOW THAT YOU HAVE BEEN THROUGH THE BASICS OF MAKING JAM, YOU WILL PROBABLY WANT TO ACTUALLY MAKE SOME. I WILL START WITH A SIMPLE RED FRUIT JAM AND WILL THEN PROVIDE SOME RECIPES FOR JAMS YOU WILL NOT TYPICALLY SEE IN THE STORES, OTHERWISE YOU MIGHT AS WELL BUY THEM OF COURSE.

BASIC RASPBERRY JAM

For approx. 8 x 250 ml (1 cup) jars
1 kg (2 lb/10 cups) raspberries or other red fruit (also frozen)
1 kg (2 lb/4½ cups) jelling sugar or use granulated sugar and pectin (add pectin according to instructions on the package)
juice of ½ lemon

Add all ingredients to a large thick-bottomed pot. Stir well and slowly bring to a boil. Using a wooden spoon (a metal one gets too hot), crush a portion of the fruit against the side of the pot, in order to release the pectin. This is necessary for the jam to set. Allow the jam to simmer for approx. 15 minutes. Scoop a spoonful of jam onto a saucer and briefly place in the refrigerator to test whether it sets. If not, continue to cook briefly. Using a skimmer, scoop the foam from the jam in the pan. In the meantime, boil the jam jars and lids in another pot for 10 minutes. Remove them from the water using tongs and drain on a clean towel. Scoop the jam into the jars, allow to set briefly then stir the mixture in each jar using a clean spoon in order to spread the fruit. Tighten the lids and store the jars upside-down to cool.

BLACKBERRY, RASPBERRY AND BASIL JAM

For approx. 10 x 250 ml (1 cup) jars
1 kg (2 lb/10 cups) blackberries
500 g (1 lb/5 cups) raspberries
150 ml (5 fl oz/⅔ cup) grapefruit or orange juice
150 ml (5 fl oz/⅔ cup) lemon or lime juice
1.5 kg (3 lb/7 cups) jelling sugar or use granulated sugar and pectin (add pectin according to instructions on the package)
1 bunch basil

Allow mixture, except for the basil, to cook for approx. 20 minutes. Briefly purée the jam and check it has thickened sufficiently. Remove from the heat, add the basil leaves and purée the jam again. Fill the clean jars.

COVER THE LID WITH A PIECE OF FABRIC AND GIVE IT AWAY AS A PRESENT..

home made jam

PEAR AND STAR ANISE JAM

For approx. 12 x 250 ml (1 cup) jars
3 kg (6 ½ lb) peeled, cubed pears
2 kg (4½ lb/9 cups) jelling sugar or use granulated sugar and pectin (add pectin according to instructions on the package)
2 handfuls of star anise
750 g (26 oz/5 cups) mixed raisins

Cook all ingredients for at least one hour on low heat until the jam is reduced and turns an attractive brown. Very briefly purée the jam using a hand blender but don't make it too smooth!

APRICOT-ALMOND JAM

For approx. 8 x 250 ml (1 cup) jars
1.2 kg (2½ lb) apricots
1 kg (2 lb/4½ cups) jelling sugar or use granulated sugar and pectin (add pectin according to instructions on the package)
¾ cup blanched almond halves
few drops of almond flavouring

Halve the apricots, remove the stones and cut the halves into smaller chunks. Fold in the sugar and leave the jam to simmer for approx. 30 minutes. Do the refrigerator test to check the jam is thick enough. Coarsely chop the almonds and add to the jam with the flavouring. Pour into clean jars and tighten the lids. Store upside down to cool.

CONFIT DE VIN

This is actually not a jam but a jelly. After having made it once, you will be sold. Serve with a cheeseboard, for example. We also eat the confit on toast with aged cheese.

The type of wine you choose matters: this recipe calls for white wine, but red wine is also fine. Adjust your spices and use those that are warmer and fuller in flavour: cloves, mandarin peel and star anise, for example.

You can also vary the types of wine: a sauvignon blanc will result in a different jelly from a muscat.

For approx. 4 x 250 ml (1 cup) jars
2 vanilla beans
1½ bottles white wine
1 kg (2 lb/4½ cups) jelling sugar or use granulated sugar and pectin (add pectin according to instructions on the package)
6 cardamom pods
juice of 1 lemon
zest of ½ lemon
zest of ½ orange

Cut open the vanilla beans, scrape out the seeds and combine with all other ingredients in a large pot (seeds, beans and pods). Bring to a boil and allow to simmer for approx. 30 minutes. Check if the jelly sets properly by pouring a teaspoon on a saucer and briefly placing it in the refrigerator. If it is nice and stiff it can be poured into clean jars. First remove the cardamom pods and vanilla beans. Tighten the lids on the jars and turn the jars upside down, allowing them to cool.

ELDERBERRY APPLE JAM WITH BAY

For approx. 8 x 250 ml (1 cup) jars
2.5 kg (5½ lb) ripe elderberries
2 cups chopped apples
2.5 kg (5½ lb/11 cups) jelling sugar or use granulated sugar and pectin (add pectin according to instructions on the package)
juice of 1 lemon
6 bay leaves (preferably fresh)

Stem the berries and wash. Bring the berries to a boil in enough water to cover the bottom of a large pot. Immediately pour through a sieve and push through using a wooden spoon. Discard the peels and seeds. Return the pulp together with the apple chunks and bay leaves to a boil and add the sugar. Allow the jam to reduce for 30 minutes. Do the refrigerator test and fill clean jars. Tighten the lids and store upside down to cool.

RHUBARB JAM WITH GINGER

For approx. 8 x 250 ml (1 cup) jars
1 kg (2 lb) rhubarb, washed and cut in lengths of approx. 2.5 cm (1 inch)
1 kg (2 lb/4½ cups) jelling sugar or use granulated sugar and pectin (add pectin according to instructions on the package)

600 ml (20 fl oz/2½ cups) water
some slices of fresh ginger
juice of 1 orange and 1 lemon
100 g (4 oz) preserved ginger in syrup, in chunks

Bring all of the ingredients, except the preserved ginger, to a boil. Allow to simmer for approx. 15 minutes, stirring occasionally. Add the preserved ginger and leave the jam to cook until clear. Do the refrigerator test, skim the foam from the surface and pour the jam into clean jars.

ORANGE MARMALADE WITH LAVENDER

For approx. 8 x 250 ml (1 cup) jars
1 kg (2 lb) oranges
1 lemon
2 litres (8 cups) water
2 kg (4½ lb/9 cups) jelling sugar or use granulated sugar and pectin (add pectin according to instructions on the package)
2 tbsp dried lavender flowers

Peel oranges and lemons. Carefully cut in half and squeeze out the juice. Cut the peel in thin strips. Place the peel, juice and water in a heavy pot and bring to a boil. Allow to gently simmer for approx. 90 minutes (or longer). Stir in the sugar until dissolved. Add the lavender and allow the mixture to cook for approx. 10 minutes. Do the refrigerator test. Leave the marmalade to stand for 30 minutes and then pour into clean jars.

Note: dried lavender can be easily bought or you can pluck it from your own garden and leave it to dry for a few days.

17

BREAD WITHOUT KNEADING

BAKING YOUR OWN BREAD SEEMS DIFFICULT, BUT AFTER A MINOR INVESTIGATION HERE AT HOME AND ON THE INTERNET I CAME UP WITH A RECIPE FOR BREAD THAT YOU DON'T EVEN HAVE TO KNEAD. OH WELL, ONLY TEN TIMES, WHICH IS NEXT TO NOTHING. THE RESULT IS AMAZING! THE ONLY THING YOU NEED IS A LITTLE BIT OF PATIENCE. > PREPARING IN THE EVENING AND BAKING THE NEXT DAY. THE BREAD IS BAKED IN A HEAVY HEAT-RESISTANT PAN PLACED IN THE OVEN. PROFESSIONAL OVENS ARE FITTED WITH STEAM GENERATORS, WHICH IS WHY PROFESSIONALLY BAKED BREAD HAS SUCH A GREAT CRUST. WE HAVE ACHIEVED THE SAME EFFECT BY MAKING THE OVEN SMALLER – BAKING THE BREAD IN A HEAVY POT. THE HOT MOIST AIR REMAINS AND THE BREAD COMES OUT OF THE OVEN PERFECTLY. I WILL EXPLAIN IN A FEW STEPS: (RECIPE ON NEXT PAGE).

PREPARE ALL INGREDIENTS.

IN A BOWL, IMMEDIATELY COMBINE >

INTO A BALL.

COVER WITH PLASTIC WRAP AND SET ASIDE FOR 8 TO 18 HOURS.

AFTER SOME 12 HOURS THIS IS WHAT IT LOOKS LIKE AT OUR HOUSE!

DUST THE COUNTERTOP WITH FLOUR AND REMOVE THE BALL FROM THE BOWL.

KNEAD THE DOUGH EXACTLY 10 TIMES.

MOULD INTO A NICE BALL OR OVAL SHAPE.

PLACE THE BALL ON A PLATE ON A LARGE SHEET OF BAKING PAPER.

PLACE A HEAVY POT IN THE OVEN AND PREHEAT THE OVEN WITH THE POT TO 190C (375F/GAS 5).
CAREFULLY LIFT THE BAKING PAPER WITH THE DOUGH ON IT, PLACE IT IN THE POT AND COVER IMMEDIATELY.

LOOSELY COVER WITH PLASTIC WRAP AND LEAVE TO STAND FOR 2 MORE HOURS.

SPRINKLE WITH A LITTLE FLOUR AND SCORE THE TOP.

LOWER THE TEMPERATURE TO 175C (340F/GAS 4) AND BAKE THE BREAD FOR 30 MINUTES.
REMOVE THE LID FROM THE POT AND BAKE FOR ANOTHER 20 MINUTES, APPROXIMATELY.

CONGRATS! THE BREAD TURNED OUT WELL! THAT WAS NO TROUBLE AT ALL!

BREAD WITHOUT KNEADING (WELL ALMOST)

I promised you the recipe on the previous page, here are the quantities:

425 g (approx. 14 oz/2¾ cups) plain (all-purpose) flour (I used rye here)
¼ tsp yeast
2 tsp salt
250 ml (9 fl oz/1 cup) water
100 ml (approx. 3 fl oz/½ cup) beer
1 tbsp vinegar

See previous pages for preparation.

LET'S GET GOING...

BY NOW YOU HAVE OBVIOUSLY ACQUIRED A TASTE FOR BREAD BAKING...
I WILL THEREFORE PROVIDE YOU WITH A SLEW OF RECIPES, ALLOWING FOR SOME VARIETY. THEY DO FEATURE RECIPES THAT REQUIRE KNEADING. THEY ALSO INCLUDE RECIPES FOR BREAD WITHOUT YEAST, SUCH AS SCONES OR FLATBREAD.

COUNTRY BREAD WITH HAZELNUTS & ROASTED CUMIN

500 g (1 lb/3⅓ cups) wholemeal (whole-wheat) flour
250 ml (9 fl oz/1 cup) lukewarm water
dab of butter (2 tbsp) pinch of salt
1 sachet yeast (7 g/¼ oz/2¼ tsp)
75 g (2½ oz/½ cup) unsalted hazelnuts
4 tbsp roasted cumin seeds, plus 1 tbsp for garnish

Make the dough from the first four ingredients. Knead for 10 minutes on a countertop dusted with flour. Allow to rise for an hour in a warm place covered with plastic wrap. Knead the dough again and also fold in the nuts and cumin seeds. Shape the dough into a long ball. Grease a cake tin and place the ball in it. Allow to rise again for 30 minutes and in the meantime

preheat the oven to 180°C (350°F/ Gas 4). Wet the surface of the dough with some water and sprinkle with the remaining cumin seeds. Using a sharp knife, score the bread and bake for approx. 30 minutes. The bread is baked as soon as it makes a hollow sound when tapped. Allow to cool for 5 minutes on a rack before slicing.

TURKISH POGACA

These are brioche-like buns, but much easier to make. You can also turn it into a large flatbread, but I often make pointed balls with it.

For approx. 8 buns
2 sachets yeast (14 g/½ oz/5½ tsp)
5 tbsp lukewarm water
500 g (1 lb/3⅓ cups) plain (all-purpose) flour
pinch of salt
250 g (8 oz/2 sticks) butter at room temperature
2 eggs, + one extra

Dissolve the yeast in the warm water and leave to stand for 10 minutes. Add the flour and salt to a large bowl and fold in the butter. Make a 'well' in the flour and pour in the yeast and water. Add the eggs and knead the mixture

into a pliable ball. Place in a greased bowl, cover with plastic wrap and allow to rise for one hour. Knead again and divide the dough into 8 equal portions. Roll into balls and press the dough on either side between thumb and index finger to create 'eye-shaped' buns. Using a sharp knife, score the top of the dough. Lay on greased baking tray and leave to stand for approx. 30 minutes. In the meantime preheat the oven to 200°C (400°F/Gas 6). Brush the buns with beaten egg. Bake until done and golden brown in approx. 20 minutes.

HOME MADE FOCACCIA WITH OLIVES AND ROSEMARY

500 g (1 lb/3⅓ cups) plain (all-purpose) flour
300 ml (10 fl oz/1¼ cups) lukewarm water
pinch of salt
2 sachets yeast (14 g/½ oz/5½ tsp)
200 g (7 oz/1½ cups) mixed olives, cut in rounds
small bunch of rosemary, needles removed from twigs and cut in half
olive oil
2 tbsp coarse sea salt (optional)

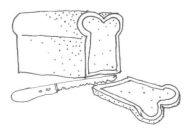

Thoroughly knead the flour, water, salt and yeast in a bowl or food processor, at least 10 minutes, creating a smooth and pliable dough. Fold in half of the olives and chopped rosemary. Allow the dough to rise for an hour in a greased bowl covered with plastic wrap. Thoroughly grease a baking tray using plenty of olive oil, knead the dough again and roll into a slab that more or less fits into the baking tray. Press the dough into the corners of the tray using your fingers. Do not worry about any unevenness. Cover with olives and rosemary leaves and drizzle generously with olive oil. Press everything in place using your fingers. Lastly, sprinkle some coarse sea salt on the bread and allow to rise for another 30 minutes or so. In the meantime preheat the oven to 180°C (350°F/Gas 4). Bake the focaccia until golden brown in approx. 30 minutes.

SAFFRON BREAD WITH PISTACHIO NUTS

few strands saffron
1 sachet yeast (7 g/¼ oz/2¼ tsp)
300 ml (10 fl oz/1¼ cups) lukewarm water
500 g (1 lb/3⅓ cups) plain (all-purpose) flour
pinch of salt
dab of butter (2 tbsp)
75 g (2½ oz/½ cup) roasted and peeled pistachio nuts

Leave the saffron and the yeast to soak in water for 10 minutes. Add flour, salt and butter to a large bowl. Create a 'well' in the middle and add the yeast, water and pistachio nuts. Knead thoroughly. Dust flour onto the countertop and spread the dough on it. Knead for another 10 minutes until pliable. Add some water if it is too dry. Add some flour if it is too wet. Place the dough in a greased bowl, cover with plastic wrap and allow to rise for another hour. Knead the dough again and place in the greased tin in which you plan on baking the bread. Leave to rise for another 30 minutes. Bake the bread in an oven preheated to 180°C (350°F/Gas 4). The bread is ready as soon as it sounds hollow when tapped. Great with a drink, served with sausage and olives.

THREE-COLOURED PLAITED BREAD

500 g (1 lb/3⅓ cups) plain (all-purpose) flour
300 ml (10 fl oz/1¼ cups) lukewarm water
2 tbsp olive oil
1 sachet yeast (7 g/¼ oz/2¼ tsp)
pinch of salt
2 tbsp homemade! pesto
8 sundried tomatoes in oil, finely chopped
2 garlic cloves, crushed

Make the dough from the first five ingredients. Thoroughly knead for 10 minutes. Allow to rise for 1 hour in a warm place. Knead the dough again and divide it into three equal parts. Knead the pesto through the first part. Knead the finely chopped sundried tomatoes through the second part. Knead the garlic through the last part. Roll all parts into equal 'sausages' and braid them. Pinch the ends and brush the braid with a little beaten egg. Place the braid on a baking tray and allow to rise for at least 30 minutes. In the meantime preheat the oven to 180°C (350°F/Gas 4). Bake the braid until done in approx. 35 minutes. The bread must sound hollow when tapped on the bottom.

RED CHERRY AND THYME BREAD

I sometimes make bread as follows: partially replace the water in the recipe with red cherry juice from a can of preserved cherries in syrup. Also knead a handful of cherries and a little thyme through the dough. The result is not a very sweet bread, but of a pretty pinkish red colour and great with fresh fillings such as cottage cheese and spring onion.

270 g (9 oz) tin cherries in light syrup and a little water
500 g (1 lb/3⅓ cups) plain (all-purpose) flour
2 sachets yeast (14 g/½ oz/5½ tsp)
pinch of salt
small bunch of thyme, leaves stripped from the twigs

HEY THAT ISN'T A PLAIT!

YUP, IT SURE IS!

Pour the cherries through a strainer and collect the moisture in a measuring cup. Top up the fruit juice with water to 250 ml (9 fl oz/1 cup). Combine the flour, yeast, salt and thyme in a bowl. Add the cherry syrup.

Knead the mixture into a pliable dough for at least 10 minutes. Allow to rise covered in a warm place for 1 hour. Knead the dough again and fold in the cherries. Create a nice ball. Place the ball on a baking tray and allow to rise for at least another 30 minutes. Bake the bread until done in a preheated oven, below the middle at 180°C (350°F/Gas 4) for approx. 30 minutes. Carefully tap on the bread to hear if it sounds hollow; if it sounds dull, briefly return to oven.

PUMPKIN BUNS

These buns are of course best while still warm, tied in a dish towel. Serve during a picnic with portions of thyme butter, wrapped separately in baking paper.

200 g (7 oz) pumpkin (winter squash), peeled, in cubes
1 tsp chilli powder
1 tsp ground paprika
1 tsp nutmeg
125 ml (approx. 4 fl oz/⅔ cup) milk
30 g (1 oz/¼ stick) butter
1 sachet yeast (7 g/¼ oz/2¼ tsp)
300 g (10 oz/2 cups) plain (all-purpose) flour
250 g (8 oz) aged cheese, grated: reserve a little for the garnish
pinch of salt
1 handful of pumpkin seeds (pepitas) to garnish, briefly roasted in the pan

Preheat the oven to 180°C (350°F/Gas 4). Grease a baking tray with olive

oil and arrange the pumpkin on it. Sprinkle with the chilli and ground paprika, nutmeg, salt and pepper. Bake the pumpkin until done, (approx. 30 minutes). Leave to cool. Purée in a food processor and blend in the other ingredients. Carefully add the milk, maybe you won't need all of it, maybe a little more, depending on the pumpkin's moisture content. Continue to knead into a pliable dough. Grease a bowl with some oil and place the dough ball in it. Cover with plastic wrap. Allow to rise for an hour in a warm draft-free place. Thoroughly knead the dough again and divide into approx. 16 equal portions. Shape into balls and place on a greased baking tray. Loosely cover with plastic wrap and allow to rise for approx. 30 minutes. Preheat the oven to 180°C (350°F/Gas 4), brush the buns with a little water and sprinkle with the pumpkin seeds and reserved cheese. Bake the buns until done and golden brown in approx. 30 minutes. Serve with thyme butter.

THYME BUTTER

handful of thyme, thoroughly washed and the leaves stripped from the twigs
200 g (approx. 7 oz/2 sticks) butter at room temperature
1 tbsp salt flakes
freshly ground pepper

Place all ingredients in a bowl and thoroughly stir. Roll into a sheet of plastic wrap and shape into a sausage. Place in the refrigerator for approx. 3 hours to firm. Cut the butter roll into slices and if necessary wrap individually to take out. Store in the refrigerator.

MULTIGRAIN MUESLI BALLS

500 g (1 lb/3⅓ cups) multigrain flour (whole-wheat flour is also good)
300 ml (10 fl oz/1¼ cups) lukewarm water
1 tsp salt
1 sachet yeast (7 g/¼ oz/2¼ tsp)
100 g (approx. 4 oz/½ cup) raisins or mixed dried fruit
100 g (approx. 4 oz/½ cup) nuts, pumpkin seeds (pepitas), sunflower seeds
a mixture of crushed oat flakes and bran to garnish

Make the dough from the first four ingredients. Knead for 10 minutes on a floured surface. Allow to rise for an hour in a warm place covered with plastic wrap.

Knead again and fold in the raisins, chopped dried fruit and nuts. Divide the dough into approx. 12 balls, place on a greased baking tray and cover with plastic wrap. Leave to rise for 30 minutes.

Preheat the oven to 180°C (350°F/Gas 4). Wet the tops and sprinkle with oat flakes. Bake until golden brown, (approx. 25 minutes).

SMALL BUNS WITH WALNUTS AND FENNEL SEED IN SMALL FLOWER POTS

250 g (8 oz/1⅔ cups) plain (all-purpose) flour
75 g (2½ oz/⅓ cup) sugar
2 tsp baking powder
pinch of salt
100 g (approx. 4 oz/1 stick) cold butter, cubed + extra
2 egg yolks
125 ml (approx. 4 fl oz/⅔ cup) buttermilk
75 g (2½ oz/⅓ cup) raisins, blanched
50 g (approx. 2 oz/½ cup) walnuts, coarsely chopped
1 tbsp fennel seed
1 egg, beaten with 1 tbsp. water
12 small unglazed clay flower pots

Preheat the oven to 180°C (350°F/ Gas 4). Grease the flower pots with butter, dust with flour and shake off the extra flour.
Blend the flour, sugar, baking powder and salt with the butter in a food processor until the mixture looks like coarse sand. Fold in the egg yolks and buttermilk. Remove the mixture from the food processor and blend in the raisins, walnuts and fennel seed. Gently knead the dough with floured hands into a smooth ball. Then roll the ball into a long sausage. Cut the sausage in half, then cut these two pieces in half and continue cutting until you have 12 equal pieces. Quickly roll each piece into a small ball and place each ball in its own clay flower pot. Spread beaten egg on top of each ball.

Bake until done and golden brown, (approx. 20 minutes). Serve hot with salted butter and if desired, with soft goat's cheese.

TASTY MINI MUFFINS

For 35 small muffins

175 g (6 oz/1⅛ cups) self-raising flour
50 g (approx. 2 oz/½ stick) butter
1 egg yolk
200 ml (6 fl oz/¾ cup) milk
4 dried tomatoes, finely chopped
½ bunch chives, finely chopped
1 tsp ground paprika
freshly ground pepper and salt

Preheat the oven to 180°C (350°F/ Gas 4). Combine all ingredients in a blender into a nice batter. Fill a piping bag with a tip approx. 1 cm (½ inch) in diameter. If you do not own one, you can also create balls using two tablespoons. Fill paper mini muffin cups with the batter. Place cups in the cavities in a mini muffin tray, if you do not own one, use two paper cups for strength. Bake until golden brown in hot oven for 22–25 minutes.

THOSE CACTUSES ARE VERY STRANGE INDEED...

SPINACH AND GOAT'S CHEESE BUTTER BUNS WITH PISTACHIO NUTS

For six 150-g (5-oz) bread moulds

1 egg
125 ml (approx. 4 fl oz/⅔ cup) milk
350 g (12 oz/2⅓ cups) plain (all-purpose) flour
1 sachet yeast (7 g/¼ oz/2¼ tsp)
pinch of salt
250 g (approx. 8 oz/2 sticks) cold butter, cubed
100 g (approx. 4 oz/¾ cup) pistachio nuts
150 g (5 oz) goat's cheese
200 g (7 oz) spinach

Beat the egg with the milk. In the food processor combine the flour, yeast, salt and cold butter into coarse crumbs. Add the milk-egg mixture slowly, since you might not need all the milk, or perhaps you will need a little more. Also fold in half the pistachio nuts. Do not beat for too long, the dough must be well blended, but not too smooth. Cover with plastic wrap and place in the refrigerator for at least 4 hours or overnight. Allow the dough to reach room temperature and thoroughly knead for a few minutes. Divide into six equal balls. Grease the baking moulds and place the balls in them. Fry the spinach in a wok, squeeze out the moisture, distribute over the buns. Crumble the goat's cheese over with the remaining pistachios. Allow to rise again for 90 mins. Preheat the oven to 180°C (350°F/Gas 4) and bake until golden brown, (approx. 30 minutes).

Joris

GINGER COFFEE

YESSS → JUST MAKE COFFEE THE OLD-FASHIONED WAY, BY HAND!

COMBINE THE GROUND COFFEE WITH 1 TBSP GROUND GINGER

POUR HOT WATER ONTO IT → FOR A STRONG CUP!

NICE, EH? A CHANGE OF PACE! AND IF YOU DON'T LIKE GINGER, USE CARDAMOM, CLOVES OR ALLSPICE. →OR EVEN MIXED SPICES OR CINNAMON!

IRISH BROWN SODA BREAD

For this bread you do not need yeast and it is also ready in about 30 minutes. A good recipe for a Sunday morning! While the bread is baking, boil the eggs and squeeze some oranges. Still warm from the oven and with slightly salted melted butter on top, I can easily eat an entire loaf...

500 g (1 lb/3⅓ cups) wholemeal (whole-wheat) flour
500 g (1 lb/3⅓ cups) strong flour (pure white bread-making flour)
1 tsp salt
2 tsp bicarbonate of soda (baking soda)
approx. 1 litre (4 cups) buttermilk

Preheat the oven to 200°C (400°F/Gas 6). Sieve the dry ingredients into a bowl. Add nearly all of the buttermilk to the mixture. If necessary add more buttermilk or more flour. Rapidly knead the mixture into a smooth dough, since the acid in the buttermilk will work immediately. Kneading too long will result in stiff and unleavened bread. Quickly shape into a large ball and score a large cross in the middle using a knife. Immediately bake the bread in the middle of a hot oven for approx. 30 minutes. The soda bread is ready when it sounds hollow when tapped on the bottom. If you wrap the bread in a dish towel immediately after baking, the crust will soften.

TIP Make white bread by replacing the wholemeal flour with strong flour. You will probably need a little more buttermilk.

TIP Add a generous handful of raisins to the batter. The Irish call this bread 'spotted dick'.

SCONES

For 8–10 easy peasy scones

450 g (15 oz/3 cups) plain (all-purpose) flour
2 teaspoons baking powder
50 g (approx. 2 oz/⅓ cup) icing (confectioner's) sugar
pinch of salt
125 g (4 oz/1 stick) cold butter, cubed
approx. 150 ml (5 fl oz/⅔ cup) milk or buttermilk

Preheat the oven to 200°C (400°F/Gas 6), i.e., hot! Combine all ingredients, except for the milk, in a food processor or large bowl. Knead briefly but thoroughly until the butter and the flour turn into coarse grains. In Ireland they do it with two knives, in order not to warm the butter with their hands, but I really don't think this is practical. Doing it fast is best, chop, chop…
Add the milk and knead the mixture into a smooth ball. Perhaps you will need less milk, or perhaps more. Dust the countertop with flour. Roll the ball of dough into a 2 cm (¾ inch) thick slab. Cut out the scones, using a biscuit cutter or glass. Knead the remaining dough into a 2 cm (¾ inch) thick slab and continue cutting until all the dough is used up. Spread milk over the scones and place on a greased baking tray or on a sheet of baking paper in a hot oven. Bake until done and golden brown, (approx. 15 minutes), depending on size.
Serve with jam, slightly salted butter or unsweetened whipped cream.

Scones with raspberry jam, recipe on page 16 .

HOME MADE MUESLI

Making crunchy muesli is easier than you think. This recipe is for a large jar, i.e., 1 litre (4 cups) content. Store the muesli in a sealed jar and it will have a shelf life of about two to three months.
As soon as you have mastered this recipe, you can add your own favourite ingredients, since this recipe is only a start.

500 g (1 lb/4 cups) regular muesli (I make it up myself: in organic stores you can buy all kinds of grains, bran, crushed oat flakes and nuts that you can blend into your own mixture)
250 g (8 oz/1⅔ cups) unsalted mixed nuts, walnuts, sliced almonds, pecan nuts, etc. Chop the large nuts coarsely, not too finely!
3 tbsp sunflower oil
6 tbsp honey
100 ml (approx. 3 fl oz/½ cup) organic apple juice
pinch of salt
100 g (approx. 4 oz/½ cup) raisins

Preheat the oven to 180°C (350°F/Gas 4). Cover a baking tray with baking paper and coat with a little sunflower oil.
Mix the muesli and the nuts in a bowl. Beat the honey and the oil, the apple juice and the salt and fold into the muesli.
Spread the muesli as thinly as possible on the baking tray and place in the oven.
Bake for approx. 25 minutes until the mixture is golden brown. Thoroughly stir the muesli every 6–7 minutes. Allow to fully cool and only then fold in the raisins.

In the restaurant we serve this with organic sheep's yoghurt and lots of fresh fruit.

CROQUE MONSIEUR

Serves 4

For the béchamel

20 g (⅔ oz/4 teaspoons) butter

25 g (approx. 1 oz/2 tbsp) plain (all-purpose) flour

250 ml (9 fl oz/1 cup) thick cream

1 egg

8 slices tasty bread

8 slices raw ham

250 g (8 oz) Swiss cheese or emmental, grated

ground paprika

Preheat the oven to 180°C (350°F/Gas 4).

First make the béchamel sauce: melt the butter in a thick-bottomed pot. Fold in the flour and cook briefly. Stir carefully, blend in the cream until the mixture thickens. Simmer briefly while stirring. Remove from heat, season with salt and pepper and beat in the egg. Cover the bread slices with a thick layer of béchamel. Place them on a greased baking tray. Cover with the raw ham and generously sprinkle with the grated cheese. Place in the oven and wait 10 minutes or until the cheese bubbles. Sprinkle with ground paprika and serve.

WELSH RAREBIT

Serves 4

8 slices firm bread (preferably sourdough), toasted

400 g (14 oz/4 cups) grated aged cheese

5 tbsp beer

3 tbsp butter

2 tbsp spicy mustard

200 g (7 oz/3⅓ cups) breadcrumbs

parsley to garnish

Spread the bread slices on a baking tray covered with baking paper, neatly fitting them in. Mix cheese, beer, butter and mustard in a saucepan on low heat. Fold in the breadcrumbs and blend into a thick sauce. Pour this sauce over the toast slices on the baking tray. Heat the grill to its highest setting. Grill until the cheese bubbles and has light brown patches. This will happen quite quickly. Serve with a little parsley sprinkled on top.

TOASTED CAMEMBERT SANDWICH WITH APRICOT JAM

Serves 4

4 slices light sourdough bread

dab of butter

4 slices camembert

2 tbsp apricot jam

Spread the butter on the bread slices. Turn the buttered side down and cover the other side with the camembert and a dab of apricot jam. Cover with a slice of bread. Cook the sandwiches in a grill pan or in a regular frying pan. Make sure the camembert does not run from all sides!

Toasted camembert sandwich with apricot jam (top); Welsh rarebit and croque monsieur (bottom).

OEUF COCOTTE

This is really nothing more than a small bowl from the oven with an egg in it that cooks in the sauce. There are endless variations, so delicious and ready in a jiffy. As a starting point, for one serving you will require:

dab of butter
freshly ground pepper and salt
1 tbsp thick cream
1–2 tbsp filling (see below)
1 egg
chopped chives or parsley or other topping (grated cheese, for example)

Preheat the oven to 180°C (350°F/Gas 4). Grease a small oven-proof bowl with butter. Sprinkle with pepper and salt. Fill the bottom with cream and cover with filling, which can be ham, salmon or a pre-cooked vegetable. Break the egg on it. You could also add some spices on it. Place the bowl with the egg in a gratin dish, or another shallow dish, place on the oven grill and pour (preferably boiling) water into the dish to halfway up the egg bowls.
Bake the egg for 10–15 minutes, or to taste. The egg white must be solid, the yolk is up to you. This is the basic recipe. Now you can make variations. On the page opposite you will see a number of variations, but you can probably think of more. Sometimes it is good to add leftovers from the previous day. Always reserve a little filling to garnish the egg. Serve your oeuf cocotte with croutons.
Right: Various cocottes for inspiration. (Some cocottes are double.)

SOFT GOAT'S CHEESE

Replace the thick cream with goat's cheese, as fresh and soft as possible.
Garnish with chives.

RATATOUILLE

Make ratatouille with 1 eggplant (aubergine), 1 zucchini (courgette) and 2 tomatoes, all cubed. Fry for approx. 30 minutes in a generous splash of good-quality olive oil, season with salt and pepper and possibly also some garlic. Cover the bottom of the bowl with the ratatouille and thick cream.

RAW HAM, CURRY CREAM AND EMMENTAL

Stir a teaspoon of curry powder through the thick cream with some salt and pepper. Cover with strips of raw ham, reserving some to garnish. Break the egg on top and sprinkle with a generous amount of grated emmental.

FRIED MUSHROOMS, SPRING ONION & PARSLEY

Fry some tasty mushrooms with a sliced spring onion and some flat-leaf parsley in a frying pan. Season with salt and pepper. Reserve some parsley to garnish.

EGGS BENEDICT

This dish is for the fairly experienced cook. You will need some skill, but since it tastes so good, you will make it more often and you will automatically become an expert!

For the hollandaise sauce
250 g (8 oz/2 sticks) butter, in small pats
2 egg yolks
2 tbsp water
2 tbsp white wine vinegar or lemon juice

And also:
8 eggs, preferably freshly laid
dash of vinegar
8 slices fried ham, or cured side of pork, or smoked salmon, I even used smoked trout here
8 English muffins or other thick round toasted buns
a few leaves of chives or parsley, chopped

First make the hollandaise sauce: in a large pot, bring a layer of water to a boil. Beat in the egg yolks with the water and vinegar into a metal bowl that fits into this large pot, but doesn't touch the water (in other words a bain-marie). Using a whisk or hand blender begin to beat the eggs. Never stop whisking, as the eggs will set on the bottom of the bowl and you will have to start again. Lower the heat and allow the water to simmer.

After a few minutes the egg mixture will thicken considerably into a firm foam (after beating for 5 to 10 minutes). While whisking, add the butter pats, one by one. Only add the next pat of butter when the previous one has melted. It sounds like quite a fuss, but you will become quicker and it gets easier. A mayonnaise-like sauce should be the result. If it is too thick, you can dilute it by adding a few drops of hot water.

Remove the bowl from the pan, cover with lid or plate and proceed to poach the eggs.

Again bring a pan with water and a splash of vinegar to a boil. Break an egg in a small strainer and allow the excess egg white to run through. Gently shake the strainer. Keep the water near boiling point and stir a 'well' into it, using a spoon. Slide the egg into the water. Allow to poach for 2 to 3 minutes and remove from the pan using a slotted spoon.

Save on a warm plate covered with aluminium foil. Continue until all eggs are poached. Once you have some practice, you can try two eggs at the same time.

Halve the muffins and toast them in the toaster or oven. Cover them with some fried or raw ham or salmon (or spinach!). Place a poached egg on each muffin and generously cover with hollandaise sauce. Sprinkle with chives or parsley.

SMOOTHIES

All smoothie recipes are for approx. 4 glasses

MORNING SMOOTHIE

3 bananas

2 punnets of strawberries or other red fruit

2 tbsp whole milk

2 tsp vanilla sugar

juice of 1 lemon

Purée mixture using hand blender.

FOR INCREASED ENERGY

2 bananas

400 g (14 oz/1⅔ cups) raspberries (frozen is OK)

2 tbsp honey

6 ice cubes

Purée mixture using food processor or blender, strain if necessary because of the seeds.

AFTER A NIGHT ON THE TOWN

100 g (approx. 4 oz/¾ cup) raspberries

1 mango, peeled and cubed

2 blanched celery stalks (ribs), clean and in chunks

1 pear, peeled and cubed

juice of 1 lime

500 ml (16 fl oz/2 cups) buttermilk

Purée mixture using a hand blender, strain if necessary because of the seeds.

MELON & LIME SMOOTHIE

1 honeydew melon (cantaloupe), clean and in chunks

250 g (8 oz/1 cup) thick yoghurt (Greek, Bulgarian)

juice and zest of 2 limes

if desired, honey, to taste

Purée mixture using hand blender.

FOREST FRUIT YOGHURT SHAKE

100 g (approx. 4 oz/¾ cup) forest fruits (from the freezer)

2 tbsp icing (confectioner's) sugar (to taste)

300 ml (10 fl oz/1¼ cups) yoghurt

300 ml (10 fl oz/1¼ cups) buttermilk

Purée mixture using food processor or blender, strain if necessary because of the seeds.

STRAWBERRIES, CURRANTS & BALSAMIC SHAKE

250 g (8 oz/1⅔ cups) strawberries, in chunks

150 g (5 oz/1 cup) currants, cleaned

2 tbsp ginger syrup (to taste)

1 tbsp balsamic vinegar

350 ml (approx. 12 fl oz/1½ cups) buttermilk

Purée mixture using food processor or blender, strain.

CUCUMBER & AVOCADO SMOOTHIE

2 cucumbers, peeled and in chunks

1 avocado, peeled and seed removed

1 small bunch mint sprigs

few chive sprigs

500 ml (16 fl oz/2 cups) low fat yoghurt

salt and pepper

Purée mixture using hand blender.

SPICY CARROT & MANGO LASSI

3 mangos, peeled and in chunks

1 carrot, grated

250 ml (9 fl oz/1 cup) low fat yoghurt

10 ice cubes

150 ml (5 fl oz/⅔ cup) skim milk

2 tbsp honey

1 tsp cinnamon and 1 tsp cardamom powder

Purée mixture using hand blender.

WATERMELON SOUP!

juice of 2 limes

1 tbsp brown sugar

2 cm (1 inch) fresh ginger, peeled and finely chopped

¼ seedless watermelon, flesh only

150 ml (5 fl oz/⅔ cup) orange juice

some mint leaves

Purée mixture using hand blender.

My cousin Joris and I run a breakfast and lunch restaurant as well as a catering business in Amsterdam.
It is called 'Aan de Amstel', which is in fact where it is located. Since we feel that Dutch people do not eat
proper lunches, and often only just a cheese sandwich and an apple, we try to treat our guests to something different.
It works out quite well since most of the time as we are packed for lunch. We serve our guests salads, pies and soups that
are as unexpected as possible. I have given you the recipes for a number of delicious dishes, but since our menu changes
on a weekly basis, it was quite difficult to make a selection.

Sophie

GOOD
FOOD
SERVED
HERE!

→ APPELTAART MET 'N
VLEUG COGNAC

GEMBER-CHOCOLATEFUDGE

ELDEN MET KANEELROOM EN

SHAKE VAN DE
DINSDAGEN:

MANGO &
SINAASAPPEL 3,-

Kelly

FRITTATA
WITH MINT, SPINACH & PECORINO

3 tbsp (approx. ¼ cup) olive oil
500 g (1 lb) spinach, washed
1 tbsp lemon juice
8 eggs
150 ml (5 fl oz/⅔ cup) thick cream
freshly ground pepper and salt
1 small bunch of mint sprigs, washed and finely chopped
50 g (approx. 2 oz/½ cup) grated pecorino cheese

Preheat the oven to 170°C (340°F/Gas 3).
Heat a tablespoon of olive oil in a wok and fry the spinach with the water still clinging to it for a few minutes,
until cooked. Add the lemon juice, stir and season with salt and pepper. Beat the eggs with the cream, grind in some pepper
and salt and fold in the mint. Grease a (preferably square) brownie baking tin or six small tins with 2 tablespoons
of olive oil and cut a sheet of baking paper to the fit the bottom. Grease. Spread the spinach on the bottom of the tin
and cover with the egg mixture. Shake the tin slightly in order for the egg to even out and blend with the spinach.
Generously sprinkle with pecorino and reserve a little to garnish. Place the frittata in the middle of the hot oven for approx.
15 minutes. It is ready when the top starts turning light brown and feels firm. Leave to cool and cut in diamond
or block shapes. Garnish with the reserved pecorino. Serve with a small green salad.

OTHER FILLINGS:

• Grilled pumpkin, goat's cheese and sage.
• Stewed kale, pancetta and olive oil.
• Eggplant (aubergine) with oregano and cheese (e.g. taleggio, port salut).
• Parma ham and blanched green asparagus.
• Artichoke hearts, slices of boiled potatoes and aged goat's cheese.
• Truffle paste, slices of prosciutto (Coppa di Parma).
• Roasted zucchini (courgette) and eggplant (aubergine) with basil.
• Strips of salmon (raw or smoked), coriander (cilantro) and lime zest.

TABOULEH WITH POMEGRANATE

Eat as a main meal with white wine or a delicious rosé.

400 g (14 oz/2¼ cups) coarse burghul/bulghur (available from Arab delicatessens or organic supermarkets)

2 kg (4½ lb/11 cups) fresh broad (fava) beans

400 g (14 oz/2 cups) green beans

4 large bunches of herbs:

> parsley (preferably flat-leaf)
>
> basil
>
> lots of mint, dill or tarragon

2 pomegranates

juice of 2 lemons

150 ml (5 fl oz/⅔ cup) high-quality olive oil

freshly ground pepper and salt

Bring 600 ml (20 fl oz/2½ cups) water to a boil, add salt and burghul. Cook on low heat for 2 minutes and remove from heat to allow the burghul to further simmer. Stir occasionally to loosen any grains. The grains must be nice and *al dente*. If they are still too hard, add a little boiling water, if they are too wet, put the pan back on the heat and stir until all the water has evaporated.

Pod the broad beans and blanch briefly in salted water. Rinse them in cold water. Pod the broad beans again to remove the grey 'skin' from the bean by making a cut in the side and squeezing out the green bean. Blanch the green beans, rinse in cool water and cut in three pieces.

Coarsely chop all herbs. Cut the pomegranates into sections and fill half a large bowl with water. Remove the seeds from the peel under water. The bitter white peel will float and the arils will sink. Remove the white pulp and arils from the water. Once the burghul is fluffy and fully cooled, fold in all the ingredients.

Season the salad with lemon juice, olive oil, salt and pepper.

You can easily prepare this salad in advance. It can only get better.

AUTUMN SALAD WITH HAZELNUTS, FRIED MUSHROOMS & YOGHURT-NUT DRESSING

4 small artichokes, or 1 tin artichoke hearts, quartered

½ lemon

100 g (4 oz) mixed salad leaves

75 g (2½ oz) spinach leaves

2 tbsp (approx. ⅛ cup) olive oil

250 g (8 oz/2⅔ cups) mixed forest mushrooms, cut up or torn

2 tbsp (approx. ⅛ cup) white wine vinegar

1 tbsp honey

2 spring onions (scallions), cut in rounds

15 g (½ oz/1 tbsp) hazelnuts

15 g (½ oz/1 tbsp) walnuts

10 g (⅓ oz/2 teaspoons) pine nuts

For the dressing

1 tbsp honey

100 ml (approx. 3 fl oz/½ cup) white wine vinegar

125 g (4 oz/½ cup) yoghurt

75 ml (2½ fl oz/⅓ cup) walnut oil or as much as needed

freshly ground pepper and salt

Cut off the tips of the artichokes. Peel away the hard outer leaves. Using a sharp knife, trim away the base and stem. Rub with lemon. Cook in boiling water until done, approx. 25 minutes. Scoop from the pot and rinse in cool water. Quarter. Mix the salad with the spinach leaves and arrange over four plates. Cover with the artichoke hearts.
Heat the olive oil in a frying pan. Briefly sauté the mushrooms, sprinkle with salt and pepper and add the vinegar. Pour a tablespoon of honey over the mixture and briefly sauté. Fold in the spring onion rounds. Spread the mushrooms over the salad. Wipe the pot clean and swiftly roast the nuts. Sprinkle them over the salads.
Beat the dressing by dissolving the honey in the vinegar and folding in the yoghurt. Lastly, add the walnut oil and beat into a nice thick dressing. Season with salt and pepper and pour over the salads.
Serve immediately with tasty bread.

MINI FOCACCIAS WITH GOAT'S CHEESE, CAPSICUM AND JALAPEÑO

For the focaccia
500 g (1 lb/3 ⅓ cups) plain (all-purpose) flour
1 sachet dried yeast (7 g/¼ oz/2¼ tsp)
pinch of salt
3 tbsp (approx. ¼ cup) olive oil
300 ml (10 fl oz/1¼ cups) lukewarm water
1 tbsp coarse sea salt
3 sprigs rosemary

For the goat's cheese mix
500 g (1 lb/4 cups) soft goat's cheese
1 red capsicum (bell pepper)
a few sprigs of fresh mint and small mint leaves to garnish
4 tbsp (or more, to taste) jalapeño peppers (sliced, from a jar)

First, make the dough by kneading all ingredients, except the sea salt and rosemary, into a pliable dough in a bowl. Continue to knead the dough on a floured surface for approx. 10 minutes. This is necessary as all the kneading will help the dough rise better. Pour a dash of olive oil into a bowl, rotate the bowl so that all sides are coated with oil. Place the dough ball in the bowl and cover with plastic wrap. Put in a warm place. Allow to rise for one hour or until the volume has doubled.
Light one gas burner on your stove top and place the capsicum on it. Allow the skin to turn black. Turn the capsicum over every once in a while so that all sides are scorched. Place in a plastic bag and set aside for about 30 minutes. Remove the capsicum from the bag and rub off the skin under running water. Quarter and remove the seeds. Place the capsicum with the goat's cheese, mint leaves and jalapeño peppers in a food processor and blitz.

Remove the dough from the bowl and knead again. Grease a baking sheet with olive oil and roll out the dough into a flat square 'pizza'. Use your hands to push it out further. This untidy 'imprecise' aspect is part of the deal. Place the dough on the baking sheet and using your fingertips make a lot of 'dents' in the dough. Sprinkle the bread with coarse salt and rosemary. Leave to stand for 30 minutes and bake for approx. 25 minutes, or until golden yellow, in an oven preheated to 180°C (350°F/Gas 4).
Allow the bread to slightly cool off. Cut into small squares measuring approx. 4 x 4 cm (1½ x 1½ inch) and coat with the goat's cheese mixture. Garnish with a mint leaf.

SALAD WITH LAMB WRAPS FILLED WITH GOAT'S CHEESE AND DATES WITH SWEET AND SOUR CORIANDER DRESSING

For the salad

200 g (7 oz/1⅔ cups) goat's cheese

100 g (4 oz) or 8 slices of lamb gammon (or raw ham)

100 g (4 oz/⅔ cup) dates, stoned and cut into strips

100 g (4 oz/3 cups) rocket (arugula) salad

30 g (1 oz/2 tbsp) pine nuts, briefly roasted in a hot pan and cooled

olive oil for frying

For the dressing

1 small bunch of coriander (cilantro) sprigs, washed and finely chopped

½ red onion, sliced

1 generous tbsp (⅛ cup) honey

1 tsp curry powder

1 small red capsicum (bell pepper), seeds removed and finely chopped

4 tbsp (2 fl oz/¼ cup) red wine vinegar

150 ml (5 fl oz/⅔ cup) high-quality olive oil

First make the dressing by pulsing all ingredients in a food processor. The mixture can stay coarse, it does not have to be pureed smooth!

Cut the goat's cheese in four equal portions. Roll the cheese in two slices of lamb gammon, once lengthways and once crossways. Distribute the rocket salad over four plates. Arrange the date strips on the rocket salad. Heat the olive oil in a non-stick frying pan and sauté the cheese for a few minutes on both sides, until light golden brown on the edges and relatively soft.

Place a slice on each salad, top with dressing and sprinkle with the pine nuts.

Serve with warm Turkish bread from the oven.

ZUCCHINI PANCAKES WITH BASIL CREAM

For approx. 8 small pancakes

For the pancakes

1 zucchini (courgette), washed

1 tsp salt

2 egg whites

2 tbsp (approx. ⅛ cup) cornflour (cornstarch)

freshly ground black pepper

5 tbsp (¼ cup) peanut oil

3 tbsp pine nuts, roasted

5 tbsp (⅓ cup) parmesan cheese, coarsely grated

For the basil cream

125 ml (approx. 4 fl oz/⅔ cup) sour cream

15 g (½ oz/¼ cup) fresh basil, chopped

freshly ground salt and pepper

1 tbsp cold water

Grate the zucchini using a coarse grater and place in a colander. Fold in the salt and leave to stand over a bowl for 30 minutes to allow the moisture to drain. Rinse and thoroughly wring out the zucchini. Wrap the mixture in a dish towel and wring out again until it is truly 'dry'. Beat the egg whites until stiff with a dash of salt. Stir the cornflour through the zucchini and generously grind pepper on the mixture. Carefully stir in the beaten egg whites. Heat a layer of oil in a non-stick frying pan. Using two tablespoons, drop heaps of this mixture into the hot oil. Using the back of a spoon press against the pancakes to make them a little flatter. Turn them over after approx. 3 minutes or when they are golden brown. Drain on kitchen paper and continue to fry until you run out of mixture.

In the meantime, make the basil cream: blend all ingredients in a food processor, if necessary, add a tablespoon of water to make it a little thinner. Serve the pancakes on a large plate, trickle sauce on them and sprinkle with pine nuts and grated parmesan cheese.

Aan de Amstel
Lunch rush

TABOULEH WITH QUINOA, CORN, SPRING ONION AND GOAT'S CHEESE

250 g (8 oz/1¼ cups) quinoa

4 fresh corn cobs or 1 large tin of corn kernels

2 bunches spring onion (scallion) or 6 sprigs

1 bunch flat-leaf parsley

50 g (⅓ cup) cashew nuts

2 small heads little gem (romaine) lettuce

150 g (5 oz/1¼ cups) aged goat's cheese

For the dressing

2 tbsp mustard

1 garlic clove

1 tsp smoked ground paprika

50 ml (1½ fl oz/¼ cup) white wine vinegar

150 ml (5 fl oz/⅔ cup) grape seed oil or sunflower oil

Cook the quinoa for 20 minutes in a large pan with salted water. Strain through a colander and rinse thoroughly under cold running water. Leave to drain.

In the meantime cook the corn cobs for approx. 15 minutes. Also rinse under cold water and cut the kernels from the cobs. Cut the spring onions into rounds, finely chop the parsley. Cut the little gem lettuce into strips and the cheese in small dice approx. 1 x 1 cm (½ x ½ inch). Mix swiftly. Make the dressing by blitzing the mustard, garlic, ground paprika and vinegar using a hand blender. Fold in the oil until a lovely dressing is obtained. If it is too thick, add some water. Pour the dressing over the salad.

SAVOURY PIE WITH SMOKED CHICKEN AND GOAT'S CHEESE

I'm surprised how often I have to give out the recipe for savoury pie or 'quiche' to guests or friends, since I thought that by now everyone knows how to do it. But that is often not the case and that's okay. I will write it down again for you. Many people use puff pastry, instead of shortcrust pastry. I'm not a great fan of it, especially since the bottom frequently remains soft. In our restaurant we often briefly turn the pie upside down and bake it for approx. 10 minutes on a baking sheet, creating a crispy bottom. This recipe is for approx. eight small pies or one large pie.

60

For the dough
300 g (10 oz/2 cups) plain (all-purpose) flour
150 g (5 oz/1¼ sticks) butter for greasing purposes
salt
few drops of cold water

Basic mix for the filling
3 eggs
200 ml (6 fl oz/¾ cup) thick cream
freshly ground pepper and salt, to taste

This filling
1 double smoked chicken breast (fillet)
150 g (5 oz/1¼ cups) goat's cheese
few sprigs of dill

Swiftly knead the ingredients for the dough into a pliable ball. Add the water if the dough is too dry. Allow to rest in the refrigerator for 30 minutes. In the meantime preheat the oven to 180°C (350°F/Gas 4).
Cut the chicken into small cubes and the cheese into eight slices. Beat the eggs with the cream and season with salt and pepper. Divide the dough into eight equal parts. Grease eight quiche pans with butter and roll out the dough on a work surface dusted with flour. Cover the pans with the dough and trim the edges. Arrange the chicken and goat's cheese on the pies, top with the cream mixture and sprinkle with dill. Bake until golden brown for approx. 20 minutes.
Serve warm or cold.

OTHER FILLINGS:

- Slice of crottin (small round goat's cheese) with 1 tsp roasted fennel seed.
- A few slices of very young zucchini (courgette), dill and parmesan cheese.
- Grilled pumpkin, goat's cheese and spinach.
- Parma ham and blanched green asparagus.
- Gruyère and fried bacon bits.
- Leeks briefly stewed in butter, curry and cashew nuts.
- Feta, green olives and roasted capsicum (bell pepper).
- Smoked mackerel, cream cheese and dill.
- Parboiled broccoli, blue cheese (Roquefort!) and almonds.
- Onions stewed in butter for 30 minutes, anchovies and fresh thyme.

MUSSELS HORAS STYLE

When my good friend Horas heard that I was writing mussel recipes for a magazine, he immediately gave me this recipe. It was delicious and therefore I pass it on to you.

1 bunch green asparagus
200 g (7 oz) green beans
100 g (approx. 4 oz/½ cup) broad (fava) beans and/or garden peas (frozen is okay)
4 shallots, peeled and finely chopped
2 garlic cloves, also finely chopped
butter for frying and olive oil
500 ml (16 fl oz/2 cups) fish stock
500 ml (16 fl oz/2 cups) cream
approx. 40 mussels, or just a few handfuls
12 scallops (these can be found inexpensively today in large bags in the supermarket's frozen food section)

Bring a pan with water to a boil. Add a pinch of salt. Trim away the bottom hard part of the asparagus and blanch for 2 minutes. Rinse under cold running water and cut diagonally in three parts. Then blanch the green beans for 2 minutes and rinse immediately under cold running water. Blanch the garden peas and lastly, the broad beans. Broad beans will turn the water brown, which is why you have to cook them last. Remove the seeds from the pods, by making a small incision in the grey skin and pressing out the inner green beans. Thoroughly rinse all vegetables under cold running water to keep them green and crunchy.

Briefly sauté the shallots with the garlic in a pat of butter. Add the fish stock and cream and reduce the liquid by half. Wash the mussels and cook them in the reduced sauce with the lid on the pan until they open up. Add the vegetables to the sauce.

In the meantime briefly fry the scallops on both sides in a drop of olive oil and add to the mixture. Leave to heat for another minute, season as needed with salt and freshly ground pepper and immediately arrange the warm salad on four plates. Serve with bread.

RISOTTO FROM THE OVEN WITH SAUSAGEMEAT AND CAPSICUM

If you make this for an evening meal, double the quantities.

1 tbsp olive oil

4 sausages, about 250 g (8 oz)

1 red capsicum (bell pepper), cubed

1 green capsicum (bell pepper), cubed

1 small onion, peeled and finely chopped

2 garlic cloves, slivered

2–3 sprigs rosemary, chopped

Tabasco (hot-pepper) sauce, to taste

150 g (approx. 5 oz/⅔ cup) arborio rice

150 ml (5 fl oz/⅔ cup) white wine

125 ml (approx. 4 fl oz/⅔ cup) passato (smooth tomato pulp)

250 ml (9 fl oz/1 cup) chicken stock

Heat the oil in a heavy frying pan, which can also go into the oven. Preheat the oven to 180°C (350°F/Gas 4). Cut open
the skin on the sausages and crumble the sausagemeat over the hot oil in the pan. Turn over. Add the capsicums, onion
and garlic. Sprinkle with two-thirds of the rosemary and dribble with the Tabasco sauce. Fry the mixture while stirring
for approx. 5 minutes. Fold in the rice and fry for another minute. Add the wine and stir in the passato and stock. Bring the
mixture to a boil while stirring.

Cover the pan with a lid and place in the oven. Bake the risotto for 18–20 minutes until done, or until all liquid is absorbed.
Before serving sprinkle with the reserved rosemary. Serve with a small rocket (arugula) salad.

SALAD WITH SPELT, BARLEY, FOREST MUSHROOMS AND GRILLED PUMPKIN

For the pumpkin

500–600 g (16–20 oz) butternut pumpkin (butternut squash)

150 ml (5 fl oz/⅔ cup) olive oil

1 garlic clove, crushed

2 tbsp (approx. ⅛ cup) fresh thyme

½ tsp each cumin, ground coriander and cayenne pepper

1 tsp salt

For the forest mushrooms

500 g (1 lb/5 cups) mixed mushrooms

2 tbsp fresh thyme

2 garlic cloves, coarsely chopped

1 tsp salt and freshly ground pepper

75 ml (2½ fl oz/⅓ cup) olive oil

And also:

150 g (5 oz/¾ cup) spelt (organic store)

150 g (5 oz/¾ cup) barley (organic store)

approx. 75 ml (2½ fl oz/⅓ cup) red wine vinegar

a little fresh thyme

Peel the pumpkin, quarter and remove the seeds. Cut the pulp into large chunks approx. 2 x 2 cm (¾ x ¾ inch). In a bowl, mix all the other ingredients and pour over the pumpkin cubes. Stir thoroughly. Place a sheet of baking paper on a baking sheet and arrange the pumpkin on it. Bake the cubes in an oven preheated to 180°C (350°F/Gas 4) for 30 minutes until done or until the edges turn dark.

In the meantime cook the spelt and barley in salted water until done (approx. 40 minutes). Rinse in cool water.

Clean the mushrooms, tear or cut them coarsely into pieces and place them in an oven-proof dish. Sprinkle with all ingredients on the list. Stir and place in the oven under the pumpkin. The mushrooms will be ready after 8–10 minutes. Remove from oven and leave to cool.

When all ingredients are ready they can be loosely mixed in a large bowl including any liquid from the mushroom oven dish. Season the salad with red wine vinegar. Sprinkle with the remaining thyme leaves.

TIP: This salad can be served lukewarm or cold.
You can easily make it a day in advance.

SALAD WITH LENTILS, APPLE AND CORIANDER

200 g (7 oz/1 cup) lentils, (use small greyish green [Puy] lentils that stay firm after cooking and do not become mushy)

1 whole celery, stalks (ribs) washed, leaves can be removed (or used in soup)

2 handfuls sultanas

2 stalks chicory (witlof/Belgian endive)

1 lemon

2 red crunchy apples, suitable for baking

1 bunch of coriander (cilantro), leaves pulled

For the dressing
1 garlic clove

75 ml (2½ fl oz/⅓ cup) red wine vinegar

freshly ground pepper and salt

200 ml (6 fl oz/¾ cup) grape seed oil or mild olive oil

Cook the lentils in plenty of unsalted water for approx. 20 minutes until done, drain them in a colander and rinse under cold running water. Cut the blanched celery on a slicer, mandolin or in the food processor in very thin diagonal slices. Place them in a tray of ice-cold water until used, which will make them hard and crunchy. Soak the sultanas in warm water, drain in colander and save until used. Trim away the ends of the chicory, quarter and then cut in two or three, remove the bitter core. Add the chicory to the blanched celery in the iced water then add the juice of a lemon. Place the garlic and vinegar in a tall bowl and purée using a hand blender. While puréeing add the oil until a thick dressing develops.

If necessary add a little water if the dressing is too thick and season with salt and pepper.

To serve:
Cut the apple, skin and all, into thin strips. Drain the celery and chicory, add the apple and lentils. Mix quickly. Stir in half of the coriander leaves, cover with the dressing and sprinkle the salad with the remaining coriander leaves.

EXTREMELY DELICIOUS DUCK BREAST SALAD WITH RICE

BOIL 300 G
(10 OZ / 1½ CUPS)
BROWN OR WILD RICE
FOR 40 MINS. (BE
CAREFUL RICE DOESN'T
DRY OUT)
ALLOW TO COOL

RUB 2 DUCK BREASTS
WITH PEPPER & SALT
AND FRY ON BOTH
SIDES UNTIL GOLDEN
BROWN AND MEDIUM
RARE. I DO THIS IN
½ BUTTER & ½ OLIVE
OIL ⟶ SLICE!

CUT 3 SMALL GEM (COS)
LETTUCE INTO STRIPS.
COMBINE WITH THE RICE.
ADD 75 G. (3 OZ / ⅔ CUP)
HAZELNUTS,
200 G. (7 OZ / 1¼ CUPS)
RAISINS & ONE COARSLEY
CHOPPED BUNCH OF PARSLEY

WHISK
THE DRESSING WITH

2 CLOVES OF CRUSHED GARLIC
4 TBSP. (2 FL OZ / ¼ CUP)
WHITE WINE VINEGAR
ZEST & JUICE OF 1 LIME
PINCH OF CURRY POWDER
1 TSP CARAWAY SEEDS
2-3 TBSP APRICOT JAM
150 ML (5 FL OZ / ⅔ CUP)
OLIVE OIL &
75 ML (2½ FL OZ / ⅓ CUP)
SOUR CREAM

⟶ ARRANGE THE
SALAD ON 4
PLATES & COVER
WITH THE DUCK
SLICES.

TEA ANYONE?

MAKING TEA

MAKING TEA IS VERY EASY AND FUN, SINCE YOU CAN MAKE UP YOUR OWN INGREDIENTS AS YOU LIKE THEM AND YOU WON'T HAVE TO DEPEND ON WHAT THEY PUT IN THOSE BOXES IN THE SUPERMARKET. YOU CAN MAKE TEA FROM FRESH PLANTS AND LEAVES OR FROM DRIED ONES. YOU CAN ALSO MAKE TEA FROM SPICES. YOU CAN MAKE REFRESHING ICED TEA FOR A HOT SUMMER DAY OR A MEDICINAL TEA FOR YOURSELF IF YOU FEEL A LITTLE UNDER THE WEATHER. TEA IS ALWAYS GOOD, ESPECIALLY WITH CAKE, BUT THAT COMES LATER. HERE IS A STEP-BY-STEP GUIDE TO SEVERAL TEAS. I WILL START OUTDOORS, IN THE PARK OR IN THE GARDEN: MAKING TEA FROM FRESH HERBS AND PLANTS.

PLUCK PLANTAIN, DANDELION (WITH LEAF), NETTLES, GOLDEN RODS, HIBISCUS, HOLLYHOCK, HONEYSUCKLE BLOSSOMS,

VIOLETS, ROSE PETALS OR ELDERBERRY BLOSSOMS. IT IS JUST LIKE MAKING MINT TEA:

PLACE YOUR OWN MIXTURE IN A GLASS OR POT. COVER WITH HOT WATER AND ALLOW TO BREW BRIEFLY. HERE: PLANTAIN-ELDERBERRY BLOSSOM TEA.

MAKE A SPICE MIXTURE. FOR EXAMPLE, CINNAMON, FENNEL SEED AND STAR ANISE,

AND PLACE TEA IN SMALL BAGS. THESE TEA BAGS ARE AVAILABLE FROM TEA AND COFFEE STORES.

OR DRY SPICES TO ENJOY LONGER: FOR EXAMPLE, THYME, ROSEMARY, CAMOMILE, LIME. TEA TIME!

LET'S GET GOING ...

TEA IS HIGHLY VERSATILE. I WILL GIVE YOU A NUMBER OF TEA RECIPES THAT MAKE ME HAPPY, BUT EXPERIMENT AWAY. ALL RECIPES ARE FOR A 1-LITRE (4-CUP) TEAPOT, UNLESS INDICATED OTHERWISE.

SAGE & LEMON TEA

Sage can be used everywhere. It acts as an antiseptic and is therefore good for a sore throat or pain in your mouth or around your teeth. Sage calms the nervous system and also controls blood pressure and promotes digestion.
All the more reason to make a cuppa!

15 g (½ oz) fresh sage (small sprig)
zest of ½ lemon
1 generous tbsp honey

Bring 1 litre (4 cups) of water to a boil. Add the ingredients and simmer on low heat for a few minutes. Remove from the heat and allow the tea to brew for at least 20 minutes. Strain before pouring.

LAVENDER & MINT TEA

Lavender: yes, you can make tea from it. Combined with mint it is delicious. Here's the recipe for fresh and dried lavender.

2–3 tbsp (approx. ¼ cup) fresh lavender leaves or 1–2 tbsp dried ones
15 g (½ oz) mint leaves (small sprig)

Bring water to a boil. Pour over the spices in a pot and allow to brew for 10 minutes. Strain into a cup, flavour with honey or sugar, as needed. You can also strain into a pot, flavour it with honey or sugar, and leave to fully cool. Serve in tall glasses over ice cubes and with fresh mint leaves for show.

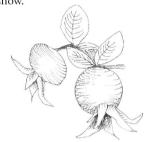

ROSE HIP & LEMON TEA

For this tea you will have to work a little first: plucking and drying rose hips. The peels of a few lemons also have to be dried. However, stored in a glass jar, this tea looks very attractive! Here's a recipe that will make a considerable volume.

100 g (4 oz) dried rose hip
30 g (1 oz/2 tsp) dried lemon peel

Crush the rose hips in a mortar, thus releasing the seeds. Mix with lemon peel. For one pot you will need one generous tablespoon of this mixture. Use a tea strainer or place the mixture in a teabag.
Allow to brew for 10 minutes.

THYME, VERBENA & TARRAGON TEA

If you have access to fresh verbena, this tea is highly recommended. It also works well with dried verbena. But do use fresh tarragon and thyme.

25 g (approx. 1 oz) fresh verbena or 1 tbsp dried verbena
15 g (½ oz) fresh tarragon (few leaves)
15 g (½ oz) fresh thyme (small sprig)

Bring 1 generous litre (4 cups) water to a boil with the spices and remove from the heat. Allow the tea to brew for 10 minutes before pouring it. Add honey, to taste. You can also sweeten the tea with honey and leave it to fully cool, serve over ice cubes on a hot day.

ANOTHER NAME FOR TARRAGON IS DRAGON'S WORT!

EUW...

FRUIT TEA WITH CRANBERRIES & SPICES

This tea is truly heart-warming. The longer you leave it to brew, the better. It almost tastes like lemonade.

250 g (8 oz/1½ cups) fresh cranberries
2 cinnamon sticks
2 cloves
3 juniper berries
300 g (10 oz/1⅓ cups) sugar
500 ml (16 fl oz/2 cups) orange juice
500 ml (16 fl oz/2 cups) pineapple juice
juice of 1 lemon

Bring 1 litre (4 cups) of water to a boil with the cranberries, cinnamon sticks, cloves, juniper berries and sugar. Stir occasionally until the sugar is dissolved and remove from the heat when all berries have burst. This only takes a few minutes. Leave to brew for a few hours. Strain and bring to a boil again. Add the juices, heat them briefly and serve the tea in warm bowls.

FRESH ICED TEA

Tea for a hot summer day.

zest and juice of 1 lemon
juice of 2 limes
1 handful or a small bunch fresh mint leaves
approx. 6 slices cucumber
honey, to taste
1 tray ice cubes

Bring a kettle to a boil and pour water over the fresh mint in a heat-proof glass jug. Leave the mint tea to slightly cool. Grate the lemon and squeeze together with the limes. Stir the zest and juice through the tea. Add the cucumber slices and stir in the honey, until dissolved. Store the tea in the refrigerator to fully cool until used. Immediately before serving add half of the ice cubes to the jug and fill four large glasses with the other half. Pour the iced tea into the glasses through a tea strainer. You can garnish the glasses with a sprig of fresh mint and some extra cucumber slices.

ELDERBERRY BLOSSOM TEA

Elderberry blossom can be used in multiple ways. I will give out further recipes with elder blossoms or berries later. Elder blossoms are good against colds and they lower fever.
If you pluck a lot of blossoms, dry them upside down in a dark and warm place. Dried elder blossoms are also available in organic food stores.

Basic tea for 1 litre (4 cups)
4 umbels elder blossoms
nectar or sugar, as needed

Allow the elder blossoms to brew for 10 minutes in boiled water.
As a variation on the basic tea, add mint leaves, a clove or two, 1 tbsp dried verbena or some fresh lemon balm leaves.

SPICY GINGER TEA

Good for the throat and improves blood circulation.

piece of ginger the length of a large thumb
½ cinnamon stick
1 sprig thyme
juice of 2 mandarins
freshly ground black pepper

Cut the ginger in fine slices. Pour the water into a saucepan and add the ginger, cinnamon and thyme. Allow to brew for approx. 20 minutes on very low heat. Squeeze the mandarins and strain the juice. Remove the tea from the heat and add the juice, flavour the tea with a little black pepper. Drink hot and flavour with high-quality honey, as needed.

RHUBARB ICED TEA

To be totally honest I actually did not want to include a recipe with store-bought tea to this section, but I will make an exception for this tea. A friend of my mother's gave me this recipe years ago and I have given it my own twist. Oh, so good.

10 stalks rhubarb
400 g (14 oz/3½ cups) sugar
4 tea bags Earl Grey tea
1 vanilla bean
2 star anise
extra sugar (to taste)
lots of ice cubes

Wash the rhubarb and cut the stalks into sections. Place on heat with the sugar in 1 litre (4 cups) water. Simmer for 2 hours on low heat until a syrup develops. Leave to fully cool. In the meantime bring 1 litre (4 cups) of water to a boil. Cut the vanilla bean open lengthways, scrape out the seeds and add them to the water with the bean. Also add the star anise. Lastly, add the tea bags. Brew on low heat for 10 minutes and remove the tea bags.
Allow the tea to cool. Store in the refrigerator to fully cool.
Before serving, first pour the rhubarb syrup into an attractive glass jug. Add the tea and stir. Add extra sugar to taste. Serve with lots of ice cubes.

FRESH CITRUS & CAMOMILE TEA WITH CATNIP

Just like the previous recipe this one is also delicious as iced tea.
I bet that you had never thought of catnip, but it is delicious and readily available.
Catnip also cleanses the blood, which is another benefit.

5 g (a few small leaves) catnip
10 g (⅓ oz/1 tsp) camomile flowers
½ lemongrass stalk, crushed
15 g (½ oz/1 tsp) lemon balm
5 g (a few small leaves) fresh mint

Combine all spices in a glass teapot and cover with boiling water. Allow to brew for 5 minutes and strain. If you dry all the spices first, you will need less than half. Crumble the dried spices in your hands, make a nice mix and store sealed until used.

gingerbread muffins

PREHEAT THE OVEN TO 200°C
(400°F / GAS 6)

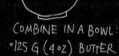

COMBINE IN A BOWL:
- 125 G (4 OZ) BUTTER
- 125 G (4 OZ / APPROX ½ CUP) SUGAR
- 2 EGGS →
- 125 G (4 OZ / APPROX 1 CUP) SELF-RAISING FLOUR
- 1 TSP VANILLA EXTRACT
- 1 TSP CINNAMON
- 1 TSP MIXED SPICE
- A PINCH OF SALT
  & 50 ML (1½ FL OZ / ¼ CUP) MILK

GREASE MUFFIN TRAY
OR LINE WITH PAPER
CASES

BAKE THE MUFFINS FOR
15-20 MINS UNTIL
LIGHT BROWN.
LEAVE TO COOL

MIX THE
ICING IN
ANOTHER BOWL

- 2 PACKS CREAMCHEESE (=250 G / 8 OZ) AT ROOMTEMPERATURE
- 375 G (13 OZ / 3 CUPS) ICING (CONFECTIONERS') SUGAR
- 1 TSP VANILLA EXTRACT
- ZEST & JUICE OF ½ LEMON

CAREFULLY SPREAD THE ICING
ON YOUR MUFFINS,
SPRINKLE WITH CINNAMON
AND SERVE WITH A CUP OF TEA

PEAR-HAZELNUT TART

For the dough
200 g (7 oz/1⅓ cups) plain (all-purpose) flour, plus some extra for rolling out the dough
100 g (approx. 4 oz/½ cup) sugar
100 g (approx. 4 oz/1 stick) butter
1 egg
pinch of salt

For the pears
3 firm sweet dessert pears, peeled, with the stem
1.5 litres (6 cups) water, or half water half white wine
100 g (approx. 4 oz/½ cup) sugar
1 cinnamon stick
½ lemon

For the filling
100 g (approx. 4 oz/⅔ cup) hazelnuts
50 g (approx. 2 oz/¼ cup) sugar
2 tsp vanilla sugar
50 g (approx. 2 oz/⅓ cup) plain (all-purpose) flour
50 g (approx. 2 oz/½ stick) butter at room temperature
2 eggs

Knead the dough ingredients into a nice dough and place in the refrigerator for 30 minutes wrapped in plastic wrap. Bring the water for the pears to a boil with the sugar, cinnamon stick and squeezed half lemon. Poach the pears for 30 minutes.
In a food processor, grind the hazelnuts and the sugar into a powder. Then add the other ingredients.
Preheat the oven to 180°C (350°F/Gas 4).
Roll out the dough on a floured countertop. Use to cover a greased 24-cm (9-inch) pie dish or 6 individual pie dishes.
First fill the bottom. Carefully halve the pears. Remove the cores and cut the pear halves in fan shapes, and leave the stem. Arrange the pears on the filling with the stem facing inward. Bake the tart until golden brown (approx. 35 minutes). Smaller tarts are ready in approx. 25 minutes.

TIP For a shiny effect: heat 3 tbsp apricot jam with a dash of rum, calvados or water. Press the jam through a sieve and cover the tart with it.

TIP Instead of hazelnuts you can also use almonds.

IRISH TEA BRACK

A cake I remember well. The flavour is truly Irish. It looks a little like Christmas pudding or those real Irish fruitcakes, also often used as the basis for those gorgeous wedding cakes with all that white icing. But of course, all those cakes contain a lot of alcohol and as children we were not allowed to eat them. Hence this more virtuous version, based on tea.
This recipe is for 1 cake.

400 ml (14 fl oz/1⅔ cups) boiling water
2 tea bags black tea, e.g., Ceylon or Earl Grey
500 g (1 lb/3 cups) mixed raisins, citrus or semi-tropical fruit or a mixture thereof
200 g (7 oz/1⅛ cups) raw caster (superfine) sugar
1 egg
1 tsp mixed spices (or 1 tsp cinnamon, a pinch of nutmeg and pimento)
250 g (8 oz/1⅔ cups) self-raising flour
pinch of salt

Brew strong tea with the water and teabags. Remove the teabags and stir in the raisins. Leave to steep, preferably one day (for example, before you go to work). Preheat the oven to 170°C (340°F/Gas 3). Stir the sugar, egg and mixed spices through the tea raisins. Lastly, fold in the flour and the salt. Stir briefly, otherwise the swollen raisins will break and the cake will not turn out well. Grease a bar cake tin and cover the bottom with baking paper cut to size. Grease. Pour the mixture into the tin and bake the cake for 90 minutes until done or until a skewer poked into it comes up dry.
Leave the cake to rest and turn over on a board. Allow to further cool before cutting it. The cake must be a little moist and must be easy to cut. Preferably eat in thin slices and still warm, with butter.

BANANA RUM CAKE

One of Koosje's recipes, who used to bake delicious cakes for us at 'Aan de Amstel'.

For 1 cake

100 g (4 oz/½ cup) raisins
75 ml (2½ fl oz/⅓ cup) rum
4 ripe bananas
100 g (4 oz/¾ cup) walnuts or pecan nuts, briefly toasted
175 g (6 oz/1⅛ cups) self-raising flour
½ tsp salt

125 g (approx. 4 oz/1 stick) butter, melted
150 g (5 oz/⅔ cup) sugar
1 tbsp vanilla sugar
2 eggs
zest and juice of 1 lemon

Heat the raisins and the rum for 1 minute in the microwave or in a small saucepan. Leave to steep for at least 1 hour, but preferably longer. Preheat the oven to 170°C (340°F/Gas 3). Cut the bananas into thick slices. Mix all ingredients swiftly into a firm batter. Grease a cake tin and cover the bottom with baking paper cut to size. Grease. Cover with the batter. Bake the cake for approx. 1 hour. The cake is done when a skewer poked into it comes up dry. Otherwise bake the cake a little longer. Leave the cake to rest for 5 minutes after it comes out of the oven and transfer to a rack in order to fully cool.

CHOCOLATE-GINGER FUDGE CAKE WITH PECAN NUTS AND CINNAMON CREAM

For the cake
125 g (approx. 4 oz/1 stick) butter
250 g (8 oz) dark chocolate, in chunks
100 g (approx. 4 oz/½ cup) raw caster (superfine) sugar
100 g (approx. 4 oz/⅔ cup) self-raising flour
100 g (approx. 4 oz/½ cup) grated fresh ginger
4 large eggs, beaten

For the caramel nuts
150 g (5 oz/1½ cups) pecan nuts
150 g (5 oz/⅔ cup) sugar
2 tbsp water

For the cinnamon cream
200 ml (6 fl oz/¾ cup) thick cream
2 tbsp sugar
2 tsp cinnamon

And also:
dash sunflower oil for greasing purposes
cocoa powder to garnish

Preheat the oven to 175ºC (340°F/Gas 4). Briefly melt the butter and chocolate in the microwave or over a bain-marie. Quickly mix all ingredients, just until the batter is smooth. Grease a 22 cm (8 inch) springform pan. Cut a sheet of baking paper to size and place on the bottom. Grease. Pour the batter into the tin. Place the cake in the hot oven and bake for 30 minutes.

The cake should not become completely dry, as in pound cake. Leave to fully cool on a rack. It will still sink a little, that is the idea. It is supposed to be a bit of a 'boggy' cake. During the cooling process, make the pecan nuts.

Toast the pecan nuts in a non-stick pan, when they start smelling they are done. Grease a metal tray with a dash of sunflower oil. Arrange the nuts on the tray, some distance apart. Heat the sugar and water in a heavy-based saucepan, but stay close! Do not walk away, as this melting process is fast and caramel gets very hot. When the sugar starts to colour around the edges, swirl the pan to ensure an even colour.

Carefully trickle the caramel onto the loose nuts, making sure that each nut is covered with a layer of caramel. Leave to cool and harden. Break into pieces using a hammer or pestle.

Beat the cream with the cinnamon and sugar until thick. Dust the cake with cocoa powder. Cut the cake into wedges. Serve each wedge with a dash of cinnamon cream and sprinkle with the pecan nuts-caramel chunks.

DATE & LEMON RICOTTA CAKE

120 g (approx. 4 oz/½ cup) sugar

1 kg (2 lb/4⅓ cups) ricotta cheese

340 g (12 oz) jar lemon jam (you can also use lemon curd)

2 tsp vanilla sugar

zest of 1 lemon

50 g (approx. 2 oz/⅓ cup) cornflour (cornstarch)

6 eggs

500 g (1 lb/3 cups) Medjool dates (or just regular dates)

dash Marsala wine

300 g (10 oz/1⅓ cups) jelling sugar or use granulated sugar and pectin (add pectin according to instructions on the package)

2 cinnamon sticks

6 cardamom pods

4 gelatine leaves (3 tsp powdered gelatine)

Preheat the oven to 175°C (340°F/Gas 4). Grease a springform tin approx. 24 cm (9 inch) in diameter. Cut a sheet of baking paper to size and place on the bottom. Grease. Combine the sugar, ricotta, lemon jam, vanilla sugar, lemon zest, cornflour and eggs into a smooth batter. Pour into the tin. Bake the cake until done for approx. 1 hour. Leave to stand in the tin for 15 minutes and carefully transfer the cake to a plate to cool.

Halve the dates and remove the pit. Leave to steep in the Marsala.

In a saucepan bring the jelling sugar, 200 ml (6 fl oz/¾ cup) water, the cinnamon sticks and cardamom pods to a boil. Reduce. Add the dates and the Marsala and allow to slightly thicken. In the meantime soak the gelatine sheets in cold water, squeeze and stir into the warm jelly until dissolved. Or dissolve the powdered gelatine in a tiny amount of warm water and then add to the jelly. Briefly leave the jelly to cool. Using a spoon first remove the spices and then the date halves. Arrange the dates neatly next to each other on the cake. Cover with the rest of the jelly and allow to set before slicing the cake.

ALMOND & APPLE MUFFINS

Recipe for 12 muffins

150 g (5 oz/1½ cups) almond meal (or shaved almonds)
150 g (5 oz/1 cup) plain (all-purpose) flour
180 g (6 oz/1½ sticks) butter, melted
150 g (5 oz/⅔ cup) caster (superfine) sugar
6 egg whites
pinch of salt
12 small cooking apples, but 12 chunks of any apple, pear or other fruit is also fine. Leave the peel, it looks good!

And also:
butter for greasing purposes

Combine all ingredients for the batter, except the apples. Grease 12 muffin moulds. Distribute the batter in the moulds. Press the apples into the moulds and bake the muffins for 40 minutes in an oven preheated to 160°C (320°F/Gas 3) until golden brown and done.

CHEWY CHOCOLATE RAISIN BROWNIES

You probably are familiar with brownies, but brownies with chocolate raisins are devilishly addictive.

150 g (5 oz/1¼ sticks) butter, cubed
250 g (8 oz) dark chocolate, in chunks
2 eggs
150 g (5 oz/⅔ cup) sugar
2 tsp vanilla sugar
200 g (7 oz/1⅓ cups) self-raising flour
pinch of salt
200 g (7 oz/1 cup) chocolate coated raisins

Preheat the oven to 170°C (340°F/Gas 3), grease a square baking tin.
Melt the butter and chocolate in the microwave for 2 minutes or use a bain-marie. Leave to slightly cool. Beat the eggs, the sugar and the vanilla sugar into a light airy foam. Carefully fold in the melted chocolate-butter mixture. Fold in the sifted flour with a little salt. Lastly, fold in the raisins. Pour the mixture into the tin and bake the brownies for 25 minutes until done or until a skewer poked into them comes up dry. Leave to cool and transfer to a board. Leave to fully cool and cut into equal chunks.

ORANGE POLENTA CAKE

For the cake
2 oranges
juice of 1 lemon
100 g (approx. 4 oz/½ cup) polenta
1 tsp baking powder
1 tbsp vanilla sugar
100 g (4 oz/1 cup) almonds, finely ground
6 eggs
250 g (8 oz/approx. 1¼ cups) caster (superfine) sugar

To garnish
3–4 oranges
approx. 100 ml (3 fl oz/½ cup) apricot jam or marmalade
2 gelatine leaves (1½ tsp powdered gelatine)

And also:
butter for greasing purposes

Preheat the oven to 180°C (350°F/Gas 4).

Cook the whole oranges for 1 hour in plenty of water. Leave to fully cool.

Place in food processor and blitz with the lemon juice. Stir in the polenta, baking powder and vanilla sugar and then the ground almonds. In another bowl, beat the eggs with the sugar into a fine white foam.

Carefully fold the polenta mixture into the airy egg foam and pour into a thoroughly greased 26-cm (10-inch) cake tin.

Bake the cake in a hot oven for 35 minutes. Leave the cake to cool for 5 minutes and transfer to a rack to fully cool.

Peel the oranges for the garnish. Using a sharp knife, trim the top and bottom of an orange including the pith. Place the orange in front of you on the cutting board and cut the peel from top to bottom removing all of the pith, leaving only the pulp. Cut the orange into slices. Continue until all oranges are cut.

Cover the top of your cake with overlapping orange slices.

In the meantime soak the gelatine sheets in cold water. Or dissolve the powdered gelatine in a small amount of warm water. Heat the jam in a saucepan and press through a sieve. Squeeze the water out of the gelatine leaves and stir them into the hot jam until dissolved. Or add the dissolved powdered gelatine. Spread the oranges on the cake with the jam and allow to set.

Maxance

Pat

Math

'Apéro' is short for aperitif! and really means pre-dinner drinks, which I learned all about in France. There things are not the same as in the Netherlands where everyone drinks white wine or a glass of beer. In France, everyone gets their own personalised drink as an aperitif and wine is only drunk during meals. I felt I went from 'country plain' to 'posh Parisian'. Now I have a lot of 'aperos' behind me and many different and personalised mixed drinks. I learned to make a lot of aperitifs myself from my friends in Provence, since a drink sure hits the spot after a game of boules.

MAKING DRINKS

IN THIS SECTION I NOT ONLY GIVE YOU RECIPES FOR APERITIFS, BUT ALSO DRINKS WHICH YOU CAN SERVE WITH COFFEE AFTER A MEAL.

TO MAKE THESE RECIPES YOU WILL NEED ALCOHOL, PURE ALCOHOL. IT IS NOT EASY TO FIND WHERE I LIVE IN THE NETHERLANDS, WHICH IS WHY I OFTEN REPLACE IT WITH VODKA, GIN OR BRANDY. PAY ATTENTION TO THE ALCOHOL PERCENTAGE: THE HIGHER THE PERCENTAGE THE MORE SUGAR SYRUP OR WATER YOU HAVE TO ADD TO DILUTE IT. IT IS UP TO YOU. SHOULD YOU EVER BE IN A FRENCH SUPERMARKET, TAKE A LOOK AT THE ALCOHOL AISLE: YOU WILL FIND 'ALCOOL DES FRUITS', WHICH IS 40% ALCOHOL > FANTASTIC STUFF TO MAKE LIQUEUR AND IT COSTS NEXT TO NOTHING.

I MAKE LIQUEUR: DISTRIBUTE THE ALCOHOL OVER SEVERAL BOTTLES. HERE I HAVE 1 LITRE (4 CUPS) 40% ALCOHOL, SO I HALVE IT, LEAVING ME WITH TWO BOTTLES AT 20% ALCOHOL.

ADD FLAVOURING TO EACH BOTTLE. IN THIS CASE, ROSEMARY AND TONKA BEAN.

SEAL THE BOTTLES AND ALLOW TO FERMENT IN A DARK PLACE FOR 2 WEEKS.

MAKE SYRUP: DISSOLVE 400 G (2 CUPS) SUGAR IN 250 ML (9 FL OZ/1 CUP) WATER (YOU CAN USE LESS SUGAR).

POUR THE MARINATED ALCOHOL THROUGH A SIEVE OVER A LARGE JUG.

ADD THE SYRUP AND TOP UP TO 1 LITRE (4 CUPS). IMMEDIATELY POUR INTO ATTRACTIVE BOTTLES AND SEAL.

LET'S GET GOING...

SOME LIQUEURS HAVE TO FERMENT FOR A LONG TIME, AND SOME CAN BE SERVED AFTER A DAY OR SO. TO THICKEN A LIQUEUR, ADD A TEASPOON OF GLYCERINE, WHICH IS AVAILABLE FROM THE PHARMACY, BUT IS ABSOLUTELY NOT A MUST. IT WORKS WELL WITHOUT IT TOO.

IN ANY GLASS
AS LONG AS
IT'S SMALL

COFFEE LIQUEUR

Coffee liqueur can be easily made at home and what is great is that you can drink it the same day. It's a drink for those of us who tend to be impatient.

For 1.5 litres (6 cups)
750 g (26 oz/3½ cups) sugar: ½ raw caster (superfine) & ½ granulated sugar
750 ml (25 fl oz/3 cups) water
200 ml (6 fl oz/¾ cup) very strong espresso coffee
seeds and pods of 4 vanilla beans
400 ml (14 fl oz/1⅔ cups) vodka

In a saucepan, bring the sugar, water, coffee and vanilla to a boil. Reduce for nearly 1 hour on a very low heat to a thick syrup. Allow the syrup to slightly cool. Remove the vanilla beans. Careful, they may still be hot! Swiftly add the vodka and stir into a smooth liqueur. Immediately pour through a funnel into bottles and seal. You can strain the liqueur through cheesecloth or a coffee filter if you prefer a clear liqueur.

HAZELNUT LIQUEUR

250 g (8 oz/2 cups) hazelnuts
250 ml (9 fl oz/1 cup) vodka
125 ml (approx. 4 fl oz/⅔ cup) brandy or cognac
seeds and pods of 2 vanilla beans
300 ml (10 fl oz/1¼ cups) water
125 g (4 oz/½ cup) granulated sugar
125 g (4 oz/½ cup) raw caster (superfine) sugar

Coarsely chop the nuts (in the food processor), place in a large preserving jar and cover with the vodka and brandy. Add the vanilla. Leave to stand for 6 weeks (yes, really!). Then strain through a sieve and then again through a coffee filter. Leave to stand for another two days, in order for the last residue to sink and then strain again through a coffee filter. Heat the water with the sugars and briefly boil until the sugar is dissolved. Pour the sugar syrup on the nut drink in a bottle. Leave to cool until used.

VERMOUTH

This is my version of red vermouth. Do try it with white or rosé wine and add more cinnamon, for example, to taste. A tasty recipe that makes 1 litre (4 cups)

juice and rind of ½ grapefruit
zest of 1 orange

1 tsp of: oregano, rosemary, basil, sage and thyme (whatever you have in the house)
4 star anise
1 cinnamon stick
8 juniper berries
4 cloves
pinch of saffron
250 ml (9 fl oz/1 cup) brandy, gin or vodka
sugar: 125 g (4 oz/½ cup) sugar for sweet, 75 g (2½ oz/⅓ cup) for medium dry and 25 g (1 tbsp) for dry vermouth
1 bottle red wine (750 ml/25 fl oz)

Add zests, juice, spices and flavourings to the brandy. Leave to stand for two weeks at room temperature to ferment. Shake the bottle occasionally. After this period, pour the liquid through a coffee filter or fine strainer and add the sugar. Then add the wine. Stir to dissolve the sugar. Pour the vermouth into a 1-litre (4-cup) bottle and shake a little to fully dissolve the sugar. You can drink the vermouth immediately, but the longer you leave it, the more mature the flavour. Serve on lots of ice cubes and garnish with a curly orange peel.

HEY!
I ALWAYS THOUGHT THAT 'VERMOUTH' WAS SPELLED WITH A TEE HA!

VIN DE CAMOMILLE

Camomile wine

1 bottle white wine (750 ml/25 fl oz)
100 g (4 oz) camomile, dried (from the tea store)
200 g (approx. 7 oz/1 cup) sugar
100 ml (approx. 3 fl oz/½ cup) rum
1 vanilla bean

Combine all ingredients and leave to stand in a clean preserving jar in a dark place for 14 days. Shake occasionally. Strain through coffee filter and serve on ice cubes and garnish with a slice of lemon.

CRANBERRY LIQUEUR

500 g (1 lb/3 cups) fresh cranberries
zest of ½ lemon
zest of ½ orange
350 ml (approx. 12 fl oz/1½ cups) vodka
1 cinnamon stick
1 clove
200 ml (6 fl oz/¾ cup) water
350 g (12 oz/1⅔ cups) sugar

Boil the preserving jars for 10 minutes in plenty of water and dry on a clean dish towel. You will need jars with more than 1 litre (4 cups) in volume. Finely chop the cranberries in the food processor. Place in the preserving jars and add the lemon and orange zest. Add the vodka and spices. Bring the water and sugar to a boil. Add the syrup to the jars and immediately close the lids. Leave to ferment in a dark place for 1 month. Shake the jars every

day. Place a cheesecloth or dish towel in a strainer over a large tray or jar. Strain the liquid. Thoroughly wring out the cloth, removing all moisture. If necessary, again pour the liquid through a coffee filter for an attractive clear liqueur. Pour into a clean bottle. It can be drunk immediately, but you can save it for a year.

BAY LIQUEUR

Instead of bay leaves you can also use thyme, rosemary or fresh mint. Very tasty!

500 ml (16 fl oz/2 cups) vodka
30 fresh bay leaves
1 cinnamon stick
zest of 1 lemon
500 ml (16 fl oz/2 cups) water
350 g (12 oz/1⅔ cups) sugar

Combine the vodka, bay leaves, cinnamon and lemon and leave the mixture to ferment in a clean container for two weeks. Bring the water and sugar to a boil and stir until the sugar is dissolved. Strain the bay drink and add the sugar syrup. Pour the liqueur into a bottle and leave to cool.

GINGER BEER

I call this beer (or ginger ale), since you carbonate this drink by adding yeast. It is, however, alcohol-free. And absolutely delicious!

5 cm (2 inch) piece of fresh ginger
juice of 1 lemon
approx. 750 ml (25 fl oz/3 cups) lukewarm water
150 g (5 oz/¾ cup) demarera sugar (or to taste)
¼ tsp yeast
1 clean 1.5-litre (50-fl oz) PET bottle

Grate the ginger into a fine pulp. Add to a bowl and stir in the lemon juice. Add a part of the lukewarm water and stir in the sugar and yeast until slightly dissolved (doesn't have to fully dissolve). Pour the mixture through a funnel into the PET bottle and add water to approx. 5 cm (2 inch) from the top. Leave to stand at room temperature for at least 12 hours or until the bottle feels rock-hard, which means that yeasting has taken place. Otherwise leave it a maximum of 48 hours. Immediately place the bottle in the refrigerator to cool. Be careful when unscrewing the cap! When pouring the drink you can strain it through a tea strainer: most of the pulp will end up in the first two glasses, but it isn't disgusting, you can just drink it.

ELDERBERRY SYRUP

Pick elderberries in late spring. Take scissors and a large basket with you and dive in. Make enough syrup to last you to the following spring: mixed with sparkling water this is the best tasting drink I believe I know.

60 g (2 oz) elderberry blossoms, stems roughly removed
½ lemon, sliced
1 litre (4 cups) water
500 g (1 lb/2¼ cups) sugar

Place the blossom umbels in a tall clean container, add the sliced lemon. Then add the lukewarm water. Slightly press the mixture down in order for the blossoms to be fully immersed in water. Leave to stand for 24 hours in a warm and sunny place. Then strain the liquid over a large pan. Slowly bring to a boil and add the sugar. Keep on stirring until all sugar is dissolved. Skim off and pour through a funnel into sterile jars.
You can keep the syrup in the refrigerator for a few weeks. If you soak the jars for about 30 minutes in a pan of boiling water they will have a shelf life of one year!

LEMONADE

250 g (8 oz/1 cup) sugar
250 ml (9 fl oz/1 cup) water
250 ml (9 fl oz/1 cup) lemon juice (about 4–6 lemons)

Bring the sugar and water to a boil, stir until the sugar is dissolved. Add the lemon juice. Leave to cool. Pour the lemon juice into a large jug and top up with approx. 750 ml (3 cups) cold sparkling water. Garnish with slices of lemon and ice cubes.

BLACKBERRY & THYME SYRUP

You can also make raspberry, strawberry or currant syrup.
I add thyme, but you can also leave it out. Or replace with basil or rosemary.

500 g (1 lb/4 cups) blackberries
juice of 1 lemon
1 small bunch of thyme
500 g (1 lb/2¼ cups) sugar

Wash the berries and stamp them in a large bowl using a masher. You can also blitz them briefly in a food processor. Place the fruit pulp in a large pan, add the lemon juice and thyme and bring to a boil. Leave to simmer for approx. 10 minutes until the fruit is soft. Pour through a strainer over another pan. With the round side of a ladle press out all the juice. Heat the collected juice again and add the sugar. Stir until the sugar is dissolved and skim, if necessary. Pour the syrup into clean bottles.
Make lemonade by pouring a layer into a glass and topping it up with fresh water. Or use in a cocktail.

NUT WINE (BOERENPORT)

This drink is very much like port, hence its second name. The recipe was given to me by a French farmer with whom I had become friendly and who served me this drink. Serve in tall glasses, with or without ice cubes.

You will need raw walnuts. Therefore the first thing you will have to do is find someone with a walnut tree in their garden. Pick the nuts when the hull or shell is still green.

16 raw walnuts, without dents
2 litres (8 cups) reasonable quality red wine
500 ml (16 fl oz/2 cups) cognac
500 g (1 lb/2¼ cups) sugar

Quarter the nuts. Combine with the other ingredients in a sealable bucket or clean preserving jars. Leave to stand at least 3 months. Then pour through a strainer and then through a coffee filter. Pour into clean bottles ready for use.

Verrine –

1/2 litre alcool a 40°
+ Feuilles de Verveine
Laisser Macerer
15 jours.

Sirop 1/4 d'eau
400 g sucre

POMEGRANATE PROSECCO

A great drink to welcome your guests at a party.

approx. 400 ml (14 fl oz/1⅔ cups) pomegranate juice in a carton (or juice of 4 pomegranates, see description)
250 g (8 oz/1 cup) sugar (to taste)
2.5 cm (1 inch) fresh ginger, sliced

And also:
1 bottle prosecco (Italian dry sparkling wine)
1 pomegranate

Make the pomegranate juice: wear an apron, it can get a little messy! Cut the pomegranates into sections and fill half a bowl with water. Separate arils and pulp under water. The bitter white pulp will float to the surface and the arils will sink to the bottom. Remove the pulp and strain the seeds from the water. You can now grind the seeds in a blender and then press the pulp with the round side of a spoon through a sieve over a bowl. If you don't own a blender, you can also push the seeds through the sieve by hand, it will only require a little more effort.

Top up the juice with water to 500 ml (16 fl oz/2 cups) and place on the heat with the sugar and ginger slices. Reduce the syrup by half. Leave to fully cool and remove the ginger.

Before serving,
Pour a coffee spoon (to taste) of pomegranate syrup into an attractive glass. Add prosecco to fill the glass. Garnish the glass with a few loose pomegranate seeds.

CASSIS & VERMOUTH COCKTAIL

Use your own home-made white wine vermouth for a true home-made cocktail.

For 1 glass
1 tsp crème de cassis or black currant syrup, see recipe on page 98
100 ml (approx. 3 fl oz/½ cup) white vermouth
100 ml (approx. 3 fl oz/½ cup) sparkling water
1 slice of lemon

First pour the crème de cassis into the glass, top up with vermouth and sparkling water.
Garnish with a slice of lemon.

CHAMPAGNE & CITRUS PUNCH

For approx. 20 glasses
100 g (approx. 4 oz/½ cup) sugar
100 ml (approx. 3 fl oz/½ cup) water
500 ml (16 fl oz/2 cups) juice: mix of lime, grapefruit and orange
200 ml (6 fl oz/¾ cup) cognac
2 bottles champagne, cava or prosecco (or any dry sparkling wine)
leaves of 1 bunch fresh mint

Make sugar syrup with the sugar and water by heating it in a saucepan and slightly reducing it. Leave to fully cool. Combine with the juices and cognac. Place in the refrigerator until ice-cold. Before serving pour into a large bowl (or a dash into a glass), add a lot of mint leaves and pour plenty of champagne over it.

SAWASDEE KHA

An alcohol-free cocktail, which I named after having had it in Thailand.
For 1 litre (4 cups), or approx. 6 or 7 glasses

1 carton pineapple juice, or 1 litre (4 cups) fresh pineapple juice (1 pineapple)
8 lemongrass stalks
2.5 cm (1 inch) piece of ginger, peeled
8 tbsp watermelon syrup or use grenadine syrup
maraschino cherries for a fancy garnish

Remove the outer leaves from the lemongrass. Cut the core of the lemongrass and the ginger into sections and purée with the pineapple juice in a blender. Then pour through a sieve into a tall jug. Serve the cocktail in tall glasses and pour a tbsp of watermelon syrup onto it. Such a posh alcohol-free drink surely has to be garnished with a cherry!

SAVOURY COCKTAIL NUTS

Make your own cocktail nut mix, so much tastier, since the nuts are freshly toasted. I will give you mine here. Buy unsalted nuts, you can add your own salt and spices.

50 g (approx. 2 oz/⅓ cup) cashew nuts
150 g (5 oz/1 cup) macadamias
150 g (5 oz/1 cup) pumpkin seeds (pepitas)
150 g (5 oz/1 cup) Brazil nuts
150 g (5 oz/1 cup) peanuts
250 g (8 oz/1⅓ cups) raw caster (superfine) sugar
dash chilli powder, to taste
25 g (1 oz/¼ stick) butter
leaves and some sprigs thyme and/or rosemary
pinch of sea salt

Preheat the oven to 175ºC (340°F/Gas 4). Arrange the nuts on a sheet of baking paper on a baking sheet and bake until golden brown and crunchy (approx. 15 minutes), turn over halfway through. Remove from oven but leave the oven on. Heat the sugar and 3 tbsp water in a saucepan, gently shake the pan until all sugar is dissolved. Remove from the heat and stir in the chilli powder, butter, spices and salt. Careful! It will spatter and the sugar gets very hot! Quickly fold in the nuts. Transfer them again to the baking sheet covered with the baking paper. Arrange the nuts so that they do not touch. Bake for a few minutes in the oven until golden brown. Remove from oven and allow to fully cool. Can be kept for at least one week in an airtight tin or canister.

VITELOTTE POTATO CHIPS

Making your own chips (crisps) is extraordinarily simple. Here is the recipe for Vitelotte potato chips, as they look great too. But also try other types of waxy potatoes, or use beetroot, celeriac or parsnip.

6 Vitelotte noir potatoes, washed but not peeled (bluey violet waxy potatoes originally from Peru)
oil for deep-frying
Maldon sea salt or salt flakes

Very thinly slice the potatoes on a mandolin or in the food processor. Pat dry using kitchen paper. This is very important, because if there is too much moisture in the chips there will be unbelievable spattering during frying. Heat the oil to 180°C (350°F). Always deep-fry a handful of potato slices at one time and leave to drain on kitchen paper. Sprinkle with sea salt before serving.

CROSTINI

This is a quick recipe for crostini or just toasts. Carefully select the bread you will be using. Good sourdough bread makes a very different toast from brioche bread. You can vary the spices and garlic or just use nothing at all. From an average baguette you will get approx. 40 thin slices of bread.

200 ml (6 fl oz/¾ cup) olive oil
garlic, oregano, thyme, rosemary, ground paprika as desired or to taste
freshly ground pepper and salt
1 baguette or other bread

Combine the olive oil, salt and pepper and garlic and any other spices. Arrange the bread slices on a baking sheet. Spread with the olive oil mixture. Bake for 5 to 10 minutes in an oven preheated to 180°C (350°F/Gas 4), turn over halfway through. Leave to fully cool before filling. Can be stored for at least one month in an airtight bag.

LAVASH CRACKERS

Make these crackers in large quantities, break into pieces on the table and spoon dips on them. Yummy!

1 g yeast (a pinch between index finger and thumb)
200 g (7 oz/1⅓ cups) plain (all-purpose) flour
pinch of salt
1 tbsp vegetable oil
approx. 125 ml (4 fl oz/⅔ cup) lukewarm water

For the garnish:
poppy seeds, sesame seeds, caraway seeds, ground paprika, cumin seeds, coarse sea salt

Dissolve the yeast in an eggshell full of lukewarm water and combine all ingredients, except the water. Pour the water into the mixture until a pliable dough ball is formed. Pay attention, sometimes you just need a little less water. Knead the dough for at least 10 minutes on a worktop dusted with flour or in a food processor until smooth and silky. Leave to rise for one hour. Roll the dough into a thin sheet (you might have to cut it in half), place on baking paper and then on a greased baking sheet. Lightly cover with water and sprinkle with seeds or salt to garnish. Do this in nice strips, for example. Bake the dough in an oven preheated to 175°C (340°F/Gas 4) for 12–15 minutes or until the crackers turn an even golden brown. Break into equal parts and serve with dips and sauces (see next page).

SPICY ZUCCHINI, RICOTTA & MINT SALAD

4 zucchinis (courgettes)
1 small green capsicum (bell pepper)
dash of olive oil
1–2 garlic cloves, crushed

1 bunch fresh mint
250 g (8 oz/1½ cups) ricotta
juice of ½ lemon

Wash the zucchinis and slice, cut the slices into strips and then into very small cubes. Halve the capsicum and remove its seeds. Cut into thin strips. In a large pan or wok, heat the olive oil and briefly sauté the garlic, otherwise the garlic will turn bitter. Add the zucchini and capsicum and quickly stir. Season with salt and pepper and, when the zucchini is cooked *al dente*, transfer the mixture to a large plate to cool. Wash and finely chop the mint. Add the zucchini and ricotta to a bowl. Stir well and season with lemon juice. Serve the salad on crostini.

113

APRICOT TAPENADE

250 g (8 oz/1⅓ cups) dried apricots, soaked
2 sprigs rosemary
100 ml (approx. 3 fl oz/½ cup) olive oil

juice of ½ lemon
1 garlic clove
freshly ground pepper and salt

Blitz all tapenade ingredients in a food processor. If necessary, add some oil. You can keep the tapenade in the refrigerator for some time. Make sure the tapenade is always covered with a thin layer of oil. This tapenade is great on toast, as is, or with cheese or raw ham.

FIG BUTTER

200 g (7 oz/1 cup) dried figs
1 tsp cinnamon
½ tsp nutmeg

Blitz the dried figs, without the hard stem, in a food processor, add the spices and a pinch of salt. Roll mixture into a round 'pipe' in plastic wrap. Leave to cool in the refrigerator and cut into attractive slices.

BROAD BEAN MINT DIP

500 g (1 lb/2½ cups) broad (fava) beans (frozen)
4 tbsp grated parmesan or pecorino
2 garlic cloves
approx. 100 ml (3 fl oz/½ cup) olive oil
3 tbsp chopped mint

Cook the broad beans for 5 minutes in salted water and drain. Pod again, leaving you with nice bright green beans. Grind in a vegetable chopper with the other ingredients into a coarse pesto.

SARDINE SALAD

2 x 125 g (4 oz) tins sardines
2 tomatoes, seeds and skin removed, cubed
75 ml (2½ fl oz/⅓ cup) mayonnaise, page 380
50 ml (1½ fl oz/¼ cup) sour cream
few sprigs of parsley, chopped
few drops of lemon juice

Drain the sardines and remove the bones. Combine the fish meat and the other ingredients, season generously with pepper and a pinch of salt.

GRILLED SOFT PEPPERS FILLED WITH GOAT'S CHEESE, PRESERVED IN OLIVE OIL

Cut into thick slices these are delicious snacks with a drink. Dip the bread in the remaining oil.

6 green, orange and/or red pointed peppers (sweet peppers, available from Turkish stores and supermarkets)
250 g (8 oz/1½ cups) soft goat's cheese
2 tbsp parsley, finely chopped
2 tbsp fresh oregano, finely chopped and a few sprigs for the jar
freshly ground black pepper
generous amount of high-quality olive oil, approx. 1 litre (4 cups)
3 dried peppers, or more if you love them
a few garlic cloves, peeled and blanched for 10 minutes
clean sealable jar, approx. 1 litre (4 cups)

Place a grill pan on the heat. Put the peppers in it and regularly turn them over until cooked. This is a relatively fast process and takes approx. 10 minutes. Leave to cool. Trim away the stems and remove the seeds and membrane from the peppers using a sharp knife. Combine the goat's cheese, parsley and oregano, cover generously with black pepper. Fill the peppers with the cheese using a small spoon. Wash your hands in between so that the peppers stay clean on the outside. Fill a tall preserving jar with the peppers and cover them with olive oil. Add the dried peppers, garlic and a few sprigs of oregano, which will sink to the bottom.
These can be kept for more than a week or two. The flavour will become increasingly spicy.

BLACK OLIVE MINI BLINIS WITH PINK MASCARPONE, SALMON AND PRESERVED BEETROOT

You will want to make these snacks simply because they look so good. Don't you agree?

For the blini batter
100 g (4 oz/¾ cup) pitted black olives
50 g (2 oz/⅓ cup) buckwheat flour (organic store)
50 g (approx. 2 oz/⅓ cup) plain (all-purpose) flour
1 egg
1 sachet dried yeast (7 g/¼ oz/2¼ tsp)
250 ml (9 fl oz/1 cup) lukewarm semi-skim milk

For the filling
1 small beetroot (beet), parboiled
100 ml (approx. 3 fl oz/½ cup) raspberry vinegar
1 tbsp honey
100 g (4 oz/⅓ cup + 1 tbsp) mascarpone
100 g (4 oz) smoked salmon

And also:
butter or oil for frying

Grind the olives in a food processor. Add all of the flours, egg and yeast. Fold in the milk in a trickle while stirring. Add a pinch of salt. Cover the batter with plastic wrap and leave to rise for 1 hour in a warm place.
Cut or slice the beetroot in very fine slices. Collect the red juice, by cutting it over a bowl. Combine the vinegar and honey, season with salt and pepper and pour over the beetroot slices. Set aside.
Stir the collected red juice into the mascarpone and season the cream with salt and pepper. Heat a pancake griddle, butter the cavities and pour a spoonful of batter into each cavity. If you don't own a pancake griddle you can also pour small spoonfuls into a shallow frying pan. You may find it easiest with a squeeze bottle if you have one available. Cook until slightly risen and done in a few minutes.
Cover the blinis with a layer of pink cream, a slice of salmon and a slice of beetroot.

DRUNKEN AVOCADO SOUP SHOT

A small shot of soup (hot or cold) is often a fun change of pace, whenever you serve several different snacks. It is also a good way to get rid of leftover soup. Make sure to season regular soup (the one from last night), as such a small glass has to make an impression!

For 6–8 small shot glasses
2 ripe avocados, quartered, peeled and pitted
75 ml (2½ fl oz/⅓ cup) milk
250 ml (9 fl oz/1 cup) chicken stock
juice of ½ lemon
1 diced shallot
1 tsp Tabasco sauce, to taste
1–2 tbsp good quality sherry
2 tbsp sour cream, slightly beaten
some chive sprigs, finely chopped
pinch of ground paprika

Place the avocados in a blender or food processor and purée with the milk and stock, lemon juice, shallot, Tabasco and sherry. Taste to check if it needs more salt and pepper and place the soup in the refrigerator to fully cool for at least 4 hours. Serve in small shot glasses topped with a teaspoon sour cream, plenty of chives and ground paprika.

SMALL CHESTNUT SOUP

This recipe is for approx. 6 shot glasses. If you want to make it as a main course serving four, double the quantities and dilute with stock to the desired consistency.

75 g (2½ oz) chestnuts, vacuum-packed: peeled and cooked (delicatessens, but these days maybe also in the supermarket)
75 ml (2½ fl oz/⅓ cup) white vermouth
150 ml (5 fl oz/⅔ cup) thick cream
150 ml (5 fl oz/⅔ cup) chicken stock
2–3 small chestnut mushrooms
2 tbsp olive oil, for frying
freshly ground pepper and salt
few drops of hazelnut oil

Cook the chestnuts for approx. 15 minutes in the vermouth, cream and stock. Purée the soup until smooth and add salt and pepper, to taste. Leave to fully cool in the refrigerator. If too thick add a little water.
Before serving, thinly slice the mushrooms and briefly fry in a little olive oil in a non-stick pan. Leave to drain on kitchen paper. Pour the cold chestnut soup into small shot glasses. Place a mushroom on each glass as well as a drop of nut oil.

POLENTA BISCUITS WITH SAGE, GOAT'S CHEESE & PARMA HAM

For at least 20 biscuits

approx. 750 ml (25 fl oz/3 cups) water

salt

150 g (5 oz/¾ cup) polenta

60 g (2 oz/½ stick) butter

350 g (12 oz/3 cups) goat's cheese, crumbled

75 g (2½ oz) Parma ham, finely chopped

few sage sprigs, finely chopped

Bring the water to a boil with a generous pinch of salt and trickle in the polenta while stirring. Lower the heat and leave the polenta to simmer for 30 minutes. Lastly, stir in the butter, goat's cheese, ham and sage and melt the butter and cheese. Pour the polenta on a baking sheet to cool. If you own a mini muffin tray, you can also fill these moulds. Leave to fully cool for a couple of hours. Cut out rounds using a cutter. Preheat the grill to 180ºC (350°F/Gas 4) and grill the polenta biscuits for 10 minutes until golden. Serve immediately.

POLENTA MUFFINS FILLED WITH SALMON IN CHAMPAGNE AND PUMPKIN PICKLES

For 24 mini muffins

100 g (approx. 4 oz/⅔ cup) self-raising flour

2 tbsp cornflour (cornstarch)

½ tsp baking powder

80 g (approx. 2½ oz/½ cup) polenta

1½ tbsp sugar

175 ml (approx. 6 fl oz/¾ cup) milk

1 egg

25 g (approx. 4 teaspoons) melted butter

250 g (8 oz) nice raw salmon

1 glass champagne or prosecco (dry sparkling wine)

approx. 6 tbsp pumpkin pickles, recipe on page 162

and a mini muffin tray

Place the salmon in a bowl and cover with the champagne, sprinkle with salt and pepper. Cover with foil and place in the refrigerator until used.

Beat the muffin ingredients into a batter, lumps are allowed. Grease the muffin moulds with baking spray or oil and bake the polenta muffins in an oven preheated to 180°C (350°F/Gas 4) for 12 minutes until golden brown. Leave to cool. Cut the salmon into thin slices. Make a deep incision in the polenta muffins and top with a slice of salmon and some pumpkin pickles, serve immediately.

CRAB CAKES WITH FRESH LEMON AND TOMATO MAYONNAISE

For the crab cakes

1 tbsp butter

1 onion, chopped

2 stalks blanched celery, cleaned and finely chopped

1 small tin of crab (approx. 170 g/4 oz)

200 g (approx. 7 oz/2 cups) fresh or dry breadcrumbs, but fresh ones taste much better

125 g (4 oz/½ cup) crème fraîche

few sprigs chives, finely chopped

1 egg

light oil for frying

For the mayo

1 egg yolk

juice and rind of 1 lemon

1 tbsp spicy mustard

sufficient sunflower or maize oil (approx. 500 ml/16 fl oz/2 cups)

2 tomatoes, seeds removed and peel cubed

pinch cayenne pepper

Melt the butter in a frying pan, add the onion and celery while stirring for approx. 4 minutes.
Leave to slightly cool on a plate. Open the crab tin, drain and shred. Blend with the onion-celery mix from the pan, half of the breadcrumbs (from old bread in the food processor), the crème fraîche, the chives and the egg. Season the mixture with salt and pepper. Roll into approx. 12 small balls. Slightly flatten and dip in remaining breadcrumbs.
Heat a thin layer of oil in a non-stick frying pan. Fry the cakes on both sides until golden brown. Drain on kitchen paper.
Make the mayonnaise: in the food processor beat the egg yolk, lemon juice, rind and mustard into a foamy mixture. Add the oil in a thin trickle until it becomes a thick mayonnaise. Briefly pulse the tomato cubes and season with cayenne pepper and salt. Serve with the cakes.

LAMB BALLS WITH SESAME & CORIANDER SALSA

For 30 balls

1 kg (2 lb) lamb mince (ground lamb)

1 egg

3 tbsp ground cumin

2 tbsp cinnamon

2 tbsp ground paprika

2 tbsp mustard

3 tbsp soy sauce

100 g (approx. 4 oz/⅓ cup) sesame seeds

and a little oil to grease the baking sheet

For the coriander salsa

1 large bunch coriander (cilantro), at least 70 g (2½ oz)

1 red onion

1 garlic clove

2 tbsp white wine vinegar

1 generous tbsp honey

5 tbsp olive oil

Preheat the oven to 175ºC (340°F/Gas 4). Combine the mince with all spices and flavourings and roll into approx. 30 balls, each the size of a walnut. Slightly grease a baking sheet with olive oil. Pour the sesame seeds into a plate and roll a few balls at the same time through the seeds until all balls end up coated with a layer of seeds. Arrange on the baking sheet and bake in the oven until done (approx. 20 minutes). Pulse all ingredients for the salsa on the pulse setting on the food processor to coarsely chop the mixture. Season the salsa with salt and pepper. Serve with the hot balls.

SHISH KEBAB WITH YOGHURT SAUCE

For the marinade

1 tbsp cumin seeds

juice and zest of 2 limes

fresh ginger the length of a thumb, peeled and thinly sliced

1 tbsp ginger syrup

1 tbsp tamarind (Toko)

3 tbsp olive oil

1 tsp ground cumin

1 garlic clove, crushed

For the yoghurt dip

200 g (7 oz/¾ cup) yoghurt

2 spring onions (scallions), finely chopped

1 red capsicum (bell pepper), cut lengthways with seeds removed

And also:

400 g (14 oz) beef steak, cut into long strips

8 wooden skewers, soaked in water for 30 minutes

or metal skewers

Briefly roast the cumin seeds in a frying pan until they release an aroma. Blend with the other ingredients for the marinade and add the steak. Leave to marinate for 3 hours. In the meantime make the yoghurt dip by combining the ingredients in a bowl. Set aside. Skewer the steak strips, in and out, like a simple basting stitch, if you like. Heat a grill pan until it smokes. Sauté the steak on both sides on high heat: it can still be a little red on the inside. Serve with the yoghurt dip.

Soup, yesssss! Soup is good.
There is a soup for every weather…
Soup can make me intensely happy. The richer the better. But…is this actually the case?
I can't say no to a bowl of hot veal broth with fresh chervil and a poached egg either.

George

MAKING STOCK

ALL SOUPS ARE MADE ON THE BASIS OF A GOOD STOCK OR BROTH.
IN OUR RESTAURANT A PAN OF STOCK CAN ALWAYS BE FOUND ON THE STOVE. IN YOUR HOUSE THIS IS NOT ALWAYS THE CASE, BUT IT IS WORTHWHILE TO MAKE A PAN EVERY ONCE IN A WHILE. LEFTOVERS CAN ALWAYS BE FROZEN.
STOCK ENSURES THAT EVEN THE SIMPLEST OF SOUPS HAS MORE DEPTH, AND THEREFORE MORE FLAVOUR. HERE I'M MAKING A VEAL STOCK IN OUR RESTAURANT KITCHEN TOGETHER WITH SOPHIE. FOR A RICH COLOUR, WE FIRST ROAST THE BONES BEFORE MAKING THE STOCK.

ARRANGE ON A BAKING SHEET: VEAL BONES AND SHANKS, THYME, BAY, GARLIC, ONIONS WITH PEEL & TRICKLE SOME OIL OVER THE BAKING SHEET.

MIX THOROUGHLY.

PLACE IN AN OVEN PREHEATED TO 180C (350F / GAS 4). BAKE THE BONES UNTIL GOLDEN BROWN. (APPROX. 45 MINUTES).

REMOVE FROM THE OVEN.

TRANSFER THE CONTENTS OF THE OVEN TRAY TO A LARGE PAN.

WASH THE VEGETABLES: BLANCHED CELERY, LEEKS, CARROTS AND PARSLEY. PREPARE THE SPICES: MACE, PEPPER-CORNS, CORIANDER SEED.

ADD ALL THE INGREDIENTS TO THE BONES IN THE PAN AND TOP UP THE PAN WITH WATER.

COVER THE PAN LEAVING THE LID AJAR AND ALLOW THE SOUP TO SIMMER ON LOW HEAT FOR AT LEAST 90 MINS.

OCCASIONALLY SKIM THE TOP OFF THE STOCK.

PLACE A COLANDER OR STRAINER ON ANOTHER PAN AND COVER WITH A CLEAN DISH TOWEL.

STRAIN THE PAN CONTENTS.

VOILA! A CLEAR STOCK WHICH YOU CAN NOW SEASON WITH A LITTLE SALT AND A DASH OF SOY SAUCE OR WORCESTER-SHIRE SAUCE.

LET'S GET GOING...

I WILL INCLUDE A NUMBER OF STOCKS, ENABLING YOU TO MAKE ANY KIND OF SOUP. ONCE YOU HAVE ACQUIRED A TASTE FOR IT, YOU CAN ALSO TAKE IT FURTHER: REPLACE THE VEAL STOCK WITH GAME CARCASSES FOR GAME STOCK. REPLACE THE BOILER WITH THE CARCASSES OF PHEASANT, PIGEON OR PARTRIDGE FOR A GAME BIRD STOCK. REPLACE THE VEGETABLES IN VEGETABLE STOCK WITH DRIED AND FRESH MUSHROOMS FOR MUSHROOM STOCK. ADD SPICES, TO TASTE.

VEAL STOCK

I will give you the recipe for approx. 6–8 servings of the stock I described on the previous page. You can also use beef bones, turning it into a beef stock.

500 g (1 lb) veal bones (ask the butcher)
2 veal shanks
2 onions, with peel, halved
1 small bunch of thyme
a few bay leaves
a few garlic cloves, unpeeled
4–5 tbsp olive oil
1 stalk blanched celery, cut in three sections
2 leeks, in coarse rounds
1 carrot, scraped and roughly sliced
1 small bunch of parsley
3–4 blades mace
1 tbsp black peppercorns
2 tbsp coriander seeds
and also 2 bunches chervil, chopped

Place the bones, shanks, onions, thyme, bay and garlic in a roasting tin. Pour over a little oil and stir. Place in an oven preheated to 180°C (350°F/Gas 4) until the bones start to colour (about 30 minutes). Transfer to a large soup pan. Add at least 4 litres (16 cups) of water as well as the remaining ingredients. Bring the liquid to a boil. Lower the heat once it boils and leave the stock to simmer on low heat. During this time, carefully skim the foam from the stock using a skimmer.

If you don't do this, the stock will become cloudy. Simmer on very low heat for approx. 3 hours until reduced by half. Strain the stock or pour through a colander in which you have placed a clean(!) dish towel. Leave to cool. Place the stock in the refrigerator. As soon as it is very cold, skim off the solidified fat. Season the stock with salt and pepper.

CHICKEN STOCK

This recipe is for a good-sized pan. I will just assume that you will make a little extra for the freezer. Should you wish to make less, use chicken legs and halve the ingredients.

1 whole boiler (stewing chicken suitable for casseroles)
2 onions, with peel, halved: insert 4 cloves in the onions
½ stalk blanched celery, cut in three sections
2 leeks, roughly cut and washed
1 carrot, scraped and roughly sliced
3 garlic cloves, unpeeled
3 bay leaves
1 small bunch of parsley and thyme
1 tbsp black peppercorns
2 tbsp coriander seeds
3–4 blades mace

Combine ingredients in the largest pan you can find. Add at least 5–6 litres (20–24 cups) cold water and bring the liquid to a boil. Then lower the heat

and allow the stock to simmer. During this time, carefully skim the foam from the surface. Reduce the stock by half on very low heat for approx. 3 hours. Strain or pour through a colander in which you have placed a clean(!) dish towel. Leave to cool. Place the stock in the refrigerator. Skim off the solidified fat, as soon as it is very cold. Season the stock with salt and pepper.

FISH STOCK

approx. 1½ kg (3 lb) fish bones
2 onions, with peel, halved
½ stalk blanched celery, cut into three sections
1 bulb fennel, quartered
1 leek, roughly cut and washed
1 carrot, scraped and roughly sliced
3 garlic cloves, unpeeled
1 bay leaf
1 small bunch of parsley, dill and thyme
1 tbsp black peppercorns
2 tbsp coriander seeds
3–4 blades mace
½ bottle white wine
if desired, a dash of Pernod

Combine ingredients in the largest pan you can find. Add at least 5–6 litres

(20–24 cups) cold water and bring the liquid to a boil. Then lower the heat and allow the stock to simmer. During this time, carefully skim the foam from the surface. If you don't do this, the stock will become cloudy.

Reduce by half on very low heat for approx. 3 hours. Strain the stock or pour through a colander in which you have placed a clean(!) dish towel. Season the stock with salt and pepper. I personally like to add a dash of Pernod.

VEGETABLE STOCK

If they are available I also sometimes add turnips to the stock. The more vegetables, the better, actually.

2 onions, with peel, halved: insert
4 cloves in the onions
1 celeriac, peeled and cubed
1 stalk blanched celery, cut into three sections
2 leeks, roughly cut and washed
3 carrots, scraped and roughly sliced
6 garlic cloves, unpeeled
3 bay leaves
1 small bunch of parsley, rosemary and thyme
1 tbsp black peppercorns
2 tbsp coriander seeds
3–4 blades of mace

Combine ingredients in the largest pan you can find. Add at least 5–6 litres (20–24 cups) cold water and bring the liquid to a boil. Then lower the heat and allow the stock to simmer. During this time, carefully skim the foam from the surface. If you don't do this, the stock will become cloudy. Reduce to half on very low heat for

approx. 2 hours. Strain the stock or pour through a colander in which you have placed a clean(!) dish towel. Leave to cool. Season the stock well with salt and pepper

BISQUE À MA FACON

Bisque is one of the tastiest soups ever. It involves a lot of work, but with a bit of humour you will get through it. Do not use fresh lobster. You can find excellent frozen lobsters which you can use to make soup. If you can't find lobster, use prawn (shrimp) shells, which also work well.

approx. 1 kg (2 lb) frozen lobster/s
4 shallots, chopped
1 leek, in rounds
6 garlic cloves, crushed
1 carrot, scraped and cubed
1 celeriac, peeled and cubed
3 bay leaves
few sprigs of thyme
few sprigs of rosemary
2 tbsp fennel
2 tbsp tomato purée
200 ml (6 fl oz/¾ cup) cognac
½ bottle white vermouth (Noilly Prat)
3 litres (12 cups) rich fish stock
200 g (8 oz/2 sticks) chilled butter
cayenne pepper, to taste
1 tsp ground paprika
salt and freshly ground pepper

If raw, briefly cook the lobster(s) in a large pan with water and salt. Bring the water to a boil, add the lobsters and when the water boils again, remove the lobsters. Leave to cool and remove the tail and claws from the shell. Remove the gills from the lobster, remove the meat from the tail and claws. Set aside the meat in the refrigerator and crush the remaining shell as finely as possible. I do it first with a pestle and then in the food processor. You do need a good food processor with a strong motor. Keep the appliance steady during the grinding process! Your workplace will certainly not stay clean, but you have to remember that it will be quickly tidied up.

Sauté the crushed shells in a dab of butter in a large pan. Add the vegetables, spices, seasonings and tomato purée. Stir while frying and add cognac and vermouth. Slightly reduce the liquid. Pour in the fish stock and leave the soup to simmer on low heat for 2 hours. Do not boil, since it will make the soup bitter.

Strain the soup through a fine sieve. Return to the pan and again bring it close to a boil. Cut the chilled butter into cubes and fold the cubes into the bisque one by one. Season with cayenne pepper, paprika, salt and possibly some freshly ground pepper. Cut the lobster meat into small chunks and stir into the soup. Briefly heat and serve immediately.

129

CREAMY CELERIAC & SAFFRON SOUP

1 onion, diced
2 tbsp olive oil
1 celeriac, cleaned and cubed
few strands of saffron
dash of white wine (approx. 75 ml/2½ fl oz/⅓ cup)
1.5 litres (6 cups) chicken or vegetable stock
200 g (7 oz/¾ cup) crème fraîche
hazelnut or walnut oil

Sauté the onion in the olive oil in a heavy-based pan. Add the celeriac and saffron, stirring occasionally. Add the white wine and stock. Allow the mixture to simmer for 25 minutes, until the celeriac is cooked. Purée the soup until smooth using a hand blender.
Fold in the crème fraîche and season the soup with salt and pepper. Reduce until it slightly thickens. Pour into attractive bowls and top with a little hazelnut or walnut oil.

TIP FOR A CHANGE:

Leave the soup to fully cool and place in the refrigerator until ice-cold. Serve cold (with drinks, for example) in small shot glasses topped with a drop of quality oil.

RED CAPSICUM SOUP WITH ORANGE AND TARRAGON-BASIL OIL

This soup can be served hot in the winter or cold in the summer.

For the soup

4 red capsicums (bell peppers)

3 tbsp olive oil

1 large onion, diced

3 garlic cloves, crushed

1 tin of peeled tomatoes (400 g/14 oz)

400 ml (14 fl oz/1⅔ cups) chicken or vegetable stock

zest and juice of 1 orange

salt and freshly ground pepper

For the tarragon-basil oil

1 bunch basil

1 bunch tarragon

sea salt, to taste

150 ml (5 fl oz/⅔ cup) extra virgin olive oil

If you have a gas cooker, light the burners. Lay the capsicums on the burners and scorch the capsicums until black. Turn regularly. If you do not own a gas cooker, it can also be done under the grill. Place the blackened capsicums in a plastic bag and seal. In the meantime, put a pan on the heat. Heat the olive oil and sauté the onion. Then add the garlic and tomatoes. Pour in the stock and simmer for at least 30 minutes. Remove the capsicums from the bag and peel off the skin. This is easier under running water. Remove the seeds and cut the pulp into large sections. Add to the soup in the pan and briefly purée the mixture using a hand blender. Fold in the zest and orange juice.

Taste! Season with salt and pepper.

Leave the soup to fully cool for a warm summer eve or serve hot topped with a few drops of herb oil.

For the oil, crush the spices and salt in a mortar. Carefully add the oil and stir with the pestle into an attractive dark green oil.

CHUNKY CHOWDER

This typical main course soup from New England is one of my favourites: a rich, creamy soup with large chunks of fish, potato, corn, strips of raw or cooked ham and a lot of fresh thyme and parsley.

250 g (8 oz) raw or cooked ham, in thick slices and then cut into strips
2 tbsp butter
2 onions, diced
1 tbsp fresh thyme sprigs
2 bay leaves
4 potatoes, peeled and diced
1 litre (4 cups) fish stock
2 corn cobs
1 kg (2 lb) cod fillet or other white fish
250 ml (9 fl oz/1 cup) cream
bunch of flat-leaf parsley, washed and chopped

Heat a large heavy-based pan and fry the ham in a spoonful of butter until golden brown. Remove from the pan and set aside. Then sauté the onion, thyme and bay leaves in the remaining fat until glassy but not brown. Add the potatoes, and fry briefly. Pour in the stock. The potatoes should be under water, if this is not the case, add some extra stock. Cut the corn kernels away from the cobs and add them to the stock. Parboil the potatoes for approx. 10 minutes. Stir the pan in order for some cubes to break and others not. The soup must be thick, but have texture. Season the chowder well with salt and pepper. Make sure it is very well seasoned as when the fish is added it's best not to stir the stock much. Add the fish and ham.

Cook for approx. 5 minutes. Remove from the heat and leave the soup to stand for 10 minutes. Stir in the cream and taste to check whether it needs more salt or pepper.

Leave the chowder to stand for at least one hour. You can also store the soup in the refrigerator until the following day. Gently heat before serving, but do not boil. First scoop chunks of fish and potato into the bowl and then top with the creamy soup. Generously sprinkle with parsley. Serve with crusty bread.

HOT CUCUMBER SOUP WITH DEEP-FRIED PARSLEY

You can make this soup in advance, since it first has to be chilled, allowing for the flavours to fully develop. It is, for that matter, particularly tasty when topped with small pieces of smoked eel before serving.

1.5 litres (6 cups) vegetable stock
2 potatoes, peeled and cubed
1 onion, peeled and chopped
3 stalks of blanched celery, cleaned and chopped
1 bay leaf, few thyme sprigs, tied together
2 cucumbers, in coarse chunks
100 ml (approx. 3 fl oz/½ cup) thick cream
100 ml (approx. 3 fl oz/½ cup) milk

And also:
1 bunch parsley
oil for frying

Heat the vegetable stock and add the potatoes, onion, celery, bay and thyme. Leave to simmer for 20 minutes or until the vegetables are cooked. Remove the thyme and bay. Add the cucumbers and cook for a few minutes. Purée the soup using a hand blender. Add the cream and taste, adjust seasoning, if necessary. Leave the soup to cool until used.
Briefly deep-fry the parsley in hot oil and drain on kitchen paper. Careful! It will splatter quite a lot.
Heat the soup close to boiling point, but do not boil, add the milk and beat the soup with a hand blender. Pour into bowls and serve immediately, topped with the parsley.

SUMMER MINESTRONE FROM YOUR OWN GARDEN

I used to have a vegetable garden and in the summer we had so many vegetables that I was at my wit's end as to what to do with them. Into the soup they went. You can use anything you have on hand. And since it is great if all the vegetables remain crunchy, this soup is actually ready in a jiffy. Excellent soup!

3–4 tbsp olive oil
1 onion, peeled and chopped
3 garlic cloves, finely chopped
500–750 g (16–26 oz) vegetables from your vegetable garden, from the greengrocer or even frozen (just don't tell!): garden peas, broad (fava) beans, broccoli florets, marrowfat peas, zucchini (courgette) and capsicum (bell pepper), cubed
2 x 400 g (14 oz) tins diced tomato
1 litre (4 cups) chicken or vegetable stock, heated
250 g (8 oz) small pasta: mini penne, ditalini (small tubes), conchigliette (small shells), rotelline (small cartwheels)
1 tin cannellini beans or white beans (approx. 400 g/14 oz, or fresh from the garden, of course!)
If desired, a piece of parmesan cheese to grate over the soup

Heat the oil in a large pan and sauté the onions until light brown. Add the garlic. Then add all the vegetables that require some cooking, such as broccoli, capsicum and zucchini, fry briefly and add the tomato.
Allow to fry for approx. 5 minutes and cover with the (hot) stock and pasta. Simmer the soup for 10–12 minutes leaving the lid slightly open. Add the smaller vegetables. Roughly mash the cannellini beans, leaving some of them puréed, and some whole. Add to the soup. Briefly heat the soup and allow to slightly thicken. Add salt and pepper to taste.

Serve the minestrone in large bowls and top with grated parmesan cheese, if desired. Serve with country bread and tasty olive oil for dipping

CREAMY CAULIFLOWER SOUP WITH STILTON

Velvety cauliflower soup, with melted Stilton. I find cauliflower to be such an undervalued vegetable, you really should start eating it more often; it is especially worthwhile in soup. It also easily purées.
Serve topped with garlic crostini, on which a little Stilton combined with crème fraîche is melted.

1 onion, diced
2 stalks blanched celery, peeled and chopped
250 g (8 oz) cauliflower, cut into florets
3 tbsp butter
500 ml (16 fl oz/2 cups) veal or chicken stock
250 ml (9 fl oz/1 cup) milk, reserve 2 tbsp
1 tbsp cornflour (cornstarch)
75 g (2½ oz) Stilton, crumbled
125 ml (approx. 4 fl oz/⅔ cup) cream

For the crostini
1 ciabatta (Italian white loaf)
100 ml (approx. 3 fl oz/½ cup) olive oil
1 garlic clove, crushed
50 g (approx. 2 oz) Stilton
3 tbsp crème fraîche

Fry the onion, celery and cauliflower on low heat in the butter until the celery and onion are soft, (approx. 10 minutes). Add the stock and milk and simmer for approx. 20 minutes on low heat until the cauliflower is fully cooked. Purée the soup until smooth using a hand blender. Combine the cornflour with the reserved milk, add to the soup and briefly bring to the boil. Leave to cook for a few minutes, slightly thickening the soup. Turn down the heat, fold in the Stilton and then the cream. Leave to simmer on low heat until the cheese has melted.
Season the soup with salt and pepper.
Meanwhile, make the crostini: using a sharp knife, cut the bread into thin slices. Careful, the bread breaks easily. Preheat the oven to 180°C (350°F/Gas 4). Combine the oil and garlic and add generous amounts of salt and pepper. Heat in the microwave for 1 minute, or in a saucepan, allowing the garlic to infuse the oil and pour over bread slices. Carefully mix until all slices have absorbed some of the oil. Arrange the bread slices on an oven rack. Bake a few minutes until light brown and remove from the oven to slightly cool.
Put the oven on the grill setting. Crumble the Stilton and the crème fraîche. Stir thoroughly and place a tablespoon of mixture on each bread slice. Put briefly under the grill. Place one or two crostini with melted cheese on each bowl and serve immediately.

SWEET POTATO SOUP WITH BUTTERED CASHEWS

1 onion, diced

2 leeks, washed and cut into rounds

3 sweet potatoes, peeled and cubed

2 garlic cloves, chopped

dab of butter

1 glass white wine

1 litre (4 cups) veal or chicken stock

1 bay leaf

pinch of cayenne pepper, to taste

1 tin chickpeas, 400 g (14 oz)

few sprigs fresh oregano

Before serving

4 tbsp cashew nuts

25 g (1 oz/5 tsp) butter

sea salt

for each bowl, 1 tbsp crème fraîche

Braise the onion, leek, potato and garlic in the butter and add the white wine. Blend in the stock as well as the bay and cayenne pepper. Leave to simmer on low heat for 25 minutes. Remove half of the vegetables from the pan and purée the other half with a hand blender. Replace the removed vegetable and add the chickpeas and a few leaves of fresh oregano. Serve the soup in individual large bowls each with 1 tbsp cashew nuts briefly fried in the butter and sprinkled with a little sea salt and a generous dollop of crème fraîche.

Italian bread soup

This is my all-time favourite soup. The recipe was given to me by my friend Claartje and I still make it often. This is the basic recipe, just add whatever you have available or leave it as it is.

→ Use high-quality olive oil ←

Sauté 1 onion, add 1 garlic clove, freshly crushed, in plenty of olive oil until soft.

2 x 400 g (14 oz) cans of peeled tomatoes, a dash of vegetable stock or broth, chilli to taste & 2 handfuls of old bread, cut into coarse chunks.

Leave to gently simmer for **30** mins.

Add 1 zucchini (courgette), cubed. Leave to cook for a further 10 minutes. And add salt & pepper to taste. Serve in large bowls splashed with olive oil.

mamma mia!

CREAMY JERUSALEM ARTICHOKE SOUP WITH FRIED PARSNIP AND MUSHROOMS

I make delicious Jerusalem artichoke soup, velvety smooth, even if I say so myself. Briefly sauté the sliced artichoke with garlic, salt and pepper as well as sliced mushrooms. Serve on the soup.

1 kg (2 lb) Jerusalem artichokes
juice of ½ lemon
3 tbsp olive oil
2 shallots, diced
200 ml (6 fl oz/¾ cup) white wine
800 ml (27 fl oz/3⅓ cups) chicken or vegetable stock
125 ml (approx. 4 fl oz/⅔ cup) cream
1 parsnip
25 g (1 oz/5 tsp) butter
150 g (5 oz/1⅔ cups) mixed forest mushrooms, torn into strips
freshly ground pepper and salt

Peel the artichoke, cut in equal slices and add the lemon juice to prevent discolouration. Heat a little oil in a large pan. Sauté the shallots, add the artichoke, fry briefly and add the white wine. Slightly reduce and add the stock. Allow to simmer on low heat until the artichoke is cooked. Purée the soup until smooth using a hand blender. Add the cream and stir well. Peel the parsnip and cut into thin slices. Heat the butter and reserved olive oil in an non-stick pan and sauté the parsnip and mushroom slices on both sides until crunchy. Generously add fresh salt and pepper. Pour the soup into bowls, top with the parsnip and mushrooms.

FAST BOUILLABAISSE

Look, I understand that real bisque is much tastier, but sometimes you just don't have the time or you don't feel like making it. This recipe provides a solution. Made in no time at all and, honestly, almost as good!

1 onion, diced
2 garlic cloves, crushed
1 fennel root, cleaned and diced
3 tbsp olive oil
1 small tin tomato purée (170 g/6 oz)
a few strands saffron
100 ml (approx. 3 fl oz/½ cup) Pernod (cognac is also good, for that matter)
1 litre (4 cups) fish stock (home-made is obviously always best, but as this soup is called 'fast', bought stock is fine)
1 kg (2 lb) fish (any white fish will do)
1 handful of mussels, cockles and prawns (ask the fishmonger for a mixture)

And also:
1 baguette (preferably a little stale)
2 garlic cloves, crushed
4 tbsp mayonnaise
2 tsp harissa or otherwise 1 tbsp tomato sauce (ketchup) and a pinch of cayenne pepper, to taste

Braise the onion, garlic and fennel briefly in the olive oil until the onion turns glassy. Add the tomato puree and saffron. Keep stirring until the tomato puree begins giving off a sweetish aroma. Add the Pernod and the fish stock and leave to simmer for 20 minutes. Five minutes before the end add the fish and cook in the soup until done.

In the meantime, make the 'rouille' and the croutons. Preheat the oven to 180°C (350°F/Gas 4). Cut the baguette into thin slices, arrange on a baking sheet. Bake the croutons until golden brown, (approx. 5–6 minutes). Turn them over halfway through the process.

Grind approx. 6 croutons in the food processor. Fold in the garlic, mayonnaise and harissa and blend into a smooth sauce. First transfer the fish from the soup into 4 bowls and then cover with the soup. Serve with the rouille and the croutons.

FOAMY GARDEN PEA SOUP WITH BASIL AND AVOCADO CREAM

300 g (10 oz/2 cups) organic garden peas, frozen, but preferably fresh!
1 litre (4 cups) chicken or vegetable stock
2 to 3 spring onions (scallions), cleaned and chopped
1 bunch of basil
1 avocado
1 small garlic clove, crushed
125 g (4 oz/½ cup) crème fraîche

Cook the garden peas with the stock. Simmer for 15 minutes. Add the spring onion and half of the basil. Purée the soup for approx. 6 minutes using a hand blender. Continue until the soup is nice and smooth. Purée the avocado and the garlic and the reserved basil in a food processor. Reserve a few basil leaves to garnish. Fold in the crème fraîche and season the avocado cream with salt and pepper. Transfer the soup to four plates. With an ice cream scoop place a dollop of avocado cream in the middle of each plate and garnish with torn basil leaves.

IRISH OYSTER SOUP WITH MUSSELS AND SAMPHIRE

Ah, as a true Irish woman I didn't want to keep an oyster soup recipe from you.
I also add mussels, but you can leave them out and add an entire crate of oysters, if you wish.
Eat the soup on St Patrick's Day, but actually any other day will do too.

2 shallots, chopped

2 tbsp butter

2 garlic cloves, chopped

2 tbsp plain (all-purpose) flour

1 bottle beer (not dark beer)

2 tbsp smooth or grain mustard

750 ml (25 fl oz/3 cups) fish stock

125 ml (approx. 4 fl oz/⅔ cup) cream

2 waxy potatoes, peeled and cubed

1 carrot, peeled and cubed

200 g (7 oz) mussels, cooked, without shell (from the fishmonger)

200 g (7 oz) samphire (glasswort/seabean)

12 oysters or more (shucked)

2 tbsp chives, finely chopped

freshly ground pepper and salt

In a heavy-based pan, braise the shallots in the butter and add the garlic when the shallots have turned a golden brown. Leave to sauté for a minute and add the flour. Continue to stir until the flour has absorbed all of the butter. Slowly add the beer and stir until the mixture thickens. Fold in the mustard, followed by the stock and cream. Add the potatoes and carrot, bring the soup to a boil and turn the heat to low and leave the soup to simmer for 30 minutes. Then add the mussels and heat thoroughly. You can keep the soup in the refrigerator until served.
Heat the soup again before serving. Add the samphire, and heat briefly. Open/shuck the oysters (if necessary) and leave to poach in the hot soup for 1 minute before serving. Immediately serve the soup, sprinkled with the chives and pepper.

PRESERVING VEGETABLES

PEOPLE USED TO PRESERVE FRUIT AND VEGETABLES IN ORDER TO BE ABLE TO ENJOY THEM THROUGHOUT THE WINTER. CURRENTLY THIS FORM OF PRESERVING IS ONCE AGAIN IN VOGUE. PROBABLY BECAUSE WE LIKE TO KNOW WHAT WE EAT, WE FIND IT IMPORTANT TO KNOW WHERE OUR FOOD COMES FROM AND NO LONGER WANT ARTIFICIAL ADDITIVES. BUT IT IS ALSO JUST FUN TO DO AND OFTEN NOT ALL THAT MUCH WORK. THERE ARE MANY DIFFERENT WAYS OF PRESERVING: YOU CAN PICKLE VEGETABLES, PRESERVE FRUIT IN ALCOHOL, MAKE CHUTNEYS AND JAMS OR BOTTLE > WHEN YOU COOK THE JARS WITH THEIR CONTENTS FOR A WHILE, IMMERSED IN WATER, YOU CREATE A VACUUM. THEREFORE ALWAYS WORK WITH PRESERVING JARS (YOU KNOW, THE ONES WITH THAT RUBBER RING), OTHERWISE THE JAR WILL BURST. > A JAR OF PRESERVED VEGETABLES CAN BE KEPT FOR ONE YEAR IN A DARK COOL PLACE - STORE THE JARS IN THE REFRIGERATOR.

TO PRESERVE CAULIFLOWER: 1 CAULIFLOWER, SALT, 1 TBSP CURRY POWER, MUSTARD SEEDS, PEPPERCORNS, 1 RED ONION, JUICE OF HALF A LEMON AND 1.5-2 LITRES (6-8 CUPS) WATER.

CLEAN THE CAULIFLOWER, WASH AND CUT INTO FLORETS.

BRING A PAN OF WATER TO A BOIL AND BLANCH THE VEGETABLES FOR 4 MINUTES.

PREPARE A LARGE TRAY WITH ICE CUBES.

LEAVE THE BLANCHED CAULIFLOWER TO COOL IN IT.

PEEL THE ONION AND CUT INTO ROUNDS.

7

FILL THE JARS WITH ONION, LEMON JUICE AND CAULIFLOWER, NICE AND FULL.

8

FILL A JUG WITH APPROX. 1 LITRE (4 CUPS) BOILING WATER.

9

SEASON WITH THE CURRY POWDER AND 1 TSP SALT PER LITRE (4 CUPS) WATER.

10

COVER WITH THE MUSTARD SEEDS AND PEPPERCORNS.

11

IF DESIRED, ADD A BAY LEAF AND COVER WITH THE LIQUID.

12

CAREFULLY SEAL THE LID.

13

FILL A PAN WITH WATER. PLACE THE JARS IN IT. THEY NEED TO BE IMMERSED.

14

COOK FOR SOME 45 MINUTES AND DO THE VACUUM TEST:

15

IF THE RING IS STUCK, IT'S A SUCCESS! OTHERWISE CONTINUE TO COOK.

LET'S GET GOING

STICK TO A FEW BASIC PRINCIPLES AND YOU WILL BE ABLE TO CREATE YOUR OWN VARIATIONS. FIRST, A NUMBER OF BASIC RECIPES. ALWAYS MAKE SURE TO WORK WITH STERILE JARS. NOT ALL RECIPES USE THE SAME PRESERVING METHODS, SINCE FRUIT AND VEG CAN BE PRESERVED IN ALL KINDS OF DIFFERENT WAYS.

PICKLED CUCUMBER

Instead of cucumbers, you can also use gherkins (pickles). You will find fresh gherkins in the summer in organic food stores.
This recipe is for 1 kg (2 lb) vegetables

1 kg (2 lb) cucumbers
plenty of salt
few sprigs of dill
approx. 500 ml (16 fl oz/2 cups) vinegar
approx. 500 ml (16 fl oz/2 cups) water
350 g (12 oz/1⅔ cups) sugar
4 cloves
1 tbsp caraway seed
12 peppercorns
2 bay leaves

Place the cucumbers in a baking tin or serving tray and generously rub them with salt.
Leave to stand in a cool place for 24 hours. Wash thoroughly.
The salt bath is necessary to slightly strengthen the peel and ensure that the pulp is tough and well-seasoned. Quarter the cucumbers lengthways. Then cut to size, to fit nicely in the jars. Insert the dill sprigs.
Bring the vinegar, water, sugar and all spices to a boil. Reduce for 10 minutes and cover the cucumbers in the jar with the liquid. Seal the lid. Sterilise the jars of pickled cucumber for 20 minutes close to boiling point.

PRESERVED LEMONS

For approx. 2 preserving jars (1–1.5 litres/4–6cups)

12 organic lemons, (unsprayed and without wax coating)
approx. 300 ml (10 fl oz/1¼ cups) lemon juice
boiling water and plenty of sea salt

Thoroughly wash the lemons, generously rub them with salt and divide them between the jars. Sprinkle 3 tbsp salt over each jar of lemons. Distribute the lemon juice over both jars and top up with boiling water. Seal the jars and leave to rest in a dark place for 2 to 4 weeks. Thoroughly rinse the lemons before use.
Use the preserved lemons in stewed dishes; in Arab cuisine it is an essential ingredient. The peel cut into strips is also very good in salads or with chicken. The lemon water remaining in the jar is tasty as flavouring for your dressings!

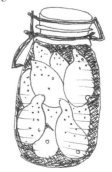

CRANBERRY, WALNUT & PEAR CHUTNEY

Almost any fruit and vegetable is fine in a chutney. This chutney can be kept for approx. three months - store in the refrigerator. After filling, turn the jars upside down to allow them to create a vacuum.
(You have no doubt read the section on jam making.)

This recipe is for 4 jars or 1 litre (4 cups)

75 ml (2½ fl oz/⅓ cup) cider vinegar
75 g (2½ oz/⅓ cup) grated ginger
3 onions, peeled and chopped
zest of ½ lemon and 1 orange
1 cinnamon stick
1 handful of walnuts
1 dried capsicum (bell pepper)
300 g (10 oz/1⅔ cups) cranberries
2 pears, peeled and cubed
125 g (approx. 4 oz/½ cup) raw caster (superfine) sugar

Reduce the vinegar, ginger, onion, lemon and orange zest, cinnamon stick and pepper for approx. 10 minutes, on medium heat. Roast the walnuts in an non-stick pan until they release an aroma. Transfer to a board and coarsely chop.
Add them to the vinegar mixture together with the fresh cranberries, the pear cubes and the sugar. Allow to simmer for 30 minutes.

Taste and add salt and pepper, to taste. Fill 4 clean jars. Turn them upside down and leave to stand for 24 hours before consuming.

PICCALILLI

For approx. 2 litres (8 cups)

2 zucchinis (courgettes), diced
1 cauliflower, in small florets
250 g (8 oz/2 cups) green beans, sliced
500 g (1 lb) fresh pearl onions, peeled
1 cucumber, peeled and diced
300 g (10 oz/¾ cup) salt
150 g (5 oz/⅔ cup) sugar
1 litre (4 cups) vinegar
2 tbsp plain (all-purpose) flour
3 tbsp mustard seeds
1 tbsp ground ginger

Mix all the vegetables. Generously cover the bottom of a large bowl with the mixture. Sprinkle with salt. Cover with another layer of vegetables and also sprinkle with salt. Continue until all vegetables are used. Cover the bowl and leave to stand for 24 hours. Drain the released moisture from the vegetables and rinse well under running water. Place in a large pan and add the sugar and 750 ml (25 fl oz/3 cups) of the vinegar. Bring to a boil and simmer for approx. 15 minutes. Stir the remaining vinegar through the flour, add the spices and, while stirring, pour onto the vegetables in the pan.
Bring to a boil and heat through for 3 minutes. Remove from the heat and immediately pour into clean jars. Turn the jars upside down and leave to cool until used.
You can keep your home-made piccalilli for approx. 2–3 months. Once opened keep in the refrigerator!

RHUBARB COMPOTE

Oh, this is so good.

1.5 kg (3 lb) rhubarb, cleaned and cut into pieces of approx. 1 cm (½ inch)
750 g (26 oz/3½ cups) sugar, or more
2 cinnamon sticks
8 cardamom pods
2 vanilla beans, split with the seeds scraped off
3 mandarins

Fill a large baking tin with the rhubarb, sugar, cinnamon, cardamom, vanilla beans and seeds. Halve the mandarins, squeeze them over the rhubarb and add the peels. Stir thoroughly and cover with aluminium foil. Place in an oven preheated to 180°C (350°F/Gas 4) for approx. 20 minutes and stir occasionally. Fill two 1-litre (4-cup) preserving jars with the hot compote and sterilise for another 20–30 minutes or until the vacuum is created. If you want to eat the rhubarb immediately, leave the jars in the oven for another 10 minutes. Before serving, remove the mandarin peel and the spices.

APPLE-DATE CHUTNEY

For 4 jam jars or 1 litre (4 cups)

1 dab butter
1 kg (2 lb) tart/sour apples (Granny Smith)
120 g (approx. 4 oz/½ cup) raw caster (superfine) sugar
1 piece of ginger the length of a thumb, peeled and finely chopped
250 ml (9 fl oz/1 cup) white wine or cider vinegar
250 ml (9 fl oz/1 cup) water
1 cinnamon stick
1 tbsp cumin
2 tbsp ground cardamom
1 garlic clove, crushed
300 g (10 oz/2 cups) pitted dried dates, cut into chunks
150 g (5 oz/1 cup) sultanas

Heat the butter in a heavy-based pan and fry the apple cubes together with the sugar and ginger on all sides. Add the vinegar and water and, together with the spices and garlic, slowly bring to a boil. Add the dates and sultanas. Leave to cook for 15 minutes. Fill 4 clean jam jars with the chutney and seal with the lids. The chutney can be kept for at least 2 months. Serve as an appetiser with some pâté or after a meal with cheese.

PINK PEARS IN SYRUP

For the syrup

1 bottle red wine

2 cinnamon sticks

3 star anise

1 vanilla bean, cut open with the seeds scraped out

4 cloves

250 g (8 oz/1 cup) sugar

1 sliced orange

rind of 1 lemon

and of course also

4–6 ripe pears (Comice)

Bring all the ingredients for the syrup to a boil, stir gently until the sugar is dissolved and lower the heat, allowing the mixture to infuse. Peel the pears and add to the syrup. Allow them to cook for 30 minutes and then remove them. (The longer you let them stay in the syrup, the darker they will become). Strain the syrup and reduce to at least half its volume, or until you like its consistency as a sauce, but note that once cooled it will thicken considerably more. Leave to cool. You can also preserve the pears in this syrup: add at least 7–8 uncooked pears in a sterilised 2-litre (8-cup) preserving jar. Add the unreduced syrup. Cover with the lid and cook the jar immersed in a tall pan for approx. 30 minutes. Pears can be processed both savoury and sweet. A savoury example is provided below, and when sweet they taste good with vanilla cream, a little syrup from the jar and almond biscuits (recipe on page 362).

SALAD WITH SPINACH, PEAR, STILTON AND RAW HAM

For this salad you can use the pears you have already preserved (see above).

For the dressing

6 tbsp white wine vinegar

1 generous tsp Dijon mustard

6 tbsp. hazelnut oil or other nut oil

6 tbsp olive oil

50 g (approx. ½ cup) hazelnuts, chopped

For the salad

1 tbsp olive oil

200 g (7 oz) raw ham, sliced

2 ripe pears (Comice)

150 g (5 oz) Stilton, crumbled

1 red onion, cut into thin rings

500 g (1 lb) spinach leaves, washed

Fill an empty jar with all the ingredients for the dressing and cover with the lid. Shake well, taste for salt and pepper and save the dressing until used. Heat a non-stick pan and add a teaspoon of olive oil. Fry the raw ham on both sides until crunchy and drain on kitchen paper. Do not fry too many slices at the same time, but two by two, keeping them whole. Quarter the pears and remove the core. Cut into strips. Combine the cheese, onion rings and ham with the spinach leaves. Transfer the salad to a plate, arrange the pears and top with dressing. Serve with pumpkin buns (page 24) and eat immediately.

PUMPKIN PICKLES

200 ml (6 fl oz/¾ cup) white wine vinegar

300 ml (10 fl oz/1¼ cups) water

3 tbsp sugar

6 cloves

1 blade mace or a pinch of freshly grated nutmeg

1 cinnamon stick

6 cardamom pods

1–2 red capsicums (bell peppers)

500 g (1 lb) butternut pumpkin (butternut squash), peeled and cubed (1 x 1 cm/½ x ½ inch)

Bring all ingredients to a boil, except the pumpkin, in a saucepan. Reduce for 10 minutes on low heat. Add the pumpkin cubes and cook for 5 minutes.

Transfer the mixture to a preserving jar and sterilise the pickles for approx. 40 minutes. Leave to stand for at least 3 days before consuming, but preferably longer. Serve the pickles with meat, vol-au-vent, fish or on a snack, as on page 120. Store in the refrigerator.

VEGETABLE TERRINE

Vegetables can be kept for a long time when preserved in oil. By applying pressure the moisture is pressed out and you are left with flavour. A perfect appetiser for approx. 10 people and served with leftovers for a tasty lunch.

For the terrine
3–4 eggplants (aubergines)
2–3 zucchinis (courgettes)
500 g (1 lb) roasted red capsicums (bell peppers), if you roast them yourself you will need 2–3
generous splash of good olive oil

For the basil oil
approx. 350 ml (approx. 12 fl oz/1½ cups) olive oil
1 bunch basil
2 garlic cloves
juice of ½ lemon

For the cottage cheese
2 tbsp chives
2 tbsp parsley
2 tbsp dill
300 g (10 oz/1 cup) low fat cottage cheese
freshly ground pepper and salt

Cut all vegetables as thinly as possible on a mandolin or with a large sharp knife. Preheat the oven to 180°C (350°F/Gas 4). Grease 1 or 2 baking sheets with olive oil, rub with salt and pepper and cover with the eggplant slices. Trickle olive oil on the eggplants and sprinkle with salt and pepper. Bake for 8–10 minutes until done. Repeat this process until all eggplant slices are baked.

Make the basil oil: blitz all ingredients using a hand blender in a tall container. Taste and add salt and pepper, as needed. Generously cover an oblong cake tin with plastic wrap allowing the edges to hang over the rim. Then cover the tin with a layer of eggplant slices: arrange them overlapping in the tin. Continue to fill the tin with layers of raw zucchini and roasted capsicums. Every three layers, cover with a dash of basil oil. End with a layer of eggplant. Fold the plastic wrap closed over the terrine. Place something heavy (tins, carton of milk) on the terrine and place in a deep bowl, to prevent leaking, for at least one day in the refrigerator.

Make the cottage cheese with herbs immediately before serving: finely chop all spices, stir through the cottage cheese and season with salt and pepper.

Remove the vegetable terrine from the refrigerator. Thoroughly drain all oil. Open the plastic wrap at the top. Cover with a plate and transfer the terrine by turning it over onto the plate. Be careful, since moisture will be released from the dressing and vegetables. Pat the plate dry with kitchen paper. Cut the vegetable terrine into thick slices (use a sharp knife!) and serve with a dollop of cottage cheese with herbs.

LENTIL SALAD

You can serve this salad immediately, as you can the previous ones, but you could also make more and preserve it, saving some for days that you do not feel like cooking. Fill the preserving jars with more chicken stock and sterilise for 30 minutes. If preserving, store it in the refrigerator.

For the lentil salad
1 small carrot
½ bunch blanched celery: some 6–8 stalks
1 leek
2 shallots, diced
3 garlic cloves, chopped
approx. 500 ml (16 fl oz/2 cups) chicken stock or broth
3 tbsp olive oil
250 g (8 oz/1 cup) lentils (good quality grey/green [Puy] lentils)
150 ml (5 fl oz/⅔ cup) white wine
1 bunch flat-leaf parsley, chopped
And also:
350 g (12 oz) smoked sausage
butter or oil for frying

For the green spice oil
1 small bunch of chives and parsley
250 ml (9 fl oz/1 cup) high-quality olive oil

Peel the carrot and all the vegetables. Finely dice all vegetables (this is called 'brunoise'). Heat the stock in a large pan. Heat the oil in a wide pan and add all vegetables, except the parsley, pour in the lentils and stir-fry until hot, just as for risotto. Add the wine and continue to stir. Add the stock slowly and continue to stir until the lentils are cooked *al dente*. Remove from the heat. Taste and add salt and pepper, as needed. Chop the parsley and add to the mixture.

In the meantime, make the herb oil: heat the oil close to boiling point. Coarsely chop the spices and add them to a tall container or jug. Blitz with a hand blender and add the hot oil in a thin trickle. Season with salt and pepper and set aside until used.

Cut the sausage into thin slices. Heat the butter in a frying pan and swiftly fry the sausage slices on both sides until golden brown. Transfer the lentil salad into a ring mould on the plate, remove the ring. Add the sausage and garnish the lentil salad with a nice sprig of parsley. Trickle the herb oil on the plate and serve with mustard. This appetiser is also good as a main course served with boiled potatoes.

BRUSCHETTA WITH MARINATED EGGPLANT AND MINT

Immersed in oil, the preserved eggplant can easily be kept for 2 weeks. It will, however, become more oily but the flavour will be more intense!

2 eggplants (aubergines)
approx. 250 ml (9 fl oz/1 cup) extra virgin olive oil and a little extra
2 tbsp honey
120 ml (approx. 4 fl oz/⅔ cup) red wine vinegar
1 green capsicum (bell pepper)
1 bunch of fresh mint leaves cut into strips
4 slices of coarse Italian bread
1 garlic clove

Cut the eggplants into slices approx. ½ cm (⅛ inch) thick. Heat a grill pan until it smokes. Cover the slices on both sides with a thin coat of olive oil. Grill the eggplant on both sides until done. Save until used.
Stir the honey through the vinegar. Beat in a trickle of olive oil until the dressing thickens. Season with salt and pepper. Halve the capsicum, remove the seeds and finely chop. Stir two-thirds of the mint through the dressing. Stir the dressing into the eggplant and leave to stand for at least 30 minutes.

Before serving, heat the grill pan. Grill the bread slices on both sides until brown. Trickle with olive oil and rub the garlic clove on the bread. Cover with a few eggplant slices. Garnish with the fresh mint and freshly ground pepper and serve with the remaining eggplant.

TIP Good served with seasoned labneh balls, see recipe on page 298.

GREEN VEGETABLE SALAD

For serving I will give you a recipe for a dressing and will recommend what to have with it. It is a good lunch or appetiser. In our restaurant we also often serve it as a side dish. You can also preserve the salad and keep it in the refrigerator.

For the salad

2.5 kg (5½ lb) green vegetables: green beans, broad (fava) beans, dried peas, snow peas (mangetouts), green asparagus, or a mixture thereof

4 stalks of blanched celery, washed and sliced diagonally in 2-cm (approx. 1-inch) slices

1 bunch parsley, tarragon, mint and dill, or a mixture thereof, coarsely chopped

2 sterile preserving jars of approx. 1 litre (4 cups) or smaller ones (see page 12 for sterile jars)

For the yoghurt-dill dressing

100 ml (approx. 3 fl oz/½ cup) yoghurt

juice of 1 lemon

1 tbsp nectar (apricot or peach)

1 spring onion (scallion), finely chopped

1 garlic clove, crushed

1 tbsp dill, finely chopped

50 ml (1½ fl oz/¼ cup) hazelnut oil

freshly ground pepper and salt

As a dressing or side dish, as an appetiser or lunch dish, calculate 40–50 g (approx. 2 oz) of the following ingredients per person. For the salad use tasty crumbles such as goat's cheese or feta, ham, smoked fish, wafer-thin smoked chicken or thinly sliced beef loin described on page 256.

Cut the long vegetables, such as green asparagus or green beans in half. Blanch all vegetables for 2 minutes, in turn, in a pan with plenty of boiling water. Finish with the broad beans, since they will colour the water purple. Rinse everything immediately under cold running water. Mix the vegetables, stir in the herbs (reserve some for the garnish if you do not preserve the salad, but will serve it later that day) and scoop into two 1-litre (4-cup) preserving jars. Top up the jars with hot water and 1 tablespoon salt per litre (4 cups) of water used. Make sure all beans are immersed. Sterilise the jars for 30–40 minutes. You can keep this salad in the refrigerator for 12 months.

If you do not preserve the salad, make the dressing straight away.
Thoroughly blend all ingredients, except the oil. Lastly, beat in the oil in a thin trickle.
Distribute the bean salad over the plates and garnish with cheese, meat or fish, or serve as is, as a side dish. Trickle the dressing on the salad and sprinkle with some of the reserved chopped herbs.
You can keep the leftover dressing carefully covered in the refrigerator for about a week.

PRESERVED BEETROOT SALAD WITH ASH COVERED GOAT'S CHEESE

Serve this beetroot salad as an appetiser with smoked fish or as a side dish with meat. Here I serve it with a goat's cheese. You can also serve it with a small green salad. The recipe for the beetroot salad makes about 4 litres (16 cups). So you had better clear some shelves in the refrigerator! If you want to make less, just halve the quantities.

1.5 kg (3 lb) sweet/sharp apples, peeled and cut into slices or sections

2 red onions, peeled and in rings

3–4 slices fresh ginger, leave the skin

1 tsp cinnamon

pinch nutmeg

2 tbsp mustard seeds

300 ml (10 fl oz/1¼ cups) raspberry vinegar, otherwise red wine vinegar

250 g (8 oz/1 cup) sugar

3 kg (6½ lb) parboiled beetroot (beet), in slices or sections

For an appetiser, 4 servings

500 g (1 lb) beetroot (beet) salad

approx. 200 g (7 oz/1½ cups) ash covered goat's cheese,

150 g (5 oz/4 cups) rocket (arugula) salad, mesclun, or a mixture thereof

In a large pan bring all ingredients, except the beetroot, to a boil and simmer for 5 minutes. Season with salt and freshly ground pepper. Add the beetroot. Stir until the beetroot is heated but be careful not to break the apples and the beetroot. Transfer the salad to four clean 1-litre (4-cup) jars or eight 500-ml (2-cup) preserving jars. Sterilise for 20 minutes. Leave to cool and store in the refrigerator until used. You can also make this salad without preserving it, but in that case, leave all ingredients to infuse (a little over an hour should be sufficient).

Serve a nice helping of preserved salad with fresh green salad, adding approx. 3 slices of goat's cheese per serving. Trickle olive oil on the salad immediately before serving.

DOLMAS FILLED WITH WILD RICE

You will make 20 dolmas with this recipe. Keep dolmas longer by covering with olive oil. Tap the bowl in which you will store the dolmas a few times on the counter, releasing as much air as possible and preventing decay. Store in a cool and dark place.

265 g (9 oz) jar vine leaves (I use the Drossa brand, available from the supermarket)
2 tbsp olive oil
1 onion, peeled and finely chopped
150 g (5 oz/¾ cup) white and wild rice (mixture)
200 ml (6 fl oz/¾ cup) water
100 g (approx. 4 oz/½ cup) raisins, coarsely chopped
100 g (approx. 4 oz/⅔ cup) pine nuts
2 tbsp parsley, finely chopped
2 tbsp mint, finely chopped
1 generous pinch of ground cinnamon
2 peeled tomatoes (tinned), in chunks
juice of 1 lemon, plus 1 extra lemon for garnish

For the dressing
200 ml (6 fl oz/¾ cup) yoghurt
juice of ½ lemon
½ garlic clove
pinch of cayenne pepper, to taste

Carefully rinse the vine leaves under running water. Fry the onion in the oil until golden brown. Add the rice and fry for 3 minutes while stirring. Add the water, salt, raisins and pine nuts. Stir briefly and cover the pan. Leave the rice to cook on very low heat for 15 minutes until nearly done, and all the water is absorbed. Stir, transfer to a large tray and leave to slightly cool. Stir in the parsley, mint, cinnamon and tomatoes. Taste the mixture and add salt and pepper, as needed.

Fill the vine leaves with 1 generous tablespoon of the rice mixture. Roll up the leaf like an envelope (by first placing the sides on the filling and then rolling it). They are most attractive if the dolmas are of equal size. Arrange the rolls next to each other in an oven tray and completely cover with water. Add the lemon juice. Cover the tray with aluminium foil and place in an oven preheated to 180°C (350°F/Gas 4) for 1 hour. Occasionally check whether there is enough water to cover the bottom of the oven tray. It should not boil dry. Leave to cool.

In the meantime make the dressing by mixing the ingredients into a smooth sauce using a hand blender. Season with salt and pepper. Serve three or four dolmas per person, drizzle with the dressing and serve with slices of lemon and crusty bread.

SALAD WITH CELERIAC, GOAT'S CHEESE, POMEGRANATE & TARRAGON

For the salad
1 celeriac
juice of 1 lemon
1 bunch blanched celery: reserve two stalks for the dressing
150 g (5 oz/1¼ cups) goat's cheese, crumbled
seeds of 2 pomegranates (read how to release them on page 102)
1 bunch flat-leaf parsley
1 bunch tarragon

For the dressing
2 stalks blanched celery
1 garlic clove
½ tbsp freshly grated horseradish or 1 tbsp from a jar
50 ml (1½ fl oz/¼ cup) red wine vinegar
100 ml (3 fl oz/½ cup) grape seed oil (or otherwise sunflower oil)

Peel the celeriac. Wash and slice, cut the slices into strips and then into matchsticks. If you are the proud owner of a food processor or mandolin with chip cutter, it will take you even less time. Save the matchsticks immersed in a container with water with the squeezed lemon juice until used. You can also add the squeezed lemon halves. Bring a pan with plenty of water to a boil and briefly blanch the celeriac.

Immediately rinse under cold running water or in ice water. Wash the blanched celery stalks. Cut into thin strips, more or less the same size as the celeriac. Mix the blanched celery matchsticks with the celeriac matchsticks. Place in clean preserving jars, fill with broth (follow the preserving instructions on pages 156–157) and sterilise for 30–40 minutes.

If serving the salad immediately, make the dressing using a blender or hand mixer in a tall container. Coarsely cut the reserved blanched celery, cook until done (15 minutes) and purée with the other ingredients into a smooth dressing, taste and add salt and pepper, as needed. Trickle half of the dressing on the salad and leave to stand for 1 hour, allowing the flavours to infuse.

Make the salad: chop the spices and add them, together with the pomegranate seeds, lightly through the salad. Transfer a good size to each plate. Distribute the goat's cheese over the salads and trickle with some extra dressing.

PRESERVING

MEAT & FISH

MAKING TERRINE

MY GOOD FRIEND FLORIS TAUGHT ME HOW TO MAKE EXCELLENT TERRINES. TOGETHER WITH DINY HE NOW RUNS HIS OWN SHOP IN AMSTERDAM. THEY MAKE THE TASTIEST (AND BEST LOOKING) FRENCH CHARCUTERIE I HAVE EVER HAD. >>> PRIOR TO THAT, FLORIS WORKED FOR US IN THE KITCHEN. WE OFTEN TRIED OUT ALL MANNER OF DISHES AND DISCOVERED THAT A SIMPLE PÂTÉ OR TERRINE IS ACTUALLY EASY TO MAKE. ONCE YOU HAVE MASTERED THE BASICS, YOU CAN MAKE ENDLESS VARIATIONS. I INCLUDE MORE THAN NORMAL HERE, ALLOWING YOU TO LEARN HOW IT'S DONE! IT'S IMPORTANT THAT YOU GRIND THE MEAT: NOT AS FINELY AS NORMAL, BUT A LITTLE COARSER. USING A GRINDER. IF YOU DON'T OWN ONE, USE A GOOD FOOD PROCESSOR, PROVIDED YOU CUT THE MEAT INTO SMALL CHUNKS FIRST. YOU CAN ALSO JUST ASK YOUR BUTCHER TO GRIND THE MEAT. THIS IS ACTUALLY THE EASIEST AND IT MAKES A HUGE DIFFERENCE IN TERMS OF WASHING UP.

NEEDED FOR 1 TERRINE DE CAMPAGNE:

250 G (8 OZ) PORK SHOULDER
450 G (15 OZ) PORK LOWER JAW
400 G (14 OZ) PORK LIVER

AFTER CLEANING AND GRINDING YOU WILL BE LEFT WITH 1 KG (2 LB).

FOR THIS RECIPE YOU WILL NEED:
10 G (1.5 TSP) PINK SALT AND
6 G (1 TSP) REGULAR SALT.
>>> WEIGH VERY PRECISELY!!
1 SHALLOT
1 DAB OF BUTTER, FAT OR LARD
1 SPRIG THYME
1 TBSP JUNIPER BERRIES
4 DRY BAY LEAVES
1 TBSP BLACK PEPPER
1 SMALL GLASS COGNAC
2 EGGS
PIECE OF LAMB'S STOMACH FAT OR
300 G (10 OZ) BACON STRIPS

START BY DICING THE SHALLOT AND...

GRIND THE BAY LEAVES, JUNIPER BERRIES AND PEPPER INTO POWDER.

SAUTÉ IT VERY SLOWLY IN A LITTLE BUTTER. ADD SOME THYME SPRIGS.

FLORIS SAYS A TERRINE MUST BE FATTY, COARSE, SLICEABLE! IMPORTANT STUFF!

CUT THE PORK SHOULDER AND LOWER JAW INTO STRIPS THAT NEATLY FIT INTO THE GRINDER.

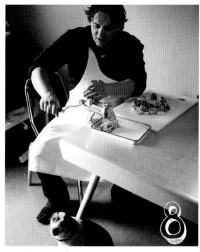

COARSELY GRIND THE MEAT. BUT YOU CAN ALSO ASK THE BUTCHER TO DO IT FOR YOU.

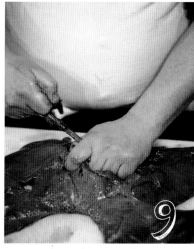

PULL OUT LIVER BILE DUCTS (TOUGH THREADS THAT MAKE THE TERRINE BITTER). COME ON, YOU ARE UP FOR IT!

COARSELY GRIND THE LIVER IN THE FOOD PROCESSOR (OR GRINDER).

COMBINE EVERYTHING; CAN YOU SEE THE AMOUNT OF FAT? THAT'S OK!

NOW YOU CAN ADD THE OTHER INGREDIENTS, EXCEPT THE SALT.

WASH YOUR HANDS AND START KNEADING. ADD THE SALT.

KNEAD THE MIXTURE THOROUGHLY INTO A TACKY CONSISTENCY.

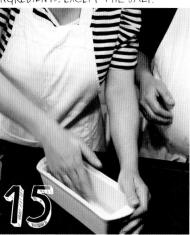

IN THE MEANTIME I GREASE THE TERRINES.

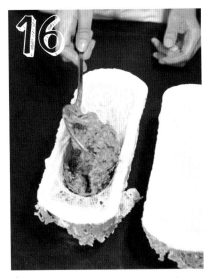

LINE THE MOULD WITH BACON STRIPS, OR LIKE HERE, WITH PORK STOMACH FAT. CREATE A LITTLE HAMMOCK. FILL WITH THE MIXTURE. PRICK THE CORNERS WITH A SPOON: ALL AIR MUST BE REMOVED!

CAREFULLY COVER THE MEAT, WITH THE PORK STOMACH. SLIDE THE DULL SIDE OF A KNIFE ALONG THE EDGES MAKING THE TERRINES NICE AND TAUT. IT LOOKS POSH.

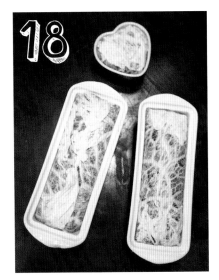

WE HAD SOME LEFT OVER; THEREFORE WE EVENTUALLY MADE 3 TERRINES. TWO LARGE ONES AND ONE SMALL ONE TO GIVE AWAY.

CAREFULLY WRAP WITH ALUMINIUM FOIL AND PLACE THE TERRINES IN A ROASTING TIN TO COLLECT THE FAT. OTHERWISE THE OVEN WILL GET VERY DIRTY. BAKE AT 120C (250F) FOR 2 HOURS.

AFTER 2 HOURS THEY WILL BE READY, BUT THEY WILL GO BACK INTO THE OVEN FOR A FURTHER 30 MINUTES TO BROWN, WITHOUT FOIL.

LEAVE THE TERRINE TO STAND FOR 24 HOURS BEFORE SLICING IT, BUT PREFERABLY FOR 1 WEEK, ALLOWING FOR THE FLAVOURS TO FULLY DEVELOP. THE TERRINE CAN BE KEPT FOR AT LEAST 3 WEEKS.

TIPS AND TRICKS:
> DO YOU OWN A MEAT THERMOMETER? TOWARDS THE END, THE TERRINES' CORE TEMPERATURE HAS TO BE 70C (158F).
> AS YOU NOTICED, WE ADDED THE SALT LAST, OTHERWISE THE SHALLOTS WOULD GET LUMPY.
> SALT EXTRACTS PROTEIN FROM THE MEAT AND PROTEINS ARE NECESSARY FOR BONDING. > FAT IS NECESSARY FOR THE FLAVOUR AND CREAMINESS OF THE TERRINE.
> ALL THE EFFORT YOU PUT INTO IT CAN BE SEEN IN THE RESULT: YOU LITERALLY REAP WHAT YOU SOW.

Floris

LET'S GET GOING

OK! I WILL GIVE YOU A FEW MORE RECIPES FOR HOME-MADE TERRINES AND PÂTÉS. A LITTLE BIT OF EVERYTHING, SO THAT YOU CAN TRY THEM. SERVE WITH YOUR OWN HOME-MADE CHUTNEYS OR PRESERVED VEGETABLES.

AUTUMN PASTY

150 g (5 oz) mixed mushrooms
a little olive oil for frying
250 g (8 oz) game fillet or steak
750 g (26 oz) beef mince (coarsely ground please!)
3 tbsp mustard
5 tbsp soy sauce
5 tbsp tomato sauce
2 to 3 sprigs fresh rosemary, both leaves and stem, finely chopped
1 tsp chilli powder
1 tsp nutmeg
1 tsp cinnamon
1 tsp ground ginger
1 egg
salt and freshly ground pepper
fresh breadcrumbs
6 sheets all-butter puff pastry (frozen)
1 egg yolk
flour to dust the countertop
and olive oil to grease

Preheat the oven to 180°C (350°F/ Gas 4). Place the pastry sheets on the counter next to each other and allow to thaw. Wipe the mushrooms clean and tear them roughly into pieces. Fry them while stirring on a very high heat in a little olive oil and season with salt and pepper. Transfer to a plate to cool. Grind the game in a food processor or ask the butcher to do it for you. Combine the mince mixture with the remaining ingredients and knead into a firm ball. Add as much breadcrumbs as necessary, the mixture must remain creamy, not too wet, but not too dry

either. You can test it by rolling a small soup ball of the mixture, and heating it for 2 minutes in the microwave to taste whether it is okay. You can decide whether it needs more salt. You have to season mince more than you think, since once fried, it loses a lot of its flavour. Create an oval ball with the mince. Stack the pastry squares. Dust the countertop with flour. Roll out the stack into a long sheet, 2 times bigger than the meat ball. Place the meat ball on one side of the pastry and fold the other side over it. Brush water on the edge and press firmly in place. If you are a little handy you can decorate the pasty: for example close it along the top with a frill made with your fingers.

Place the pasty on a greased baking sheet and using an apple corer or large fork, make decorative holes in the dough: they will be necessary later to allow the fat to drain. Brush the pasty with lightly beaten egg yolk. Bake the pasty until golden brown, (approx. 45 minutes). Leave to fully cool before slicing. Serve with the cranberry, walnut & pear chutney described on page 158.

CHICKEN LIVER PATE

Serve with a drink and gherkins, pearl onions and home-made canapés...

2 shallots, diced
3 tbsp butter
500 g (1 lb) chicken livers
500 ml (16 fl oz/2 cups) cream
1 tbsp cognac or brandy
150 g (5 oz/1¼ sticks) butter
sprig of thyme

Sauté the shallots in the butter until glassy. Place in the food processor bowl. Fry the chicken livers in portions in the same pan for approx. 5 minutes. They have to stay pink on the inside! Place in the food processor. When they are all cooked, add the cream, cognac and butter to the bowl and finely grind. Press the pâté with the round side of a spoon through a sieve into a bowl below. Transfer the pâté to a dish in which you want to serve it. In the meantime, melt the butter on low heat in a saucepan. Only pour the clear part of the melted butter over the pâté to neatly seal it. Finish with a sprig of thyme. Leave the pâté to set for at least 4 hours.

BEEF AND PARSLEY TERRINE

1 kg (2 lb) pork steaks
400 g (14 oz) beef steak
2 bunches of flat-leaf parsley
100 ml (approx. 3 fl oz/½ cup) sweet white wine or port
2 tbsp cognac
4 shallots, finely chopped
2 garlic cloves, finely chopped
2 tsp salt
plenty of freshly ground pepper
½ tbsp allspice
2 tbsp olive oil
2 bay leaves
some thyme sprigs

Cube all the meat. Rinse the parsley, pat dry and chop. Pour the wine and cognac into a bowl. Add the meat, parsley, shallots, garlic, salt, pepper and allspice and lastly, the thyme and bay. Stir thoroughly and sprinkle with oil. Cover the meat with plastic wrap and leave to marinate in the refrigerator for 3 hours. Preheat the oven to 150°C (300°F/Gas 2).
Remove the thyme and bay from the marinade and grind all ingredients in a mincer or food processor. Press the mixture into a clay pot, smooth it out and garnish with a bay leaf and a few thyme sprigs. Cover with a lid or aluminium foil and bake the terrine in the oven for 1 hour. Leave the terrine to cool and keep in the refrigerator for 24 hours before serving.

SALMON AND PRAWN TERRINE WITH BROAD BEANS AND PORTOBELLO MUSHROOMS

20 large peeled prawns (shrimp)
2 slices day-old bread
200 ml (6 fl oz/¾ cup) milk
600 g (21 oz) salmon fillet
1 handful broad (fava) beans
2 portobello mushrooms
4 eggs
400 g (14 oz) white fish fillets
200 ml (6 fl oz/¾ cup) cream
1 small bunch chives, finely chopped
salt and freshly ground pepper
little oil for frying

Cut the prawns in half lengthways and set aside. Cut the bread in cubes and soak in the milk. Preheat the oven to 120°C (250°F/Gas ⅓). Cut the salmon into thin strips and set aside. Blanch the broad beans in boiling water for 3 minutes and rinse under cold water. Slice the mushrooms and fry briefly on both sides in a frying pan. Sprinkle with salt and pepper and set aside. Separate the egg whites from the yolks. Cut the white fish into chunks and add them to the food processor bowl. Add the drained, soaked bread and egg yolks and blend into a coarse purée. Pour the purée into a bowl and add the cream. Add the prawn halves and the chives. Beat the egg whites until stiff in another bowl and carefully stir through the white fish mixture to keep it airy. Season the mixture with salt and pepper. Generously line an oblong cake tin with plastic wrap and allow the edges to hang over. Cover the bottom with half the salmon strips. Pour half of the white fish mousse over the salmon. Arrange the mushroom slices and broad beans on the fish. Cover with the remaining mousse. Top the mousse with the rest of the salmon. Cover the terrine with the overhanging plastic wrap and place in a larger oven dish. Fill that bowl with water halfway up the terrine and bake in the oven for 75 minutes. The terrine must feel firm when pressed, otherwise briefly return to the oven.
First leave the terrine to slightly cool then place in the refrigerator for at least 12 hours. Serve with horseradish sauce on page 195. or green herb oil on page 166. or with a small green salad and mustard dressing.

185

HAM PIE

In this recipe I use sausagemeat, available from any butcher. In Holland, I typically buy 'saucisson' and remove the skin. Sausagemeat is nice and fatty and well-seasoned. Therefore it gives a good creamy flavour and texture to this pie.

500 g (1 lb) pork mince (ground pork)

300 g (10 oz) sausagemeat

200 g (7 oz) ham, cubed

6 sage leaves, chopped

1 small onion, finely chopped

few drops of Tabasco sauce

450 g (15 oz/3 cups) plain (all-purpose) flour and a little extra for dusting purposes

2 tsp salt

4 tbsp milk

100 g (approx. 4 oz/1 stick) butter and a little extra for greasing purposes

1 egg, lightly beaten

Combine the pork mince with the sausagemeat, ham, sage and onions in a large bowl. Season with salt and pepper and a few drops of Tabasco sauce. Grease a 20-cm (8-inch) springform tin and dust with flour. Mix the remaining flour with 2 tsp salt. Combine the milk and butter in a pan with 150 ml (5 fl oz/⅔ cup) water and heat until the butter melts. Add the flour and stir well into a firm ball. Remove from the pan and knead into smooth dough on the countertop. Line the springform tin with baking paper. At the top allow the baking paper to slightly extend beyond the pan. Roll two-thirds of the dough into a round sheet approx. 30 cm (12 inch) diameter. Line the pan and leave some dough to hang over the edge. Fill the pan with the meat mixture and press down thus eliminating any air bubbles. Roll out the rest of the dough into a sheet that fits on the pie and cover the pie with it. Brush some water on the edges and press into a decorative pattern, if you are able to do so. Make 3 holes in the cover, using an apple corer, for example. Trim the edges and roll out the remaining dough. Cut out 3 rounds of which the diameter is the same as the holes you have made with the apple corer. Place the rounds on the holes, filling them. Brush the beaten egg on the dough. Bake the pie for 30 minutes in an oven preheated to 180°C (350°F/Gas 4) and then turn down the heat to 160°C (320°F/Gas 3). Bake the pie for another hour. Leave to fully cool.

Serve with grainy mustard or with the cranberry, walnut & pear chutney from page 158.

MARINATED SALMON IN FENNEL SEED AND PERNOD

This recipe is for at least 25 servings, a great party dish. Making less is also possible of course. Use a smaller piece of salmon, but preferably keep the skin on it. A side of salmon weighs approx. 1.5 kg (3 lb). Adjust other ingredients proportionally to make a smaller quantity.

2 whole sides of salmon, with skin
100 g (approx. 4 oz/¾ cup) fennel seeds
1 generous bunch dill, chopped
300 ml (10 fl oz/1¼ cups) Pernod
300 g (10 oz/1⅓ cups) sugar
500 g (1 lb/1 cup) salt

Line a large container with plastic wrap, allowing a wide rim to hang over the edges. Combine salt and sugar. Sprinkle two handfuls of this mixture on the bottom. Place one side of salmon on the mixture, skin side down. Sprinkle with a portion of the sugar-salt mixture, fennel seeds, dill and half the Pernod. Also sprinkle the other piece of salmon (reserve a little sugar-salt mixture) and place it on the other side of the tray. Sprinkle the top of the fish with the remaining salt mixture and cover the entire salmon tightly with the plastic wrap. Place the fish in a cool place and place a number of heavy objects on it to press it down. Tins, for example, or something similar. Leave the fish to marinate for at least 24 hours, but preferably 48 hours.
Remove the plastic wrap, scrape the salt from the salmon using a knife and cut the salmon into thin slices.
Serve with a salad of thinly sliced fennel and lemon juice.

SALMON TARTARE

You will always have leftovers from the marinated salmon on the previous page. Since you have marinated it in salt and alcohol, it will keep for a few days. Wrap well and place in the refrigerator. Never throw anything out!
And then just use it up in the following recipe serving 4, as an appetiser, for example.

300 g (10 oz) marinated salmon (see previous page)
1 small bunch rocket (arugula) salad, mustard greens or watercress, or a mixture thereof
1 tbsp dill, finely chopped

For the oil
3 sprigs parsley
150 ml (5 fl oz/⅔ cup) olive oil
few drops of lemon juice

Before serving
4 tbsp horseradish sauce, see recipe on page 195
a little coarse sea salt (Maldon, if you have it)
4 slices dark brown bread, toasted
It is fun if you own a 'ring', but it isn't necessary.

Chop the marinated raw salmon with a sharp knife and mix thoroughly, add the dill. Heat the oil, not too hot, just warm.
Add the parsley to a tall container. Finely chop the parsley using a hand blender and, while grinding, add the warm oil.
Season the oil with some lemon juice, pepper and salt.
Prepare the plates: arrange the salmon tartare in a ring on the plate. Remove the ring. Garnish the tartare with a little salad rolled in your hands into a small ball. Spread a dollop of horseradish sauce on the plate and add a swirl of the green oil around the tartare.
Sprinkle the green salad with some coarse sea salt, if desired. Serve with thinly sliced and toasted dark brown bread.

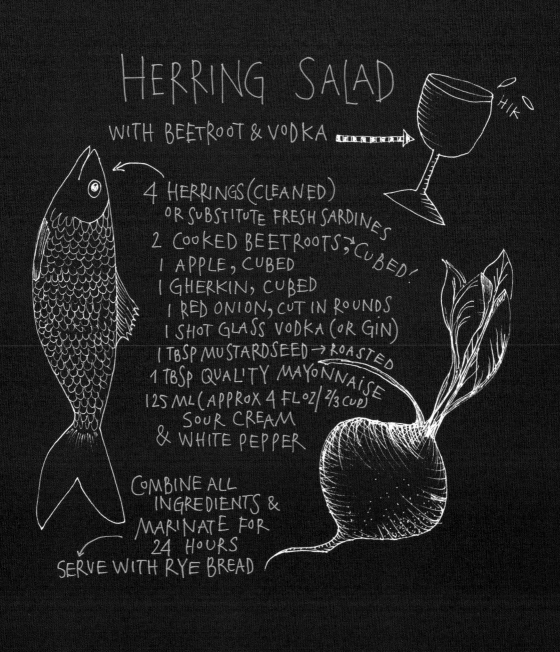

HERRING SALAD

WITH BEETROOT & VODKA ⟶

HIK

4 HERRINGS (CLEANED)
   OR SUBSTITUTE FRESH SARDINES
2 COOKED BEETROOTS, CUBED!
1 APPLE, CUBED
1 GHERKIN, CUBED
1 RED ONION, CUT IN ROUNDS
1 SHOT GLASS VODKA (OR GIN)
1 TBSP MUSTARDSEED → ROASTED
1 TBSP QUALITY MAYONNAISE
125 ML (APPROX 4 FL OZ / 2/3 CUP)
   SOUR CREAM
& WHITE PEPPER

COMBINE ALL
INGREDIENTS &
MARINATE FOR
24 HOURS
SERVE WITH RYE BREAD

AAN DE AMSTEL'S NOW FAMOUS PORK BELLY

In our restaurant we make pork belly every week. It was actually supposed to be on the menu for a short while, but, due to its huge success, it was never removed. It is a perfect 'hangover cure' on a Saturday morning: briefly bake the bacon slices in a hot oven, until the fat is crispy. Serve on bread with (fresh) horseradish sauce or fresh potato salad.
We use an entire pork belly, but you can also easily make it at home with a smaller bacon cut.
Once laid in salt and baked, you can keep the bacon in the refrigerator up to two weeks.
The recipe below is for four people.

¼ piece pork belly bacon, without rind (ask your butcher), approx. 1 kg (2 lb)
1 generous handful of coarse sea salt
1 handful fennel seeds
at least 12 bay leaves, as fresh as possible

For the horseradish sauce
1 piece fresh horseradish the length of a thumb (or 2 tbsp from a jar)
100 ml (approx. 3 fl oz/½ cup) sour cream
juice and rind of ½ lemon

Score the fat on the pork belly with a sharp knife to make an attractive check pattern. Rub the entire piece with salt and fennel. This is a rough job, do not skimp on the ingredients. Press bay leaves into the grooves and inside the meat. Wrap in a clean dish towel, place in a suitable dish in the refrigerator and cover with a heavy object. Leave to stand for 24 hours, but two days is even better. By processing it in this way, the meat acquires flavour, but the salt also extracts moisture from the meat, which will make the pork crispier later.
Heat the oven to 170°C (340°F/Gas 3), place the pork belly in a baking tin and bake for at least one hour in the oven, or until the top is crispy and golden brown and the meat is fully cooked.
In the meantime, make the horseradish sauce: peel the horseradish with a vegetable peeler and grate it on a fine grater. Or better still, use a food processor as fresh horseradish is very sharp and will make your eyes water! Once blended with the other ingredients the fumes will disappear. Season the sauce with salt and freshly ground pepper. Serve with the meat.

24,50

CONFIT DE CANARD

1 AILE, 1 CUISSE

900 g

A consommer de préférence avant la date figurant sur le couvercle

18,40

760g
Poids net

Poids net
égoutté

425g

sur le couvercle
ner rapidement.

"A la Ville de Rodez"
eille du Temple 75004 PARIS
Tel : 01.48.87.79.36

anard
es

Poids net
760g
Poids net
égoutté
425g

couvercle
apidement

50

oureux"

Pâté

Conf

INGRÉDIENTS :
manchons de canard, g

CONSERVATION
consommer de préfére
après ouverture, à con

NGRÉDIEN
manchons

CONSERVA
consomm
après ouve

DUCK CONFIT

This recipe is for 8 legs, but while you're at it and have purchased such a large jar of goose fat, you might as well make more. It is not that much work and once preserved, you will enjoy it for an entire winter. Whatever you don't consume, you can put in a sealable jar. Ensure the duck is well immersed in fat, allowing you to make lots of legs at the same time. The only thing is that you will probably have to borrow a large pan from a friendly local restaurant.

8 duck legs, approx. 180 g (6 oz) each
approx. 10 tbsp coarse sea salt
6–8 bay leaves
few sprigs of fresh thyme
4 garlic cloves, crushed
2 litres (8 cups) goose fat (available at specialist food stores)

Put the legs in a bowl 24 hours in advance, rub them with the sea salt, bay, thyme and garlic. Cover and put in a cool place.
Heat the goose fat in a large heavy-based pan. Wipe the legs clean and slide them into the hot fat.
Leave the pan with the lid slightly open and simmer on very low heat for 2–2½ hours so that bubbles come to the surface every so often. The meat is cooked when it easily falls off the bone. Leave the legs to fully cool in the fat.
You can place those legs that you will not consume straight away in suitable clean jars and cover with the hot goose fat. Carefully seal the jars and place in a dark cool place until used.
If you would like to eat them immediately: ladle a few spoonfuls of cooled fat into a frying pan. Fry the confit duck legs on both sides until crunchy, about 7–8 minutes. Drain on kitchen paper and serve immediately.
The goose fat, in which you have fried the legs, can be used again: strain and leave to set. Save in the refrigerator. It's great to use for frying potatoes. Just continue to use it until you have no more!

POTTED PRAWNS

Just like goose fat for duck confit, butter works as a preservative for the prawns. Peeling them is a little bit of a chore, but you will need the shells to flavour the butter. Look at it as a relaxing job.
We used to like eating this in Ireland and in our restaurant it is also often served as lunch or appetiser.
You can keep the potted prawns in the refrigerator at least 10 days.

500 g (1 lb) unpeeled prawns (shrimp)
250 g (8 oz/2 sticks) butter
2 blades mace (or pinch of ground mace)
pinch of cayenne pepper (to taste), use ground paprika if you don't like it hot
pinch of nutmeg

Peel the prawns. Initially it's a little bit trial and error, but later you will get the hang of it. First break off the head, pull up the first shell near the legs in order for the prawn flesh to become visible. Hold between thumb and index finger. Now you can easily remove the tail. Reserve half the shells from the prawns. Crush them briefly, with a rolling pin for example, thoroughly breaking them. Melt the butter with the prawn shells, mace, cayenne pepper and nutmeg. Leave the mixture to simmer on very low heat for 20 minutes and strain over a bowl. With the back of a spoon, press all the juice from the shells. Return the collected juices to the pan. Add the prawn meat and season with salt and pepper. The prawns will be cooked in a jiffy in the hot butter. You can leave the heat off. Pour the mixture into small single portion jars or bowls and ensure that the prawns are fully covered with butter. Then leave to set in the refrigerator.

Before serving we briefly place the jars in a pan of hot water, thus slightly melting the butter and the prawns can be easily spooned from the semi-hard butter.

We serve potted prawns with two lemon segments, thin slices of brown toast and a green salad with watercress, rocket (arugula) and/or butter lettuce. Sprinkle some sea salt on the salad.

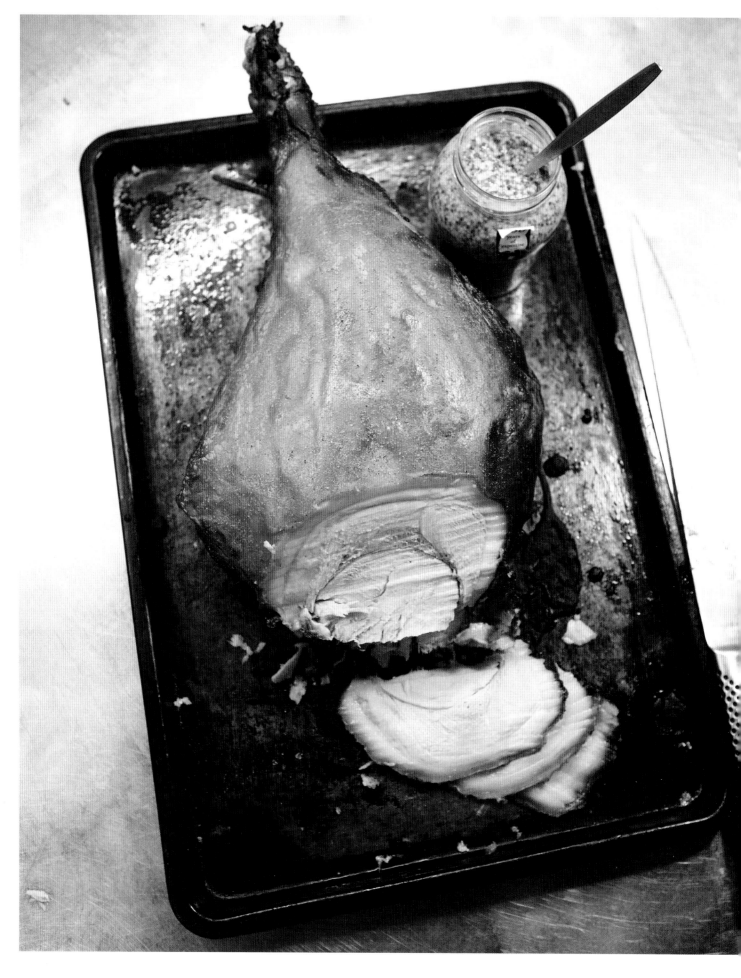

BOILED HAM WITH MUSTARD-HONEY CRUST

This recipe is for 10 people at least, since you will obviously prepare a whole ham. Boiled ham can be kept for more than a week in the refrigerator. Always wrap neatly and with clean material.

1 large leg of ham (can be ordered from the butcher). Ask him to leave in the bone. Here in the photo I used a suckling pig ham, but this is by no means a must!
4 tbsp salt
2 onions, coarsely chopped
1 carrot, clean and in chunks
4 blanched celery stalks, clean and in coarse chunks
¼ celeriac, clean and cubed
3 garlic cloves, unpeeled
some thyme sprigs
3 bay leaves
2 cloves
1 tbsp juniper berries, crushed
2 tbsp honey
4 tbsp spicy mustard
freshly ground pepper

Place the ham in a large pan. Pour 3 litres (12 cups) cold water over it, add the salt and bring to a boil. Skim off and add the onion, carrot, celery and celeriac. Crush the garlic and add to the broth with the thyme, bay, cloves and juniper berries. Allow the ham to simmer for 1½ hours until fully cooked.
Remove from the broth and leave to cool for at least 2 hours on a plate.
Stir the honey through the mustard and crush a generous amount of pepper on the mixture. Spread the honey mixture on the ham and place it in an oven preheated to 180°C (350°F/Gas 4) for approx. 25 minutes or until golden brown.
Cut into slices and serve with mustard, with drinks, add a salad as an appetiser or serve the ham with turnip greens.

MAKE YOUR OWN DUCK HAM

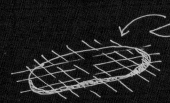 SCORE THE FAT LAYER OF 1 DUCK BREST FILLET CROSSWAYS.

 FILL HALF A TRAY WITH SALT

  GRATE THE RIND OF 1 OR 2 ORANGES, SPRINKLE ON THE DUCK BREST

 PLACE THE DUCK BREST IN THE SALT & TOP WITH MORE SALT UNTIL FULLY COVERED.

 COVER THE TRAY AND PLACE A HEAVY OBJECT ON IT. STORE IN A COOL PLACE

 WAIT 2 DAYS

TA - DA! HOME MADE HAM!

FIRST RINSE THE MEAT THOROUGHLY, PAT DRY AND CUT INTO VERY THIN SLICES USING A SHARP KNIFE

BE CREATIVE → SERVE ON A SALAD, ON SOUP → ON TOP OF RISOTTO ...

PICKLED MACKEREL

This is a good recipe as a replacement for pickled herring. That is what it most resembles, but since it's freshly prepared, it is much better than herring that has been sitting in a glass jar for weeks.

approx. 6 mackerel fillets (ask the fishmonger to fillet three mackerels for you, or maybe you can do it yourself?)

1–2 red capsicums (bell peppers), in thin strips

1 tbsp juniper berries, crushed

approx. 4 bay leaves

3 tbsp mustard seeds

1 tbsp fennel seeds

4 cloves

2 tsp salt

2 tbsp white peppercorns

200 ml (6 fl oz/¾ cup) red wine vinegar

200 ml (6 fl oz/¾ cup) water

few sprigs of oregano

Place a non-stick pan on the heat. Place the fillets, with the skin up, in the hot pan for 10 seconds to singe. Arrange them in a dish with the skin up. Heat all other ingredients in a saucepan for the marinade. At the very last moment, add the oregano sprigs. Cover the fish with the hot sauce. The fish will be soaked and curl upward. Immediately cover the dish with plastic wrap and leave to cool. Place in the refrigerator to marinate for at least 1 day (and night), but preferably 2 days. Test whether the fish is cooked. If the fish is big, it often has to be one day longer. Serve the fish as an appetiser with potato salad or on bread with a drink.

TIP You can also do this with filleted sardines, or even with prawns (shrimp).

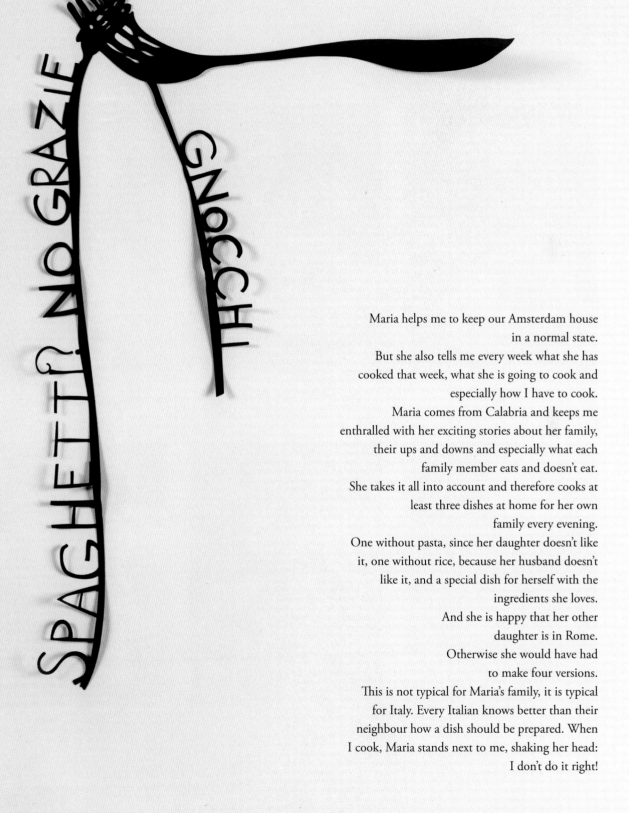

SPAGHETTI? NO GRAZIE

GNOCCHI

Maria helps me to keep our Amsterdam house
in a normal state.
But she also tells me every week what she has
cooked that week, what she is going to cook and
especially how I have to cook.
Maria comes from Calabria and keeps me
enthralled with her exciting stories about her family,
their ups and downs and especially what each
family member eats and doesn't eat.
She takes it all into account and therefore cooks at
least three dishes at home for her own
family every evening.
One without pasta, since her daughter doesn't like
it, one without rice, because her husband doesn't
like it, and a special dish for herself with the
ingredients she loves.
And she is happy that her other
daughter is in Rome.
Otherwise she would have had
to make four versions.
This is not typical for Maria's family, it is typical
for Italy. Every Italian knows better than their
neighbour how a dish should be prepared. When
I cook, Maria stands next to me, shaking her head:
I don't do it right!

MAKING GNOCCHI

I HONESTLY BELIEVE THAT GNOCCHI IS ONE OF THE BEST THINGS IN THE WORLD. MY NEIGHBOUR, CHEF SALVATORE, MAKES THE BEST, IN MY OPINION, BUT THESE DAYS I'M PRETTY GOOD TOO, WHICH IS WHY I WILL NOT EXPLAIN HERE HOW TO MAKE PASTA OR MAKE RISOTTO, SINCE YOU HAVE PROBABLY READ IT A MILLION TIMES. HOWEVER, I MEET A LOT OF PEOPLE WHO HAVE NO IDEA HOW TO MAKE GNOCCHI.

IT IS TRULY DELICIOUS WHEN IT IS HOME-MADE, SO PAY ATTENTION, HERE IT IS:

SCRUB POTATOES AND BOIL IN SKINS. FOR EACH 1 KILO (2 LB) POTATOES YOU NEED: 1 EGG, 300 G (2 CUPS) STRONG FLOUR (TYPE 00), AND A LITTLE SALT.

REMOVE THE SKIN WHILE THE POTATOES ARE STILL HOT. THIS IS EASIER IF YOU PRICK A FORK INTO THE POTATO.

MASH (I USE A POTATO RICER, ACTUALLY AN ESSENTIAL TOOL).

ADD THE FLOUR, BUT NOT ALL OF IT! MAYBE YOU WON'T NEED ALL OF IT. YOU CAN ALWAYS ADD SOME LATER. ALSO ADD A LITTLE SALT.

ADD A BEATEN EGG. AGAIN NOT EVERYTHING IN ONE GO, THE REST CAN BE ADDED LATER.

SWIFTLY KNEAD INTO A SMOOTH DOUGH. IF DESIRED, YOU CAN NOW ADD SOME FLOUR OR EGG.

THIS IS WHAT IT SHOULD LOOK LIKE.

ROLL OUT INTO A ROPE.

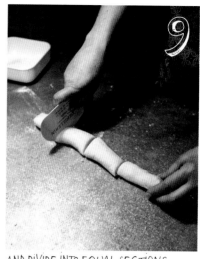

AND DIVIDE INTO EQUAL SECTIONS.

ROLL THE SECTIONS OUT INTO SMALLER 'SAUSAGES'.

CUT THESE SAUSAGES INTO SMALL CUSHIONS, AND LEAVE.

ROLL OVER A GNOCCHI BOARD.

OR ROLL OVER THE BACK OF A FORK.

SAVE GNOCCHI UNDER A DISH TOWEL, UNTIL USED,

OR COOK IMMEDIATELY: WHEN THEY FLOAT TO THE SURFACE, THEY ARE READY.

YES! LET'S GET GOING ...

GNOCCHI' IS ITALIAN FOR WHAT THE ENGLISH CALL 'DUMPLINGS', BUT THAT DOESN'T SOUND VERY ATTRACTIVE IN MY OPINION.
HERE ARE MANY VARIATIONS ON THE BASIC RECIPE AND EVEN A TRADITIONAL RECIPE CALLED GNOCCHI, THAT ARE ACTUALLY
A TYPE OF BISCUIT AU GRATIN, MADE WITH POLENTA.
NOW, I ABSOLUTELY LOVE POLENTA, SO I WILL GIVE YOU THAT RECIPE AS WELL.

GNOCCHI WITH SAGE

A small variation on the basic recipe. This recipe uses sage, but you can use any other herb, such as parsley, basil or rosemary. Great with rabbit stew, for example. Or with butter sauce and deep-fried sage. You know what, I will give you that recipe as well:

1 x basic gnocchi recipe from page 208
1 bunch (approx. 15 g/½ oz) sage

For the sauce
1 bunch (approx. 15 g/½ oz) sage
150 g (5 oz/1¼ sticks) unsalted butter

Knead the finely chopped sage evenly through the potato meal. Then make the gnocchi as described on the previous page.
Melt the butter for the sauce on very low heat. Carefully pour the clear part, which has risen to the top, away from the white protein components at the bottom of the pan. This is called clarifying. The proteins burn quite rapidly. Heat the clarified butter again; with a tablespoon remove any remaining whey from the pan.
Leave to infuse on low heat until the colour turns darker. You have now created a 'beurre noisette'. The butter will acquire a slightly nutty flavour. Remove the stems from the sage leaves. Deep-fry them swiftly, in small portions, in the hot butter and drain on kitchen paper. Serve the herb gnocchi topped with a spoonful of butter sauce and sprinkled with the deep-fried sage leaves.

WALNUT GNOCCHI

Serve these gnocchi with lots of fried mushrooms in a cream sauce with garlic and parsley, for example.

250 g (8 oz) potatoes, hot mashed
1 egg
2 tbsp walnut oil
50 g (approx. 2 oz/½ cup) ground walnuts
100 g (approx. 4 oz/⅔ cup) strong flour, type 00
freshly ground pepper and salt
2 tbsp good-quality olive oil
2 generous tbsp butter

In a large bowl, combine the mashed potatoes with the egg, oil, ground walnuts and enough flour to make a firm ball. Add more walnut oil as needed. Season with salt and pepper. Quickly roll out into a 2-cm (1-inch) thick rope. Cut it in small slices and press these slices gently on the back of a fork to create ridges. Cook in a pan with plenty of salted water and boil for 2–3 minutes until done. Rinse under cold running water and fry in a mixture of butter and good olive oil until crunchy. Serve with fried mushrooms and a cream sauce, as desired.

BUTTERNUT GNOCCHI

You can also make gnocchi from butternut pumpkin instead of potato. They will be a nice shade of orange. Great with the butter sauce described earlier or a ragu, see recipe on page 216.

1 butternut pumpkin (squash) approx.
1 kg/2 lb
1 egg yolk
approx. 100 g (4 oz/⅔ cup) strong flour, type 00
nutmeg, pepper and salt.
50 g (approx. 2 oz/½ cup) freshly grated parmesan
2 tbsp toasted pumpkin seeds (pepitas)

Preheat oven to 180°C (350°F/Gas 4). Peel the butternut squash, cut into sections and remove the seeds and threads using a small sharp knife. Cut into slices approx. 1.5 cm (½ inch) thick. Arrange on a baking sheet lined with baking paper and sprinkle with salt. Bake in the middle of the oven for approx. 30 minutes until done. Press them through a potato ricer or mash until smooth with a hand blender. Using a fork, as it can get sticky, add the flour and egg yolk and season with nutmeg, pepper and salt. Be careful, this mixture will always be a little sticky. Do not add too much flour, as the gnocchi will become tough. You will have to become a little practised at rolling these gnocchi: work on a spacious surface dusted with flour and with floured hands. Quickly roll the dough into thin ropes. Cut into small cushions with a floured knife. Save on a baking sheet lightly dusted with flour until used. Bring a large pan of water to a boil. Add the salt and cook in small quantities for 3 to 4 minutes until done. Sprinkle with grated parmesan cheese, and roasted pumpkin seeds.

IT'S PRONOUNCED 'NYOKI' NOT GNOKKI OR GNOTCHI!

GNOCCHI 'QUATTRO FORMAGGI'

1 x basic gnocchi recipe from page 208
100 g (approx. 4 oz/1 cup) gorgonzola
100 g (approx. 4 oz/1 cup) fontina
100 g (approx. 4 oz/⅓ cup) ricotta
100 g (approx. 4 oz/1 cup) grated parmesan
75 ml (2½ fl oz/⅓ cup) crème fraîche
2–3 tbsp milk, as needed
freshly ground black pepper

Prepare the gnocchi as described on the previous page. Before you cook them melt the cheeses in the crème fraîche in a saucepan. Add some milk,

if necessary. Cover with a generous amount of freshly ground black pepper. Cook the gnocchi for a few minutes until done, remove them from the water and instantly stir them through the hot sauce. Serve immediately.

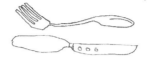

GNOCCHI ALLA ROMANA

Although these are called gnocchi there are no potatoes or other mashed vegetables in the recipe. They are made from polenta and then baked au gratin.
Delicious. Serve with fresh (spicy) tomato sauce.

500 ml (16 fl oz/2 cups) milk
125 g (4 oz/⅔ cup) polenta
nutmeg, pepper and salt
1 egg
75 g (2½ oz/approx. ½ stick) butter
75 g (2½ oz/¾ cup) grated emmental (or gruyere)
75 g (2½ oz/¾ cup) grated parmesan
olive oil

Heat the milk in a frying pan. When it starts to boil, trickle in the polenta, while stirring. Keep on stirring, thus preventing any lumps from forming. Season with nutmeg, salt and pepper. Leave to simmer for 15 minutes on very low heat. Remove from the heat and add the egg, half of the butter and half of both cheeses.
Grease a flat low pan with a little olive oil: it can be a dish or a baking sheet, it makes no difference. Cover with the mixture. Smooth out. Leave to cool. The polenta will stiffen nicely.
Preheat the oven to 180°C (350°F/

Gas 4) before serving. Cut the polenta into 4-cm (1½-inch) squares or cut them out with a round biscuit cutter. Grease an oven dish with the remaining butter. Place the overlapping gnocchi in it and sprinkle with the remaining cheese and a few dabs of butter, if you have any left.
Bake for 30 minutes and serve with raw tomato sauce, see page 212.

GNOCCHI SALAD

Hmm. I'm willing to bet that you are always left with cooked gnocchi.
No problem. They can be used in a salad.
Make a creamy dressing and complement the salad with crunchy vegetables.

Make the dressing from
75 ml (2½ fl oz/⅓ cup) white wine vinegar
60 g (2 oz/¼ cup) sour cream
1 tsp mustard
1 tsp sugar, or a little more
1 tbsp parsley, finely chopped
1 garlic clove, crushed
freshly ground pepper and salt
approx. 200 ml (6 fl oz/¾ cup) olive oil

Make the salad from blanched vegetables
green asparagus, garden peas, broad beans or green beans

(coarsely cut) raw vegetables
little gem (romaine/cos) lettuce, spinach leaf, watercress, radicchio, rocket (arugula), tomato, spring onion (scallion) rings, grated zucchini (courgette) or herbs

meat or fish
roasted sardines, parma ham, smoked salmon, smoked bacon, chicken.

BLACK SPAGHETTI WITH RAW TOMATO SAUCE

I believe there are as many recipes for fresh tomato sauce as there are people in Europe. But this very simple one we like to make in the restaurant. Be careful, this is an uncooked sauce!

For the sauce
8 good tasty tomatoes
zest and juice of ½ lemon
2 garlic cloves, crushed
1 red chilli pepper

For the oil
100 ml (approx. 3 fl oz/½ cup) olive oil, plus a little extra
1 small bunch of basil
2 balls mozzarella, torn into pieces
salt and freshly ground pepper

And also:
300 g (10 oz) black (squid ink) spaghetti, regular spaghetti is also okay of course, but this looks so ridiculously good.

Purée 6 tomatoes in a blender or food processor, together with the lemon, garlic and chilli (seeds removed, if you don't go for spicy). Taste and add salt and pepper, as needed. Quarter the remaining 2 tomatoes, remove the seeds and cut the pulp into small cubes. Stir the cubes through the sauce.

In another tall container, purée the basil with the olive oil until smooth and add a pinch of salt. Set aside. Cook the pasta *al dente* and drain. Add a dash of olive oil to keep the pasta from sticking together.

Transfer the spaghetti immediately to four bowls. Add the tomato sauce to the pasta, sprinkle with mozzarella and top with a trickle of basil oil.

Serve the pasta immediately, otherwise it will cool off quickly.

TAGLIATELLE WITH ZUCCHINI AND CARROT RIBBONS & WHITE PEPPER

You do need a pasta machine for this recipe. If you don't own one, you could use lasagne sheets, cooked and cut into strips.

For the pasta dough
300 g (10 oz/2 cups) plain (all-purpose) flour
3 eggs
salt and pepper
a little semolina (farina/cream of wheat)
If you buy pasta use 350–400 g (12–14 oz)

For the sauce
250 g (8 oz/1 cup) crème fraîche
1 garlic clove, bruised but kept whole
salt and freshly ground white pepper
2 carrots, peeled
2 zucchinis (courgettes)
some fresh chervil, if you can get it

First make the pasta: knead all ingredients into a firm ball in a food processor, or by hand. Leave the dough to rest in the refrigerator for one hour. Roll the dough into a nice slab and run through the pasta machine on the highest setting. Fold and repeat the process. Do this a few times until the dough starts getting smooth and supple. You can now reduce the pasta machine setting. Continue to pass the pasta through the machine until you have a long thin sheet and stop at the lowest setting but one. Sprinkle with semolina and fold over and over into a rectangle. Using a sharp knife, cut the rectangle into strips. If you unfold it, you should have long strings. Keep the strips in small nests. Set aside until used, sprinkle generously with semolina. In the meantime bring the crème fraîche and garlic to a boil, generously sprinkle with salt and white pepper, turn down the heat and simmer gently until used.

Heat two pans filled with water. Cut the carrot and zucchinis in thin slices and those slices in turn, into thin strips. When the water boils, briefly cook the pasta in one pan and blanch the vegetable ribbons in the other pan for a few minutes. Drain the vegetables. Then drain the pasta and rinse thoroughly under cold water. Remove the garlic clove from the cream and stir in the vegetables. Return the pasta to the pan and top with the sauce.

Stir the mixture thoroughly but carefully, in order not to break the vegetables.

Serve immediately, garnish with fresh chervil and sprinkle with salt and pepper.

PAPARDELLE WITH SPICY LAMB RAGU AND CAPERS

3 tbsp extra virgin olive oil

750g–1 kg (1½–2 lb) leg of lamb or lamb shoulder, boned and cut into chunks

1 carrot, cleaned and cubed

1 red onion, peeled and chopped

2 stalks blanched celery, chopped

1 tbsp coriander seeds, roasted

1 tbsp fennel seed

pinch cumin

2 sprigs rosemary, chopped

few sprigs of thyme, chopped

salt and freshly ground pepper

1 small tin tomato puree (70 g/approx. 2 oz)

½ bottle (375 ml/13 fl oz) full-bodied red wine

1 tin peeled tomatoes (400 g/14 oz)

approx. 500 ml (16 fl oz/2 cups) chicken stock (see page 128)

400 g (14 oz) papardelle (very wide fettucine)

2 tbsp capers

dab of butter

And also:

chunk of parmesan cheese for grating

Heat the oil in a heavy-based pan and sear the meat in equal portions on all sides. Do not fry everything at the same time, as too much moisture will be released and you will end up boiling the meat. Remove the meat from the pan and set aside on a plate. In the same frying fat, sauté the carrot, onion and celery. Add the meat, all herbs and spices and the tomato purée. Fry the mixture on high heat while stirring until the tomato purée starts to smell sweet. Add the red wine and stir. Fold in the peeled tomatoes and enough stock to immerse the meat. Leave to simmer on low heat for 1½ hours with the lid left ajar on the pan. Check occasionally whether there is enough moisture in the pan, otherwise add some hot stock. At the end taste for salt and pepper, but remember that the capers you will add later are also salty.

Bring another pan with water to a boil. Add the pasta and boil for 10–12 minutes or until the pasta is cooked *al dente*. Drain the pasta and rinse under cold water. Add the pasta to the ragu, stir in the capers, a dab of butter and a dash of olive oil, stir again, leave to stand for a few minutes away from the heat and serve immediately. Top with grated parmesan cheese.

Risotto al limone
(LEMON RISOTTO)

2 SHALLOTS / FRENCH ONIONS
400 G (14 OZ / 2¼ CUPS) ARBORIO RICE
LARGE PAN OF CHICKEN BROTH (HOT!)
150 ML (5 FL OZ / ⅔ CUP) DRY WHITE WINE
JUICE & ZEST OF 1 LEMON
SALT & PEPPER TO TASTE
2 EGG YOLKS
ABOUT 100 G (4 OZ / 1 CUP PARMESAN
   CHEESE → GRATED
100 G (4 OZ / 1 STICK) BUTTER,
   PLUS A LITTLE MORE TO FINISH

AND ALSO 2 EXTRA LEMONS

MELT THE BUTTER IN A LARGE THICK-BOTTOMED PAN.
SAUTÉ THE SHALLOTS. ADD THE RICE AND FRY ON
HIGH HEAT WHILE STIRRING UNTIL THE RICE GRAINS
ARE GLAZED, WITH A WHITE CORE.

ADD THE WINE → FOLD IN THE LEMON JUICE. ADD THE
HOT BROTH, SPOONFUL BY SPOONFUL, UNTIL IT IS ABSORBED.
CONTINUE UNTIL THE RICE IS AL DENTE AFTER 20 MINS.
SEASON WITH SALT & PEPPER.

OOH! LEMONS ARE TASTY

→ FOLD IN CHEESE, UNTIL IT IS MELTED. REMOVE FROM
HEAT. STIR IN SMALL PATS OF BUTTER & EGG YOLKS.
COVER THE PAN AND TURN ON THE GRILL (BROILER).

QUARTER THE 2 EXTRA LEMONS AND GRILL (BROIL) THEM UNTIL
THEY FORM BLACK SPECKS.
ARRANGE RISOTTO AND SPRINKLE WITH LEMON ZEST.

SERVE WITH THE BURNT LEMON QUARTERS!

THEY HAVE BECOME
NICE AND SWEET.
SQUEEZE THEM
OVER YOUR PLATE.
YEY!

RISO SALAD WITH YOUNG ZUCCHINIS, ASPARAGUS, RICOTTA AND FLOWERS

For the salad
100 g (4 oz) riso (rice-shaped pasta)
1 bunch green asparagus
2 small young zucchinis (courgettes) or 8 mini
200 g (7 oz/¾ cup) fresh ricotta
approx. 20 small edible flowers, available from specialist food stores or see the note below.

For the dressing
zest and juice of 1 whole lemon,
100 ml (approx. 3 fl oz/½ cup) olive oil
1 tbsp honey
salt and freshly ground pepper

Cook the pasta *al dente,* approx. 10 minutes and drain. Then rinse well under cold water to stop the cooking process. Cook the asparagus for 2 minutes and also rinse under cold water. Cut the zucchinis and asparagus into very thin slices. To do so, use a mandolin or shredder if you own one. Mix the riso with the vegetables and arrange over 4 plates. Top with the crumbled ricotta. Beat the dressing ingredients into a nice vinaigrette and pour over the salads. Scatter the flowers over the top and serve immediately.

NOTE

Edible flowers: geranium petals, marigold petals, nasturtium (petals and leaves), dandelion petals, daisies, hedge violets, carnation petals, rose petals, lavender, yellow iris, ground ivy, sweet woodruff and field mushroom flowers. They can all be put in the salad. Should you have herbs in your garden or on your balcony, the flowers of green leaf herbs can also be used in the salad: dill, chives, basil blossoms, rosemary, camomile, chervil, coriander (cilantro), spearmint and sage.

RISOTTO WITH BEETROOT AND TALEGGIO

50 g (approx. 2 oz/½ stick) + 100 g (approx. 4 oz/1 stick) butter, cubed
2 shallots, diced
leaves of a few sprigs of fresh thyme
400 g (14 oz/1¾ cups) arborio risotto rice
1.5 litres (6 cups) dry white wine
approx. 1 litre (4 cups) piping hot chicken stock (see page 128)
2 beetroots (beets), cooked and diced
salt and pepper, to taste
150 g (5 oz) taleggio without rind and cubed (Italian mountain cheese with an earthy flavour, which melts easily)

Melt the 50 g butter in a large heavy-based pan and sauté the shallots until glassy. Add the thyme and rice and fry while stirring until the rice looks glassy with a white core. Add the wine and keep on stirring. Fold in the hot stock, spoonful by spoonful, on high heat and continue to stir until absorbed. After 15 minutes, add the beetroot cubes. Continue until the rice is cooked *al dente* in 20 minutes. Season with salt and pepper. Stir in the cheese until fully melted and the remaining cubed butter. Turn off the heat and place the lid on the pan. Quickly transfer the risotto to four plates and serve.

TIP If you are unable to find taleggio, use a cheese with a strong 'earthy' flavour.

ROTOLO WITH LOBSTER, WILD SPINACH & ROSEMARY BEURRE BLANC

It takes some work, but the result is fabulous. A recipe for a lot of people, we like to make it for large dinners.
Serve 1 slice as a side dish or 2 as the main course. You will easily get 12 slices from 1 rotolo.

For the pasta dough

300 g (10 oz/2 cups) plain (all-purpose) flour

3 eggs

salt and pepper

a little semolina (farina/cream of wheat)

For the beurre blanc

2 shallots, chopped

1 bay leaf

small bunch rosemary

200 ml (6 fl oz/¾ cup) white wine

100 g (approx. 4 oz/½ cup) crème fraîche

200 g (7 oz/¾ stick) chilled butter, cubed

For the rotolo filling

250 g (8 oz) lobster tails

250 g (8 oz) peeled prawns (shrimp), the larger ones taste the best

100 g (approx. 4 oz/½ cup) + 200 g (approx. 8 oz/1 cup) crème fraîche

1 egg

zest of 1 lemon

a little olive oil for frying

2 shallots, diced

1 garlic clove, crushed

1 kg (2 lb) wild spinach, washed

nutmeg

For the pasta, knead all ingredients into a firm ball, in a food processor or by hand. Leave the wrapped dough to rest in the refrigerator for one hour.

Make the rotolo filling: coarsely grind the lobster, prawns, 100 g crème fraîche and egg in the food processor. Top with a little grated lemon zest and season with salt and pepper. Set aside. Heat a little olive oil in a wok or large frying pan, add the shallot and garlic and fry the spinach in portions with the water still clinging to it, until done. Leave to drain in a colander and press as much moisture out as possible. Finely chop the spinach, stir in the rest of the crème fraîche and season with salt, pepper and nutmeg.

Roll out the dough into a nice sheet that fits into the pasta machine and run it through the pasta machine on its widest setting. Fold and repeat the process. Do this a few times until the dough is smooth and supple. You can now reduce the setting on the machine. Keep passing the pasta through the machine until you have a long thin sheet and stop at the lowest setting but one. Dust the sheet with semolina and cut into three equal parts. Use some water to stick them together so that you have a large square mat of pasta in front of you. On the side closest to you, place a long rope from left to right of the seafood mixture. Spread the spinach-cream mixture over the rest of the sheet. At the end leave a 3-cm (approx. 1-inch) border. Carefully roll, beginning with the side with the crayfish mixture. Seal the clear edge with a little water. Then roll the rotolo into a clean dish towel and tie with a string just like rolled meat.

Bring a roasting tin with plenty of water and a pinch of salt to a boil. Slide in the rotolo. Cook for 20 minutes. Remove. Leave to stand and remove the string and the towel. Cut the rotolo into thick slices.

During cooking, prepare the 'gastrique' or buerre blanc: heat the shallots with bay, rosemary and white wine in a saucepan. Allow liquid to evaporate on low heat and stop when you are left with approx. 4 tbsp of moisture. Strain and return the collected moisture to the pan. Add the crème fraîche. Using a whisk, stir in the butter, bit by bit. Never allow the sauce to boil, but keep it near boiling point. When all butter is absorbed, the sauce should have thickened considerably. Spoon some sauce on a (preheated) plate, cover with a slice of rotolo and serve immediately.

SMOKING FISH

HOT SMOKING IS QUICK AND GIVES A BETTER RESULT THAN SMOKING TOO LONG WHICH IS DISGUSTING AND MAKES YOUR FOOD TASTE LIKE AN ASHTRAY. IF YOU ARE NOT SURE THE FOOD IS READY, YOU CAN ALWAYS REHEAT IT IN THE OVEN OR FRY IT IN THE PAN. YOU HAVE TO ACQUIRE SOME SKILL HERE AS YOU WILL NOTICE THAT FATTER FISH VARIETIES, LARGER CUTS OF MEAT OR FIRMER VEGETABLES HAVE TO SMOKE FOR A LONG TIME, SAY, 30 MINUTES, AND SMALL, LIGHT ITEMS, ONLY A VERY SHORT TIME: SOMETIMES 5 MINUTES WILL DO IT! SMOKERS TEND TO BE EXPENSIVE, BUT YOU CAN MAKE ONE YOURSELF FOR NEXT TO NOTHING. USE SMOKE CHIPS, WHICH YOU CAN BUY IN A GOOD FOOD STORE. BUT YOU CAN ALSO USE DRIED HERBS, TEA OR SPICES. JUST EXPERIMENT. DRIED BAY AND JUNIPER BERRY (TWIGS) ARE ANOTHER OPTION.

228

CLEAN 2 MACKERELS, OR ASK THE FISHMONGER TO DO IT FOR YOU. EITHER WAY, WASH THEM BRIEFLY AT HOME.

THEN PLACE THEM IN A TRAY WITH SALTED WATER FOR 2 HOURS. I USE 3 TBSP SALT FOR 2-3 LITRES (8-12 CUPS).

PAT THE FISH DRY, INCLUDING THE ABDOMINAL CAVITY (WHICH YOU CAN FILL WITH LEMON, OR OTHER HERBS).

PLACE THE FOLLOWING IN A ROASTING TIN OR ON A BAKING SHEET: 3 TBSP SMOKE CHIPS, 2 TBSP JUNIPER BERRIES AND 1 TBSP FENNEL SEED. TEA IS ANOTHER OPTION.

FOLD A SHEET OF ALUMINIUM FOIL IN HALF AND COVER THE SMOKE CHIPS AND HERBS.

COVER WITH A RACK THAT FITS ON OR INTO THE ROASTING TIN. THIS CAN BE AN OVEN RACK, A RACK FROM THE MICROWAVE OR A TRIVET, AS LONG AS IT IS HEAT-RESISTANT.

PLACE THE FISH ON THE RACK, LIGHT THE FLAME AND WAIT UNTIL IT STARTS SMOKING. TURN DOWN THE FLAME...

...COVER THE LOT WITH PLENTY OF ALUMINIUM FOIL. ENSURE THERE ARE NO GAPS, CAREFULLY CLOSE THE EDGES. USE AN OVEN MITT IF YOUR FINGERS ARE NOT FLAME-RESISTANT.

THIS IS A FATTY FISH AND THEREFORE I SMOKE IT FOR 30 MINUTES. I WOULD SMOKE A FISH WITH LESS FAT, SUCH AS WHITE FISH, FOR ONLY 10 MINUTES AND REHEAT IT IN THE OVEN, IF NECESSARY.

LET'S GET GOING ...

THE RULE TO REMEMBER IS THAT MEAT AND FISH WITH LESS FAT ARE SMOKED FOR A SHORTER TIME THAN THEIR FATTER FAMILY MEMBERS. SMOKING IT FOR TOO LONG WILL RESULT IN AN UNPLEASANT BITTER TASTE. IT'S PREFERABLE THAT ANYTHING IS UNDERSMOKED RATHER THAN OVERSMOKED – YOU CAN ALWAYS FINISH IT OFF IN A PREHEATED OVEN.

PICKLED AND SMOKED SALMON

Fish that is fairly fatty lends itself better to smoking, but actually any fish can be smoked. Always pickle the fish (or meat) beforehand. You can do so in a brine bath, but also by rubbing the meat with salt. You will achieve the best result if you first dry the fish before smoking it. You can do this in the refrigerator. But patting it dry with kitchen paper also works for the more impatient chefs.

500 g (1 lb) fresh salmon fillet, skinned
115 ml (approx. 3½ oz/½ cup) dark rum
100 g (approx. 4 oz/½ cup) brown sugar
50 g (approx. 2 oz) coarse sea salt
freshly ground black pepper

Place the salmon in a shallow dish. Pour the rum over the salmon and leave to stand for 30 minutes. Remove the salmon from the liquid and carefully pat dry with kitchen paper. Discard the liquid. Combine the sugar, salt and pepper. Line the bottom of a bowl or roasting tin with part of the salt-sugar mixture and place the salmon in it. Spread the rest of the mixture to fully cover the salmon. Cover with plastic wrap and leave the salmon to marinate in the refrigerator for 3 to 4 hours. Place a handful of wood chips at the bottom of the smoker and get ready to smoke. Take the salmon from the refrigerator, wipe it clean and discard the moisture and the remaining mixture. Rinse the salmon under the water and carefully pat it clean and dry with kitchen paper. Smoke the salmon until done for approx. 15 minutes. The thickness will determine how long. You can leave the salmon to cool completely and use it as sandwich filling. Delicious with the horseradish sauce on page 195.

SMOKED TOMATO SOUP

This is a very easy recipe and quite surprising. It often features on the menu in our restaurant. You can smoke any vegetable with high moisture content in this way. Think of zucchini (courgettes), large mushrooms, eggplants (aubergines) and capsicums (bell peppers). I have provided a great recipe for this on page 236.

1 kg (2 lb) tomatoes
2 x 400 g (14 oz) tins peeled tomatoes
1 tsp ground paprika
1 tsp cayenne pepper
2 cloves garlic, peeled
500 ml (16 fl oz/2 cups) chicken stock
salt and freshly ground pepper
2 tbsp smoke chips or tea

Bring a pan with water to a boil. Using a sharp knife, score a cross in the skin at the bottom of each tomato. When the water boils, add the tomatoes and blanch for ½ minute. Rinse under running water. The skin can now be easily removed. Smoke the tomatoes in a smoker for 30 minutes on low heat.
In the meantime, heat the peeled tinned tomatoes in a large pan. Add the herbs and garlic. Pour in the stock. Allow the soup to simmer for 30 minutes. Lastly, add the smoked tomatoes and purée the soup until smooth, using a hand blender. Taste and add salt and pepper, as needed. Serve the soup in large bowls with a spoonful of spreadable labneh (see page 296), or a dash of olive oil.

SPARERIBS

At first, I was unsure about including this recipe here, since I thought it should be in the barbecue section. But spareribs taste so much better if you smoke them first.

4–6 racks of spareribs
(plan 1–1½ racks per person)

For the sauce
100 ml (approx. 3 fl oz/½ cup) soy sauce
3 tbsp raw caster (superfine) sugar
zest and juice of 1 lime
1 capsicum (bell pepper), seeds removed and finely chopped
6 garlic cloves, crushed
1 piece of fresh ginger the length of a thumb
3–4 sprigs fresh thyme, finely chopped
3 tbsp oil

Combine all ingredients and stir into a thick sauce. Use it to cover the spareribs and leave to marinate for at least 3 hours, but preferably longer. Turn on the smoker and smoke on very low heat for 20 minutes. Cook them a further 1 hour covered with aluminium foil in a 180°C (350°F/Gas 4) oven. Do not forget to continue to baste them with the marinade. Remove the foil during the last 20 minutes. Serve with Oof's barbecue sauce, see page 380, or the garlic sauce on the same page. Serve with white cabbage salad with cumin, see page 261.

SMOKED GARLIC DRESSING

First smoke the garlic, smoke more than one bulb at the same time. Smoked garlic can actually be used wherever you use regular garlic. Only the flavour is surprisingly different. Store smoked garlic tightly covered in the refrigerator.

a few bulbs of good quality garlic
2 tbsp smoke chips
a few dried bay leaves

Fill the smoker with the smoke chips and bay leaves. Place the garlic on the grid and smoke on as low a heat as possible for 30 minutes. Turn off the heat and leave the garlic in the smoker for another hour or more.

For the dressing
4 cloves smoked garlic
1 tbsp horseradish or ½ tbsp freshly grated horseradish
4 tbsp sherry (wine) vinegar
100 ml (approx. 3 fl oz/½ cup) grape seed oil or another light vegetable oil
1 tbsp fresh thyme or oregano
freshly ground pepper and salt

Flatten the garlic in order to easily remove the skins. Add them with the horseradish and the vinegar to a blender or food processor and purée until smooth. Add the oil while stirring and then the herbs. Once the dressing is thick and white, season it with salt and pepper.
This dressing is delicious on boiled potatoes, on a grilled vegetable salad or served with red meat.

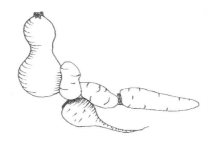

SMOKED ROOT VEGETABLES

Anything can be smoked, including root vegetables.
Contrary to meat and fish, these vegetables, which contain less moisture than tomatoes or zucchinis, for example, must be smoked longer and hotter than other recipes so far.
Cut all vegetables into chunks of approximately equal size, thus retaining the flavour everywhere.

231

2 carrots
2 sweet potatoes
2 waxy potatoes
2 parsnips
1 butternut pumpkin (squash)
all peeled and cut into chunks of the same size
2 beetroots (beets), also cut in the same size, but not peeled only washed
4 tbsp olive oil
1 tbsp thyme
freshly ground pepper and salt
3 tbsp smoke chips

Mix all vegetables in a bowl with the oil, thyme, salt and pepper. Arrange on the smoker rack and smoke for at least 30–40 minutes on medium heat. After 25 minutes, turn on the oven and preheat it to 180°C (350°F/Gas 4). Bake the vegetables for a further 15 minutes, until they take on a nice colour and are cooked *al dente*. Serve as a side dish with one-person chicken, see recipe on page 263.

SMOKED PRAWNS WITH LEMON & ROSEMARY SALT

A good snack with drinks or on a table full of small dishes.

1 kg (2 lb) large prawns (shrimp), raw
1.5 litres (6 cups) water
2 tbsp salt

For the rosemary salt
3 tbsp coarse sea salt
2 sprigs rosemary
zest of 2 lemons

Peel the prawns, but leave the tails on. Stir the salt into the water. Add the prawns and allow to soak in the brine for at least two hours.

Preheat oven to 180°C (350°F/Gas 4).

Place the prawns on the rack in your home-made smoker (see page 228) and smoke the prawns for 5 minutes. Remove from the smoker and leave to cook for another 5 minutes in the regular oven. Allow to cool.

In the meantime, prepare the rosemary salt: crush the sea salt and the rosemary leaves into a green powder in a mortar. Fold in the lemon zest.

Sprinkle on the smoked prawns and serve as a dip with some extra salt.

TIP You do not need all the herb salt for this dish, so save the rest for another time. It is delicious on steak or on fried fish or chicken.

SMOKED PORK CHOPS

4 tasty pork chops, preferably organic
2–3 tbsp salt
8 juniper berries, crushed
2 bay leaves
8 peppercorns
smoke chips, a few dried bay leaves and preferably a few dried twigs of the juniper berry bush

Dissolve the salt in a tray with water in which the chops fit neatly. Add the juniper berries, bay and peppercorns, as well as the meat. Leave to soak in the brine for 2 hours or longer if you have the time.
Heat the smoker with 3 tbsp smoke chips, a few bay leaves and perhaps eight juniper berry twigs. Pat the chops dry and smoke for approx. 8 minutes.
Heat the barbecue or grill pan and bake the chops on high heat until crisp and golden brown. They are probably nearly cooked, and therefore do not have to be baked for a long time.
Serve with stew or fried scorzonera (salsify/black oyster plant) and carrots, see page 285.

SMOKED CAPSICUMS

Tasty side dish or part of many dishes on a buffet or cocktail table.

50 g (approx. 2 oz/⅓ cup) parmesan cheese or pecorino, shaved

2 yellow capsicums (bell peppers)

2 red capsicums (bell peppers)

small flowers of an unsprayed carthamus ⋆, from the thistle (optional of course)

For the dressing
3 tbsp balsamic vinegar

1 tsp mustard

1 tbsp honey

freshly ground pepper and salt

150 ml (5 fl oz/⅔ cup) olive oil

And also:
smoke chips

1 tbsp dried rosemary or Earl Grey tea

First grill the capsicums by placing them on the stove burner and slowly burning them black.

If you do not own a gas stove, place them under a hot grill. Turn over regularly, they really have to turn black!!!

Once scorched on all sides, transfer them to a plastic bag and tie in a knot. Leave the capsicums to sweat for 30 minutes.

Remove. Using a knife, remove the skin. Rinse well under running water and pat dry. Smoke for 15 minutes in the smoker on 2 tbsp wood chips and a little dry rosemary or tea.

Make the dressing by combining the first four ingredients and then adding the oil until the dressing achieves the desired thickness.

Cut the smoked capsicums into thick strips. Arrange on a dish. Sprinkle with the shaved cheese and carthamus and top with the dressing.

⋆ Carthamus is a common yellow-orange thistle, often called the saffron thistle. It is available from some florists.

BRANDADE OF SMOKED TROUT

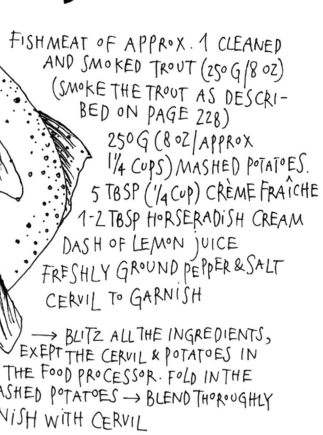

FISHMEAT OF APPROX. 1 CLEANED
AND SMOKED TROUT (250 G/8 OZ)
(SMOKE THE TROUT AS DESCRI-
BED ON PAGE 228)
250 G (8 OZ / APPROX
1¼ CUPS) MASHED POTATOES.
5 TBSP (¼ CUP) CRÈME FRAÎCHE
1-2 TBSP HORSERADISH CREAM
DASH OF LEMON JUICE
FRESHLY GROUND PEPPER & SALT
CERVIL TO GARNISH

→ BLITZ ALL THE INGREDIENTS,
EXEPT THE CERVIL & POTATOES IN
THE FOOD PROCESSOR. FOLD IN THE
MASHED POTATOES → BLEND THOROUGHLY
GARNISH WITH CERVIL

SMOKED MACKEREL WITH WATERCRESS, WHITE BEANS AND TASTY TOMATOES

For the salad

250 g (8 oz) steeped white beans or 1 jar white beans

1 whole smoked mackerel (see page 228)

250 g (8 oz) small vine tomatoes

2 bunches watercress or 2 handfuls young spinach leaves

1 small bunch parsley, washed and finely chopped

For the dressing

juice and zest of ½ lemon

1 shallot, finely chopped

100 ml (approx. 3 fl oz/½ cup) linseed oil, grapeseed oil or another light vegetable oil

freshly ground pepper and salt

Cook the beans until done, approx. 30–40 minutes, then remove from the pan and rinse under cold water. Or, if you use beans from a jar, drain well and rinse. Prepare the dressing by combining all the ingredients and lastly, stirring in the oil in a trickle. Fold the beans into the dressing. Set aside and allow to marinate. Carefully remove the skin from the mackerel and then the meat from the bone. Separate the fish into flakes over a large bowl. Wash and halve the tomatoes and add them. If you use watercress, trim away the tough stems. Mix the lettuce with the fish and tomato. Lastly, fold in the beans and dressing and garnish with parsley.

TIP Make a snack with the smoked fish leftovers, which my sister and I liked to make when we were children:

CUCUMBER ROUNDS FILLED WITH SMOKED FISH

For approx. 15 snacks

½ smoked mackerel (or 1 tin sardines)

1 tbsp butter at room temperature

2 tbsp mayonnaise, see recipe on page 380

few drops of lemon juice

pinch cayenne pepper

salt and pepper

1 whole cucumber

Mix all ingredients, except the cucumber, in a food processor or mash them in a bowl using a fork. Season with salt, pepper and lemon juice. Cut the cucumber in sections the length of the apple corer. Trim away the ends.

Using the apple corer, scoop out the seeds. You can also use a thin sharp knife, for that matter. Fill the created cavity with the fish mousse and wrap the rounds in plastic wrap. Leave to cool and set for about an hour in the refrigerator.

Cut the cucumber into thick slices with a sharp knife and enjoy!

MILLE-FEUILLE OF SMOKED AND RAW BEETROOT AND COMTÉ, WITH WATERCRESS, AND NUT DRESSING

4 parboiled beetroots (beets)

2 tbsp smoke chips

2 raw beetroots (beets)

a small handful hazelnuts, briefly toasted in a dry frying pan,

1 bunch watercress, washed with hard stems removed or fine spinach leaves

the leaves of two sprigs of fresh sage or oregano

100 g (approx. 4 oz) Comté (a cheese from the Jura, France), cubed: otherwise use parmesan cheese or goat's cheese

2 tbsp hazelnut oil

For the dressing

4 tbsp. raspberry vinegar

1 tablespoon ginger syrup or honey

8 tbsp olive oil

freshly ground pepper and salt

Smoke the beetroots for 20 minutes on low heat. Then cut all beetroots, raw and smoked, as thinly as possible on a mandolin or using a good knife. Make the dressing with the ingredients from the list and sprinkle over the beetroot slices.
Cover and leave to marinate for at least 1 hour until used.
Toast the nuts in a dry frying pan and chop coarsely.

Build the salads: stack alternating leaves and marinated beetroot slices on 4 plates.
Divide the Comté between the plates and sprinkle the salads with the hazelnuts and the sage or oregano leaves.
Trickle some hazelnut oil over each salad.

Use the leftover smoked beetroot the following day in a club sandwich: page 389.

Each time we stay in the Colombet family's orchard in the south of France, Oof will first search for large rocks near the river to build a fire in our camp.
Starting a fire is of course a lot of fun, but in this case it is also vital. We cook on it and in the evening it is our heater, since nights can get quite chilly in the country.
We stare at it together at night before we fall asleep: what will we grill on it tomorrow?

BUILDING A BARBECUE

BUILDING A BARBECUE IS OBVIOUSLY NOT DIFFICULT, FINDING A PLACE IN THE OPEN WHERE IT IS PERMITTED OFTEN IS, ALWAYS BE AWARE OF FIRE RESTRICTIONS IN YOUR AREA. SOMETIMES THERE ARE ALSO RESTRICTIONS ON GATHERING WOOD. IF ALL ELSE FAILS, USE THE BARBECUES PROVIDED IN PARKS AND CAMPING GROUNDS.
WHAT IS FUN IS OF COURSE TO BUILD A BARBECUE YOURSELF. THE SAFEST PLACE TO USE A HOME-MADE BARBECUE IS NEXT TO WATER, WHETHER IT IS A BEACH, RIVER OR A LARGE BUCKET FULL OF WATER, THE WIND CAN SUDDENLY SEND THE FLAMES IN A TOTALLY UNEXPECTED DIRECTION! >>> OOF WILL SHOW YOU, WATCH!

DIG A HOLE. SEARCH FOR ROCKS THAT NEATLY FIT AROUND IT. BUILD A BORDER WITH TWO LAYERS OF ROCKS, WHICH MAY COME IN HANDY LATER.

CHECK WHETHER THE RACK YOU BROUGHT FITS.

GATHER WOOD AND FILL THE FIRE (YOU CAN OBVIOUSLY ALSO BRING YOUR OWN LOGS WHICH CAN BE PURCHASED IN BAGS).

LIGHT THE FIRE. USE A PORTABLE FIRE LIGHTER, THE FIRE STARTED IMMEDIATELY.

NOW IT HAS TO BURN FOR A WHILE UNTIL THE FLAMES HAVE DIED DOWN AND THE WOOD SMOULDERS, IN THE MEANTIME, HAVE A DRINK AND WAIT...

PREPARE YOUR FOOD, IN THIS CASE 2 STEAKS, A BUNCH OF ROSEMARY, OLIVE OIL, PEPPER AND SALT.

BRIEFLY RUB THE MEAT WITH THE OLIVE OIL AND SPRINKLE WITH PEPPER AND SALT.

THE BARBECUE IS SMOULDERING, THE MEAT CAN GO ON IT.

WE WANT IT HOTTER, THEREFORE OOF LOWERS THE MEAT.

REMOVE THE FIRST LAYER OF ROCKS: THAT'S MORE LIKE IT!

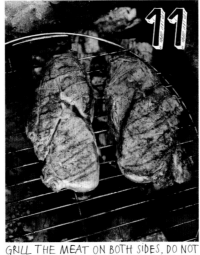

GRILL THE MEAT ON BOTH SIDES, DO NOT TURN IT CONSTANTLY.

JUST LEAVE IT BE.

OCCASIONALLY BRUSH WITH A ROSEMARY SPRIG DIPPED IN OLIVE OIL.

LEAVE TO REST FOR 10 MINUTES AWAY FROM THE FIRE.

YES! ONLY THEN CAN YOU CARVE THE MEAT. BON APPÉTIT!

OK! LET'S GET GOING ...

YOU CAN THROW MEAT OR FISH ON THE BARBECUE OR IN THE FRYING PAN AS IS, WITH ONLY SALT AND PEPPER, BUT SOMETIMES A MARINADE OR 'RUB' (DRY MIXTURE OF HERBS AND SPICES) IS A TASTY ADDITION AND YOU WON'T NEED ANY SAUCES.

STICKY MARINADE

Great for spareribs or pork, for example.

Proportions
4 tbsp red wine vinegar
150 ml (5 fl oz/⅔ cup) soy sauce
1 tbsp tomato purée
1 tsp cinnamon
1 thumb's length of peeled and grated fresh ginger
1 garlic clove, chopped
1 tbsp brown sugar

FRESH HERB MARINADE

Great with fish or chicken.

1 generous handful of chopped fresh garden herbs: tarragon, chives, basil, parsley
2 shallots, diced
2 garlic cloves, coarsely chopped
2 tbsp (white) balsamic vinegar
pinch of salt
1 tbsp. peppercorns from the mortar
100 ml (approx. 3 fl oz/½ cup) olive oil

FENNEL SEED RUB

Tasty on pork chops or on fish.

Coarsely grind in a mortar:
5 tbsp toasted fennel seeds
4 tbsp toasted coriander seeds
2 tsp coarse sea salt
2 tsp white peppercorns
1 tbsp sugar

NORTH AFRICAN RUB

Great on lamb kebabs,
lamb chops or chicken.
1 red onion, diced
3 garlic cloves, thinly sliced
2 tbsp cumin seeds, toasted
2 tbsp coriander seeds, toasted
1 cinnamon stick
1 tbsp caraway seeds, toasted
1 pinch cayenne pepper (to taste) or
1 dried chilli pepper
1 tbsp sea salt

MEDITERRANEAN MARINADE

Good with chicken, meat and fish.

juice of 1 lemon
1 chilli pepper
1 tsp coarse sea salt
2 garlic cloves
1 handful fresh basil & mint
approx. 100 ml (3 fl oz/½ cup) extra virgin olive oil

Coarsely chop the herbs and crush all ingredients in a large mortar or food processor into a coarse pesto.

SPICY SOUTH AMERICAN RUB

Great on beef
zest of 2 limes
2 garlic cloves, thinly sliced
1 pinch chilli powder
1 tbsp ground paprika
1 tbsp toasted cumin seeds
2 tbsp fresh oregano, chopped
(otherwise 1 tbsp dried oregano)
1 tsp sea salt
1 tsp ground black pepper

LOBSTER WITH LIME, SPRING ONION AND GINGER BUTTER

1 piece of ginger the length of a large thumb
2 spring onions (scallions)
150 g (5 oz/1¼ sticks) butter at room temperature
fine rind of 1 lime
salt and pepper
2 large lobsters of approx. 1 kg (2 lb) each, uncooked
extra lime

Peel the ginger and chop finely. Wash and finely chop the spring onions. Beat the ginger and spring onion into the softened butter using a fork, hand blender or food processor. Further season the butter with the lime zest, salt and pepper. Transfer the butter to a sheet of plastic wrap and roll tightly into a rope. Place in the refrigerator for approx. 1 hour to set. Precook the lobsters for 3 minutes in a pan with plenty of water. Remove from the pan and allow to slightly cool. Halve them lengthways with a sharp knife. Crack the claws with a heavy object or nut cracker. This will allow them to cook faster later and make them easier for guests to open. Place the lobster halves with the meat side up on the hot barecue. Spread some butter on the meat. Briefly cook the lobsters, until the meat is no longer glassy. You can close the lid briefly on the barbecue in order to thoroughly cook the lobster and to allow the smoked flavour to better infuse.
Serve with slices of herb butter and lime.
Great with green asparagus with parsley gremolata, see recipe on page 286.

CHICKEN KEBAB WITH HONEY, PRUNES & WALNUTS

For the marinade
3 tbsp honey
1 tbsp *ras el hanout* (North African spice mixture), or allspice, or ½ tbsp mixed spices
2 tbsp red wine vinegar
200 ml (6 fl oz/¾ cup) red wine
salt and freshly ground pepper

And also:
8 chicken thighs, the meat cut away from the bone and the cut into equal chunks
60 g (2 oz/½ cup) walnuts
250 g (8 oz/2¼ cups) dried prunes, pitted, but left whole

First prepare a marinade by combining all the ingredients. Arrange the chicken chunks in a tray and top with the marinade. Cover with plastic wrap and place in the refrigerator for a few hours, the longer the better. Thread the chicken chunks on the skewers, alternating with the prunes. Cook the marinade and the walnuts into a syrup. Grill the skewers on medium heat until done. Arrange on a dish and top with the warm marinade.
Serve with herb tabouleh and cardamom dressing, see recipe on page 282.

CHICKEN KEBAB WITH SALAD, CROUTONS AND YOGHURT DRESSING

For the marinade/sauce
100 ml (approx. 3 fl oz/½ cup) yoghurt
2 tbsp lemon juice
1 garlic clove, crushed
2 tbsp parsley, finely chopped
50 ml (1½ fl oz/¼ cup) olive oil
freshly ground pepper and salt

And also:
3 chicken legs or 4 chicken thighs, boneless
2 little gem (romaine) lettuces
½ baguette
75 ml (2½ fl oz/⅓ cup) olive oil

Make a marinade/sauce by combining all the ingredients. Cut the chicken meat into equal chunks. Stir in half of the sauce. Place in the refrigerator to marinate for approx. 3 hours. Carefully trim away the bottom of the little gem lettuces and quarter. Bring a pan with water to a boil. Add a pinch of salt and briefly blanch the lettuce. Cut half a baguette in equal 2 cm (approx. 1 inch) cubes. Season the olive oil with salt and pepper and add the bread. Thread the chicken, bread and lettuce alternatively on the skewers. Grill them on medium heat on the barbecue or grill pan until done. Serve with the remaining yoghurt dressing. Tasty with a crispy salad sprinkled with parmesan cheese.

TROUT WITH PARSLEY & FENNEL SEED BUTTER

4 trout
60 ml (2 fl oz/¼ cup) olive oil
2 garlic cloves, crushed
small bunch parsley, chopped
½ lemon, thinly sliced
125 g (approx. 4 oz/1 stick) butter at room temperature
1 tbsp fennel seeds, crushed in the mortar
salt and pepper
aluminium foil

Score the skin of the cleaned trout and rub the fish with a mixture of olive oil, 1 garlic clove, pepper, salt, and half of the chopped parsley. Fill the cavities with the lemon slices. Wrap in aluminium foil.
Make herb butter in the food processor: combine the butter, fennel seeds, reserved parsley and garlic, salt and pepper into a smooth mixture. Roll the butter in a sheet of plastic wrap and put in the refrigerator to harden for approx. 1 hour.
Cook the fish for approx. 10 minutes on a warm barbecue. Take a look after 8 minutes to check whether they are cooked! But close the foil quickly in order for the wrapping to retain the heat. Serve the fish topped with a slice of cold herb butter.

WHOLE BEEF RUMP IN SPICE CRUST
WITH ROSEMARY SALMORIGLIO
an easy recipe serving 7

Create a spice mix:

USING MORTAR & PESTLE:

2 TBSP FENNEL SEED
2 TBSP OREGANO
2 TBSP BLACK PEPPERCORNS
2 TBSP COARSE SEA SALT

PLACE 1 WHOLE RUMP
(APPROX. 1 KG / 2 LBS)
ON A SHEET OF CLING FILM

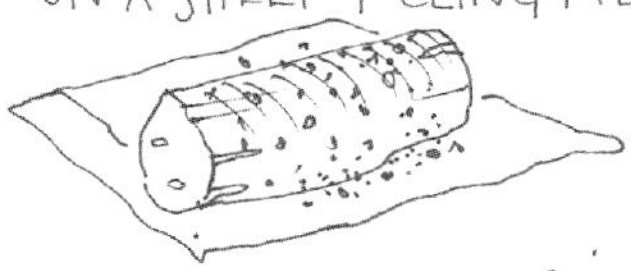

SPRINKLE WITH THE SPICES
& WRAP THOROUGHLY
STORE FOR ABOUT 1 HOUR
IN THE FRIDGE.

SAUTÉ THE MARINATED
RUMP ON ALL SIDES.
IN A LITTLE OLIVE OIL,
THIS HAPPENS
QUICKLY, JUST LIKE
ROAST BEEF.
LEAVE TO REST FOR 15
MINS UNDER ALU-
MINIUM FOIL.
CUT INTO VERY THIN
SLICES & SCOVER
WITH THE GREEN OIL
...Ready!

make salmoriglio:
IN A FOOD PROCESSOR → BLEND:

THE LEAVES OF 1 BUNCH
OF ROSEMARY
ZEST & JUICE OF 1 LEMON

½ TSP SEA SALT
FRESHLY GROUND PEPPER
100 ML (APPROX 3 FL OZ / ½ CUP)
GOOD QUALITY OLIVE OIL

Chez moi
tout est subtil

CHOUCROUTE

LEG OF LAMB WITH NETTLES & GOAT'S CHEESE PESTO

You can serve 6-8 people with a leg of lamb.

For the leg of lamb
1 whole garlic bulb
1 bunch thyme
100 ml (approx. 3 fl oz/½ cup) olive oil
salt and pepper
1 leg of lamb, deboned: approx. 1 kg (2 lb); or with bone: approx. 1.5 kg (3 lb)

For the pesto
2 handfuls or approx. 75 g (2½ oz) young nettle tops (or rocket [arugula] salad if you are not such a nature person)
2 garlic cloves
100 ml (approx. 3 fl oz/½ cup) olive oil
100g (4 oz/1 cup) grated aged goat's cheese (or pecorino)
60 g (2 oz/½ cup) walnuts, if desired

Coarsely chop the garlic. Strip the leaves from the thyme sprigs. Blend the mixture. Also add the stripped thyme sprigs. Massage the marinade into the meat, cover and leave the meat to marinate in the refrigerator preferably one night, but at least 2 hours. Allow the lamb to reach room temperature.

Preheat the oven to 180°C (350°F/Gas 4). Remove the herbs from the lamb and roast for 35–40 minutes until medium rare. A leg of lamb with bone will have to bake a little longer, say, 40–45 minutes. Leave the meat to rest under a sheet of aluminium foil for 15 minutes.

In the meantime prepare the pesto. Pulse the ingredients in the food processor into a coarse pesto, not too fine. Taste and add salt and pepper, as needed.

Cut the lamb into thin slices. Serve with nettle pesto and boiled young potatoes.

Great with lukewarm green vegetable salad, see recipe on page 171.

MACKEREL FILLETS WITH BAY, GARLIC AND CAPSICUMS

4 mackerel fillets, cleaned

For the filling
14 fresh bay leaves, cut into pieces
1 red capsicum bell pepper), seeds removed
½ red chilli
2 garlic cloves
approx. 50 ml (1½ fl oz/¼ cup) olive oil
coarse sea salt

In the food processor, make a coarse paste with the bay leaves, capsicum, garlic and red chilli. Add as much oil as needed for the mixture to stick together.
Score the skin side of the fish fillets a few times and cover with some of the paste. Grease a baking sheet. Place the fish with the filled side up and cook under a hot grill (180°C/350°F/Gas 4) for approx. 8 minutes.
Also possible on the barbecue: to do so cover the other side so that the skin side bakes on the hot grill. Thoroughly grease the skin and do not turn the fish. Bake until done just a smidge away from the highest fire.
Serve with white cabbage salad and cumin.

WHITE CABBAGE SALAD WITH CUMIN

A remarkably simple but fun salad for all seasons.

For the salad
1 quarter white cabbage, very thinly sliced, using a mandolin or in the food processor
1 bunch watercress, leaves only, or rocket (arugula) salad, or dandelion leaf (used here)
1 large bunch mint, leaves only
2 tbsp cumin seeds, roasted

For the dressing
1 garlic clove
1 tbsp cumin seeds, roasted
juice of 1 lemon
freshly ground pepper and salt
150 ml (5 fl oz/⅔ cup) grape seed oil or other light vegetable oil

Combine all ingredients for the salad. Add the first four ingredients for the dressing in a tall container and purée until smooth. Pour in enough oil to create a creamy dressing. Pour over the salad and leave to stand so the flavours infuse.

CHICKEN WITH SAGE, GARLIC AND MUSHROOMS

Along the Canal St. Martin, behind our house in Paris, a group of people, primarily students, often eat together at the end of the day as late as the summer weather allows. It is quite a bit cheaper than eating out and at least as much fun. The best urban picnic site ever.

3 whole garlic bulbs
1 bunch fresh sage, finely chopped
few sprigs of thyme
olive oil
4 cockerels or poussins (spring chickens)
1 kg (2 lb) fresh forest mushrooms: portobello, chanterelles, chestnut mushrooms, giant mushrooms,
oyster mushrooms, all cleaned

Halve the three garlic bulbs. The bottom halves will cling together nicely. Save them, peel the loose cloves and chop them finely. Fill the chickens with part of the mixture of chopped garlic, sage, thyme, salt and pepper. Rub them with olive oil, salt and pepper and place on a baking sheet. Distribute the halved garlic bulbs between them and a few of the mushrooms. Arrange the remaining mushrooms on another baking sheet, top with the remaining garlic, thyme and sage mixture. Drizzle with some olive oil and sprinkle with salt and pepper. Preheat the oven to 180°C (350°F/Gas 4). Place the chickens in it and bake for approx. 45 minutes or until done. Add the mushrooms in the last 10 minutes.
Briefly leave the birds to rest after baking.
Take them with mushrooms, garlic and all on a picnic or serve with the pumpkins au gratin from page 281 (handy, they can also go into the oven) and fried wild spinach.

MULLET WITH CHERMOULA

Plan on 2 small mullets per serving

8 mullets, cleaned and scaled (ask the fishmonger)

For the chermoula (Hassane told us you say 'Tsar-millah')
a few strands saffron
3 tomatoes, quartered, seeds removed and pulp cubed
3 roasted capsicums (bell peppers), cubed
1 small bunch coriander (cilantro)
1 small bunch mint sprigs
1 small bunch parsley (preferably flat-leaf)
juice of 1 lemon
2 tsp toasted cumin seeds, coarsely crushed in a mortar
freshly ground pepper and salt
olive oil

Preheat the oven to 180°C (350°F/Gas 4).
Prepare the chermoula: soak the saffron in 3 tbsp warm water. Combine all other ingredients. Lastly, stir in the saffron threads with the moisture and season the chermoula with salt and pepper.
Place the mullets in a greased roasting tin, cover with half of the chermoula and place in the hot over for approx. 7 minutes. Once the fish is cooked, pour the other half of the sauce over it and serve with bread and a green salad.

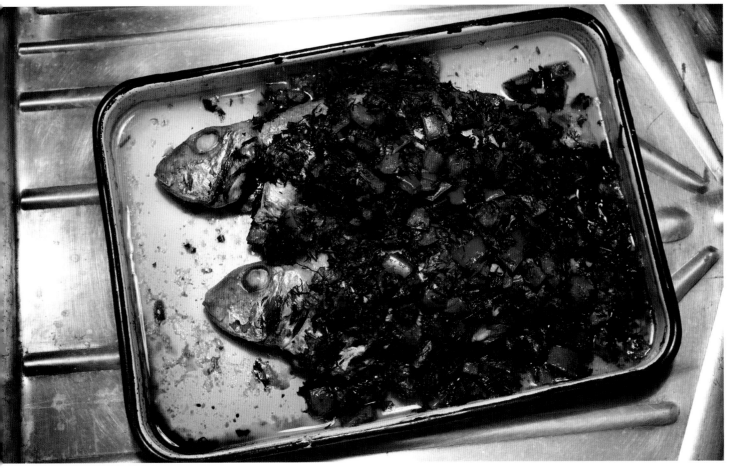

LAMB CHOPS IN A CRUST OF LEMON, MINT AND PISTACHIO NUTS

100 g (approx. 4 oz) capers
4 tbsp grated lemon zest
2 garlic cloves, crushed
4 tbsp chopped mint
75 g (2½ oz/½ cup) pistachio nuts, chopped
4 tbsp olive oil or more
4 lamb chops
olive oil for frying

Coarsely chop the capers. Mix with lemon zest, garlic, mint and chopped nuts. Add the olive oil into a smooth dressing. Pour into a shallow bowl. Pat the lamb chops dry and cut the fat, thus preventing the chop curling up on the grill. Place them in the mixture you have made in the bowl and leave to marinate for 1 hour. Remove. Ensure that all chops are well covered with the marinade. Cook on a barbecue or in a frying pan on both sides on high heat until medium rare. Serve with mint sauce.

MINT SAUCE

3 shallots, diced
1 small bunch of mint sprigs, washed and finely chopped
1 tbsp cold butter + 75 g (2½ oz/approx. ½ stick) extra, in pats
3 tbsp white wine vinegar
1 tbsp honey

Sauté the shallots with half of the chopped mint in the butter until the shallots turn glassy. Add the vinegar and then the honey. Bring the mixture to a boil and allow the acid from the vinegar to slightly evaporate. Remove from the heat, beat in the extra pats of cold butter until the sauce thickens. Season with salt and pepper.

Yvette ,
Charles & Marie

GRILLED SALAD

2 bulbs fennel
juice of 2 lemons
100 ml (approx. 3 fl oz/½ cup) good quality olive oil
50 g (approx. 2 oz/⅓ cup) pistachio nuts, halved
1 bunch fresh watercress, cleaned
1 small bunch dill, coarsely chopped
1 handful other type of lettuce, cleaned: here I used dandelion leaves, but rocket (arugula) salad or mesclun is another option
150 g (5 oz/1¼ cups) soft goat's cheese
freshly ground pepper and salt

Remove the tough outer layers from the fennel and the tips and cut them from top to bottom, as thinly as possible. Place them on the barbecue or oven rack to grill. Transfer to a large dish. Pour a portion of the lemon juice and oil over the fennel, to allow the flavours to infuse. Toast the nuts briefly in a hot dry pan until they release their aroma. Trim away the hard stems from the watercress bunch and thoroughly wash and dry the leaves. Mix them and the dill with the other salad. Arrange the salad on the plate with the fennel. Then top with the crumbled goat's cheese. Trickle some lemon juice and oil on the plate and sprinkle with the pistachio nuts. Season the salad with salt and pepper.

LUKEWARM SALAD WITH POTATOES, GREEN BEANS AND GIANT BEANS

750 g (26 oz) fine waxy potatoes, such as Roseval potatoes
250 g (8 oz) green beans, cleaned
400 g (14 oz) tin giant beans (large haricot beans), steeping a day in advance and then cooking always tastes better!

For the dressing
1 small bunch parsley, washed and chopped
1 small bunch tarragon, washed and chopped
2 tbsp pine nuts
1 garlic clove, crushed
4 tbsp extra virgin olive oil
juice of ½ lemon
freshly ground pepper and salt
50 g (approx. 2 oz/⅓ cup) parmesan cheese, freshly grated

Scrub the potatoes, cut them into approx. 3-cm (1-inch) cubes and boil until done in salted water. Cook the green beans for approx. 3 minutes. Drain and rinse briefly under cold water. Drain the giant beans and also rinse under cold water. Coarsely grind the ingredients for the dressing in a mortar or food processor. Stir into the salad and serve immediately.

GRILLED FENNEL Salad

FLATBREAD WITH CHICKPEAS AND SAGE

300 ml (10 fl oz/1¼ cups) lukewarm water
1 sachet yeast (7 g/¼ oz/2¼ tsp)
600 g (21 oz/4 cups) plain (all-purpose) flour and a little extra
400 g (14 oz) tin chickpeas, drained and rinsed
few sprigs sage, chopped
salt and freshly ground pepper

273

Stir the yeast into the lukewarm water and briefly allow to dissolve. Combine the flour and chickpeas in a food processor or in a large bowl and mix well. The chickpeas have to burst open! Combine the sage, salt and pepper and add the water. Knead thoroughly, at least some 10 minutes into a smooth dough. If necessary, add flour if it is too sticky. Dust a bowl with a little flour and place the dough ball in it. Cover with plastic wrap. Put in a draught-free place and leave the dough to rise for at least 1 hour. Dust the work surface and remove the risen flour ball from the bowl. Knead the dough again and divide the ball into equal portions the size of apricots. Sprinkle with flour and keep until used, at least one hour, on a serving tray dusted with flour. Place a grill pan on the heat. Roll the small dough balls into thin elongated pieces and fry in the grill pan until they puff up. Turn halfway through until they are cooked.

TIP You can also grill them on the barbecue! Grill them towards the end, when the fire has slightly subsided.

PIZZA BIANCA WITH FLATBREAD

For 10–12 small pizzas as a side dish or 24 mini pizzas: great when served with drinks.

250 g (8 oz/2⅔ cups) mixed mushrooms
3 tbsp olive oil, plus a little extra
few twigs fresh thyme, reserve some for garnish
1 garlic clove, chopped
freshly ground pepper and salt
1 quantity of dough, as described above
200 g (7 oz) taleggio (Italian mountain cheese with an earthy flavour, which melts easily, otherwise use raclette cheese or mozzarella)
24 drops truffle or hazelnut oil

Slice the mushrooms. Heat a frying pan with olive oil and briefly fry the mushrooms with a little thyme. Toward the end add the garlic and season with salt and pepper. If desired, save some thyme for the garnish. Set aside to slightly cool. Line a baking sheet with baking paper and grease. Make the dough as described above and create pizzas in the size of your choice. Then cover them with mushrooms and taleggio. Bake in an oven preheated to 175°C (340°F/Gas 4) for approx. 15 minutes until golden brown. Leave to slightly cool and sprinkle with a little oil. Delicious as a meal served with a beetroot salad, see page 172.

PUMPKIN & POTATO SALAD FROM THE OVEN WITH FRESH SAGE

4 small pumpkins or 2 butternut squashes
4 waxy potatoes, with skin
150 ml (5 fl oz/⅔ cup) olive oil
1 garlic clove, crushed
2 tsp ground paprika
1 bunch fresh sage, chopped (save some leaves for the garnish)
freshly ground pepper and salt

Preheat the oven to 180°C (350°F/Gas 4). Cut half of the pumpkins in two and scoop them out. Peel the remaining pumpkins using a parer. Halve them and discard the seeds. Cube all the pumpkin pulp. Cut the potatoes to the same size. Make a dressing with the olive oil, garlic, ground paprika, sage, salt and pepper.
Mix with the pumpkin and potato cubes. Line a baking sheet with baking paper. Spread the cubes on it and bake for 30 minutes until *al dente* and golden brown. Turn occasionally. Lastly, add the scooped out pumpkin shells to the oven and bake a further 10 minutes. Before serving transfer the potato and pumpkin cubes back to the hollowed pumpkins. Garnish with a few fresh sage leaves.
Great with leg of lamb, see recipe on page 258 or the smoked chops on page 235.

CARROT SALAD WITH CUMIN

3 carrots, peeled
1 garlic clove, crushed
1 tbsp cumin
4 tbsp olive oil
2 tbsp red wine vinegar
pinch cayenne pepper
a few leaves coriander (cilantro) to garnish
salt

Grate the carrots coarsely on a mandolin or in the food processor. Make a dressing with the remaining ingredients and blend them with the carrot salad. Keep the salad in the refrigerator until ready to serve. Prior to serving garnish with a few coriander leaves. Good with Arab lamb burger on page 384 or with chicken kebab on page 253.

ROSTI BISCUITS WITH ROSEMARY

6 waxy, medium potatoes
leaves of 6 twigs rosemary
sea salt
some light oil for frying

Cut the potatoes into a very fine julienne (very thin strips) in the food processor or use a good mandolin or grater. Thoroughly pat them dry. Add the rosemary and a little salt to the grated potatoes. Heat a thin coat of oil in a frying pan and fry 3 heaps of potato mixture in the oil at a time. Do not stir or touch! When the edges turn golden yellow, turn and fry on the other side. Allow to drain on kitchen paper. Can be easily made in advance: heat the biscuits for 6 minutes prior to serving in an oven preheated to 180°C (350°F/Gas 4).

JERUSALEM ARTICHOKES AU GRATIN

approx. 1.5 kg (3 lb) Jerusalem artichokes (sunchokes)
200 ml (6 fl oz/¾ cup) thick cream
300 g (10 oz/1¼ cups) crème fraîche
250 g (8 oz/2½ cups) grated gruyère
freshly ground pepper and salt
pat of butter to grease an oven dish

Peel the artichokes. Bring a pan with water to a boil and add salt. Cook the artichokes 5–7 minutes until nearly done. Swiftly rinse and cut into slices as thin as possible. This is easiest on a mandolin, but a sharp knife also works.
Beat the cream with the crème fraîche and season with salt and pepper.
Butter the oven dish and preheat the oven to 180°C (350°F/Gas 4).
Place a third of the artichokes slices in the oven dish, sprinkle with a portion of the gruyere and top with a portion of the cream. Continue until all the ingredients are used. Finish with the cheese and place the dish in the oven.
Bake the gratin for approx. 30 minutes, or until golden brown.

FRESH BEAN SALAD WITH RADISH AND CAESAR DRESSING

200 g (7 oz) green beans, cleaned and broken in half

200 g (7 oz) sugarsnap peas, cleaned

200 g (7 oz/1⅓ cups) broad (fava) beans, preferably fresh, but otherwise frozen

1 bunch radishes

1 small bunch flat-leaf parsley, coarsely chopped

For the dressing

1 garlic clove, crushed

2 generous tbsp mayonnaise

2 generous tbsp sour cream

75 g (2½ oz/½ cup) freshly grated parmesan cheese

1 tinned anchovy fillet

juice of ½ lemon

salt and freshly ground pepper

Firstly, prepare a large bowl filled with water and ice cubes. Then heat a pan with water and a pinch of salt and bring to a boil. Briefly blanch the beans, starting with the green beans, as these need the most time. Once the beans are cooked *al dente*, remove them with a slotted spoon and submerge in the ice water.

When they are ice-cold remove from the ice water and leave to drain. In the meantime, wash and clean the radishes. Quarter them and add them to the beans. Also stir in the parsley.

Make the dressing by thoroughly blending the ingredients. Taste for salt: due to the anchovy fillet and cheese it may very well be salty enough.

Blend the dressing with the bean salad. A great salad with the chicken kebab on page 253.

PUMPKINS AU GRATIN

1 butternut pumpkin (butternut squash) approx. 1 kg/2 lb

2 small pumpkins (Hokkaido pumpkins, for example)

4 tbsp olive oil

pinch cayenne pepper

pinch ground paprika

pinch nutmeg

4 eggs

250 g (8 oz/1 cup) crème fraîche

150 g (5 oz/1½ cups) grated cheese, (emmental tastes good)

Peel the butternut pumpkin, remove the seeds and cut the pulp into 2-cm (approx. 1-inch) cubes. Cut off the cap of the mini pumpkins. Scoop them out, first the seeds and then the pulp. Leave approx. 1 cm (½ inch) pulp inside the skin. Also cut the scooped out pulp into chunks. Mix all pumpkin cubes with olive oil, cayenne pepper, ground paprika, nutmeg and salt.

Arrange on a greased baking sheet and grill for 30 minutes or until the edges start turning black, in an oven preheated to 180°C (350°F/Gas 4). Leave the pumpkin cubes to cool and then purée.

Beat the eggs with a crème fraîche, stir in the pumpkin purée and then the cheese. Fill the mini pumpkins.

Preheat the oven to 180°C (350°F/Gas 4). Place the pumpkins in it. Lay the caps next to them.

Bake for approx. 40 minutes or until done.

Cut them into wedges, peel. Serve with red meat or with one-person chicken, see page 263.

HERB TABOULEH WITH CARDAMOM DRESSING

500 g (1 lb/2⅔ cups) couscous, red quinoa or burghul (bulgur)

250 g (8 oz/2 cups) mixed nuts: hazelnuts, walnuts, pine nuts, etc.

4 bunches different green herbs: coriander (cilantro), parsley, basil and mint are my favourites

100 g (approx. 4 oz/½ cup) raisins

For the dressing

1 tbsp seeds from cardamom pods, otherwise ½ tbsp cardamom powder

2 tbsp honey

1 garlic clove, crushed

juice of 2 lemons

freshly ground black pepper

salt

400 ml (14 fl oz/1⅔ cups) olive oil

Follow directions on the packaging for the couscous, which will typically recommend using one and a half parts boiling water to one part couscous. Pour over the couscous in three steps. Allow to steep briefly each time and fluff with a fork in order for the grains to separate. Transfer to a large bowl, the couscous will swell considerably. (If using quinoa or burghul, soak well until soft or follow directions on the packets.)

Toast the nuts in a dry frying pan until they begin to colour. Taste whether the couscous is cooked. Wash the herbs and chop them. Stir them through the couscous with the nuts and raisins.

Prepare the mayonnaise: crush the cardamom seeds into powder in a mortar. Combined with the other ingredients and toward the end stir the oil in a thin trickle through the dressing until it thickens.

Stir the dressing through the couscous and keep in a covered bowl until served.

(You can easily make this side dish a day in advance, but do put it in the refrigerator overnight.)

ZUCCHINI PROVENCAL STYLE

This is not even a recipe, but once prepared in this way, you will never want to eat zucchinis (courgettes) any other way. Norbert and Valerie always make this for us when we build the fire together in their back garden in the south of France. The secret is primarily in the high-quality olive oil.

Wrap whole, medium-sized zucchinis (courgettes) in aluminium foil. Place them in the hot fire, as you do when you roast potatoes. They will be cooked after 20 minutes. Do not forget to turn occasionally if you do not cook them in, but on top of the fire. Remove from the fire, open the foil and transfer the zucchini to your plate. Cut in half lengthways. Top the cooked zucchini with good quality olive oil and sprinkle with sea salt and pepper. Eat with a spoon!

FRIED SCORZONERA AND CARROT AU GRATIN WITH GORGONZOLA

750 g (1½ lb) scorzonera (long root vegetable, substitute parsnip or turnip)
100 ml (approx. 3 fl oz/½ cup) milk
3 carrots
125 ml (approx. 4 fl oz/⅔ cup) thick cream
150 g (5 oz) gorgonzola
1 garlic clove, crushed
freshly ground pepper and salt
1 sprig rosemary
2 tbsp olive oil
30 g (1 oz/¼ cup) slivered almonds

Brush the scorzonera clean under cold running water. Peel them using a parer and cut them into 4-cm (2-inch) sections.
Rinse and immediately place in a bowl with 500 ml (16 fl oz/2 cups) water mixed with the milk, reserve. Wear rubber
gloves when peeling the scorzonera, as they release a sap which will give you orange hands, which is why this vegetable
is also sometimes referred to as cook's sorrow.
Preheat the oven to 180°C (350°F/Gas 4).
Peel the carrots and cut them into sections like the scorzonera. Bring the milk-water mixture with the vegetables and
a pinch of salt to a boil and cook the vegetables for 8 minutes until nearly done. In the meantime, heat the cream with
half of the gorgonzola in a saucepan, add the garlic, pepper and rosemary and leave to simmer on low heat until used.
Using a skimmer, remove the vegetables from the cooking liquid and place them in an oven dish greased with olive oil.
Top with the sauce. Crumble the remaining gorgonzola on the vegetables and sprinkle with almonds. Bake au gratin
until golden brown for approx. 20 minutes. Serve with beef loin, for example, see recipe on page 256, and mashed potatoes.

GREEN ASPARAGUS WITH PARSLEY GREMOLATA

For the gremolata
1 generous bunch flat-leaf parsley
zest of 1 lemon
juice of nearly whole lemon
2 garlic cloves, crushed
2 tbsp olive oil
freshly ground pepper and salt
16 green asparagus (most of the time this is 1 bundle, if you have thin asparagus)

Combine all ingredients for the gremolata in a food processor into a sort of 'pesto'. Bring a pan with liberally salted water to a boil. Peel the woody bottom off the asparagus stems. Blanch for 3 minutes, they must stay green and crunchy. Rinse under cold water. Until serving, place the asparagus in a bowl with the gremolata, to allow them to marinate.
Eat cold or lukewarm.

GREEN BEANS WITH WALNUTS

For the dressing
100 ml (approx. 3 fl oz/½ cup) walnut oil
1 shallot, diced
3 tbsp red wine vinegar
salt and pepper
400 g (14 oz) green beans
75 g (2½ oz/½ cup) walnuts

Make the dressing by beating the oil in a thin trickle through the other ingredients, except the beans and walnuts.
Bring a large pan with salted water to a boil. Blanch the beans for approx. 5 minutes, until cooked *al dente*.
Drain in a colander over the sink. Toast the nuts briefly in a dry frying pan.
Place the beans in a serving dish, top with the dressing and sprinkle with walnuts.

LONG LEEK PIE

4 sheets all-butter puff pastry
3 leeks
200 ml (6 fl oz/¾ cup) white wine
pat of butter
few thyme sprigs
salt and pepper
½ cup aged goat's cheese, grated or crumbled
1 egg white, loosely beaten

Stack the puff pastry sheets and roll them out lengthways into a long and narrow strip. Using the back of a knife cut a rectangle about 2 cm (1 inch) around the inside of the pastry edge, like a picture frame.

Cut the leeks into three sections and remove the dark green leaf and the bottom. Wash carefully and then simmer until cooked in the white wine, butter, thyme, pepper and salt for approx. 20 minutes. Remove from the moisture and pat dry. Place them neatly next to each other within the rectangle you have created in the puff pastry.

Top with goat's cheese and brush the outer edges with loosely beaten egg white.

Bake the pie in an oven preheated to 200°C (400°F/Gas 6) for approx. 25 minutes. The edge will rise considerably.

Delicious with leg of lamb, see page 258 or with fennel salad as on page 270.

My sister and I often used to make cheese together.
We hung the cloth with the curds on a branch of the lilac tree in the garden and couldn't wait until it was ready.
We ate the young cheese on toast with tomatoes, actually much like cottage cheese.
As children we did not have the patience to leave the cheese to age for very long.
But you do, as I do too now.

MAKING CHEESE

ODDLY ENOUGH, TO MAKE CHEESE YOU DON'T NEED MUCH EQUIPMENT AND IT IS ACTUALLY ONLY ABOUT AS MUCH WORK AS MAKING TEA.

YOU CAN DECIDE WHEN YOU THINK THE CHEESE IS 'READY'. EACH STAGE OF THE CHEESE MAKING HAS A DIFFERENT FLAVOUR AND ANOTHER TEXTURE. BY ADDING SALT TO THE CHEESE, YOU WILL SLIGHTLY EXTEND ITS SHELF LIFE, SAY, ONE WEEK. HERE IS A STEP-BY-STEP GUIDE FOR A COW'S MILK CHEESE. BY STEP 5 I WILL HAVE MADE RICOTTA, BUT I WILL CONTINUE TO MAKE A CHEESE THAT IS MOST LIKE COW'S CHEESE. EXPERIMENT WITH GOAT'S MILK OR SHEEP'S MILK.

WITH THIS RECIPE YOU CAN MAKE A CHEESE WEIGHING APPROXIMATELY 250 G (8 OZ).

YOU WILL NEED: 1 LITRE (4 CUPS) ORGANIC MILK, 1 LITRE (4 CUPS) ORGANIC BUTTERMILK, A FEW DROPS OF LEMON JUICE AND 1 TSP SALT (TO TASTE)

292

PREPARE
ONE 400 G (14 OZ) TIN, OF WHICH THE INSIDE IS LACQUERED WHITE (AGAINST RUST, WHICH OFTEN OCCURS IN TINS), ONE OTHER TIN OR WEIGHT THAT SNUGLY FITS INTO IT, ONE PIECE OF CHEESECLOTH OR FINE FABRIC, ONE LONG PIECE OF ELASTIC, ONE SMALL PLATE.
USING A TIN OPENER, CUT THE TOP AND BOTTOM OFF THE TIN AND SAVE ONE LID FOR LATER.
PUT A LARGE PAN ON THE HEAT AND POUR IN THE MILK. SQUEEZE THE LEMON.

HEAT THE TWO MILKS IN A PAN. ADD THE LEMON JUICE.

WHEN THE MILK IS NEAR BOILING, IT WILL SEPARATE INTO WHEY AND CURD. CONTINUE TO STIR FOR 1 MINUTE.

STRAIN AND STIR UNTIL ALL WHEY HAS DRAINED.

YOU HAVE JUST MADE RICOTTA! THAT'S HOW FAST IT IS.

ADD SALT AND STIR.

NOW YOU HAVE LIGHTLY SALTED FRESH CHEESE. HIGH TIME TO MAKE ACTUAL CHEESE...

PLACE THE CLOTH IN THE TIN AND POUR IN THE CURDS.

PULL UP THE CORNERS, ALLOWING THE YOUNG CHEESE TO SINK IN.

IF NECESSARY, CUT THE CLOTH TO SIZE AND COVER WITH THE LID.

TA-DA! YOU'VE MADE AN ACTUAL CHEESE! YOU CAN NOW ROLL IT THROUGH HERBS, IF YOU SO DESIRE, OR EAT IT AS IS, WITH A TOMATO ON TOAST, FOR EXAMPLE. YOU CAN ALSO RETURN THE CHEESE TO A TRAY WITH WATER AND SALT TO THE FRIDGE (1 TSP SALT FOR 500 ML [16 FL OZ / 2 CUPS] WATER). THIS IS CALLED 'PICKLING': THE CHEESE WILL DEVELOP MORE FLAVOUR AND ALSO AN ENTIRELY DIFFERENT STRUCTURE. DO THIS FOR THREE DAYS AT THE MOST.

COVER WITH ANOTHER TIN AND PLACE THEM BOTH ON A PLATE. TIGHTLY WRAP THE ELASTIC AROUND BOTH TINS. AFTER A WHILE YOU CAN TIGHTEN THE ELASTIC. PLACE IN THE REFRIGERATOR FOR 12 HOURS.

TRUE CHEESE BOARD

From now on, you can make it yourself!

Front left, you will see the same cheese as the cheese on the right, which is sprinkled with sea salt and rosemary. Only, the first cheese has spent three days in a brine bath, giving it an entirely different structure and flavour. In terms of flavour it is fairly similar to mozzarella.

I have mixed cracked black pepper and roasted mustard seeds through the tall cheese at the back. By roasting mustard seeds, not only does the colour get darker, but the flavour changes to that of nuts, which obviously goes well with cheese.

Experiment with the shape of your cheeses. This will result in a nicely varied board.

TIP Serve with, for example:
Lavash crackers, see page 110
Crostini, see page 110
Fig butter, see page 113
Cranberry, walnuts & pear chutney, see page 58
Apple-date chutney, see page 159
Confit de vin, see page 17

LET'S GET GOING ...

MAKING CHEESE ALSO MEANS A WHOLE LOT MORE: JUST THINK OF HANGOP, A SIMPLE CHEESE, WHICH YOU CAN EAT SWEET, BUT WHICH IS ALSO TASTY SAVOURY, ON TOAST, FOR EXAMPLE.
AND THIS TOO HAS VARIATIONS: LEBANESE LABNEH IS ALSO A YOGHURT CHEESE, WHICH YOU CAN EASILY MAKE YOURSELF.
THE LONGER YOU LEAVE THE CHEESE, THE HARDER IT GETS.

HERB CHEESES

These are variations on the cheese I made on the previous page.

Before straining the cheese, stir a handful of chopped thyme, chives, nettles or parsley through it.

Add 2 tbsp briefly roasted coriander seeds to the curds.

Add 2 tbsp 'herbes de Provence' to the curds.

Add 2 chopped jalapeño peppers or harissa to the curds.

Add 1 tbsp crushed black pepper and 1 tbsp roasted mustard seeds to the curds.

Finish the cheese as described on page 293. Serve topped with (spicy) olive oil and a little sea salt, ground paprika or cayenne pepper.

> ?FROMAASH?
> THAT'S FRENCH
> FOR CHEESE

HANGOP

Hangop is the simplest cheese you can make yourself, without the use of coagulants or other additives. You cannot buy it in the store, but it is so simple that you just have to try it. Hangop is eaten as a dessert, but if you have a little left over, it is also great for breakfast!

1 litre (4 cups) yoghurt
250 ml (9 fl oz/1 cup) thick cream
seeds from a vanilla bean
zest of 1 lemon
100 g (approx. 4 oz/¾ cup) icing (confectioner's) sugar

Place a clean dish towel in a strainer. Place the strainer on a bucket. Pour the yoghurt into it and cover with plastic wrap. Set aside for one night in the basement or in a cold place in the house. The following day, whip the cream, vanilla, lemon zest and sugar. Carefully fold the yoghurt into the whipped cream and serve the *hangop* with red fruit.

SPREADABLE LABNEH

Labneh is a yoghurt cheese from Lebanon. It is very similar to hangop, but it is always salted and eaten as a savoury dish. Have it as a cheese spread on bread, on soup or salads or on toasts with a drink.

½–1 tsp salt, to taste
1 garlic clove, crushed (optional)
1 litre (4 cups) whole (full-fat) yoghurt

Mix the salt and garlic through the yoghurt. Place a clean dish towel on a colander or strainer. Pour the yoghurt on it and tie the towel with a string or elastic band. Hang over the sink or over a bucket. Or cover with plastic wrap and hang in the strainer over a bucket. Let it hang for 12–24 hours. Regularly wring the towel, the aim is for as much moisture (whey) as possible to drain from the yoghurt. You will be left with a spreadable cheese. Serve sprinkled with fresh garden herbs or sesame seeds and a little olive oil. Complement with crispy bread.

SEASONED LABNEH BALLS IN OLIVE OIL

This is a variation on the recipe for spreadable labneh on the previous page.
If you leave the yoghurt to hang longer, the labneh becomes drier and you can roll it into balls.

For approximately 25 balls

2 litres (8 cups) preferably Greek or Turkish yoghurt, but any regular whole (full-fat) yoghurt will do

2 tsp salt

1 tsp black pepper

1 garlic clove, freshly crushed (optional)

500 ml (16 fl oz/2 cups) olive oil (or more, if necessary)

a few bay leaves, some dried red chilli flakes, or something else you like, perhaps cardamom pods

1 jar dried oregano (approx. 15 g/½ oz/¼ cup)

1 jar dried thyme (approx. 15 g/½ oz/¼ cup)

Mix the salt, pepper and garlic through the yoghurt. Place a clean dish towel on a colander or strainer and pour in the seasoned yoghurt. Cover with plastic wrap and put in a cool place, or pull the corners together and tie the dish towel with a thick elastic band or string as tightly as possible around the yoghurt, thus increasing the pressure.

Make a loop in the string and hang the filled towel over a bucket or over the sink.

It is handy to turn a stool upside down, hang the towel on the cross and place a bucket under it.

Or you can hang the towel from a tree outside, if the weather isn't too hot. You'll come up with something.

Hang the towel for at least three days in a cool place. Every day try to tighten the towel a little more (as much moisture as possible has to be extracted).

Place half of the olive oil, bay leaves and other spices in an attractive tall glass container, preserving jar or clean vase.

Mix the dried oregano and thyme on a plate. With clean hands, create small balls, the size of a walnut, with the drained yoghurt, and carefully roll through the herbs. Slide them into the oil one by one and top up the container with olive oil in order for the balls to 'float'.

Eat them as a snack with a drink or serve after a meal as part of a cheeseboard.

CHEESE

BUTTERMILK HANGOP WITH CARAMEL SAUCE

A very old-fashioned Dutch recipe, and truly delicious. You will need more buttermilk than for yoghurt hangop, just because buttermilk is thinner and therefore more of it will drain away. Buttermilk hangop has a totally different structure from yoghurt hangop, it looks more like custard. This dish used to be eaten topped with crumbled bread crust, but this is no longer the case. I replace it with crunchy almond biscuits, but gingersnaps also fit the bill.

For the hangop
1 litre (4 cups) buttermilk
3 tbsp brown sugar
1 tsp cinnamon
4 crunchy biscuits (cookies): amaretti, gingersnaps
1 tbsp toasted almonds

For the caramel sauce
200 g (approx. 7 oz/1 cup) sugar
100 ml (approx. 3 fl oz/½ cup) water
50 g (approx. 2 oz/½ stick) butter
200 ml (6 fl oz/¾ cup) thick cream

Wet a clean dish towel and place it in a strainer or colander. Hang the strainer over a large bucket and pour in the buttermilk. Cover with plastic wrap or lid and leave to stand for at least two nights. Then transfer the cheese to a large bowl and beat in the cinnamon and brown sugar using a whisk or hand blender.

Prepare the caramel sauce: heat the sugar and water in a saucepan. Reduce to a syrup and remove from the heat, stir in the butter. Be careful, as it can splatter considerably. Continue to stir and return to low heat until the desired caramel colour is achieved. Remove from the heat and fold in the cream. Leave the sauce to slightly cool until used.

Transfer the *hangop* to a plate and cover with a little caramel sauce. Top with the crumbled biscuits and sprinkle with the toasted almonds.

GOAT'S YOGHURT HANGOP WITH THYME AND OLIVES

1 litre (4 cups) goat's yoghurt
100 ml (approx. 3 fl oz/½ cup) thick cream
leaves of a few sprigs of fresh thyme
pinch of crumbled dried chilli pepper (or chilli flakes)
approx. 15 Taggiasche (or other tasty) olives, pitted and halved
pinch of sea salt

Place a strainer on a bucket in a cool place. Place a clean dish towel in the strainer and pour in the yoghurt.
Cover and leave to stand for one night.
The following day, whip the cream, add the thyme, crumbled chilli pepper and olives and season with salt. Scrape the drained yoghurt from the towel and carefully fold it into the whipped cream. Place in the refrigerator in order to allow the flavours to thoroughly infuse.
Serve with crusty bread and a drink, for example.

I SCREAM
YOU SCREAM
WE ALL
SCREAM
FOR
ICE
CREAM

On the way back from Brittas Bay Beach to Dublin when I was a child, my friends and I sang this song so long and so loud
in the car that our parents sometimes gave in and eventually we were treated to an actual ice cream.
As a child I didn't like ice cream at all but it was a good song!
As an adult I married Oof who is just crazy about ice cream. He often makes ice cream just because he likes it so much
and he feeds me all kinds of flavours he came up with himself.
I ended up loving ice cream as well and now we often make it together, even more often than I would like.
Even when it's cold outside!

MAKING ICE CREAM

MAKING ICE CREAM IS EASY WITHOUT A MACHINE. EVEN IF YOU NEED TO MAKE A LOT. AN ICE CREAM LOG SUCH
AS THIS ONE IS A SOLUTION. I WILL MAKE A VERY SIMPLE ONE HERE. IT IS UP TO YOU TO DO SOMETHING WITH IT, FOR EXAMPLE.
YOU CAN ADD NUTS, RASPBERRIES OR CHOCOLATE SHAVINGS. YOU DON'T HAVE TO MAKE A MOCHA FLAVOUR AS I DEMONSTRATE
HERE. CREATE YOUR OWN.
IN THE FOLLOWING PAGES, I WILL GIVE YOU SOME VARIATIONS. YOU CAN ALSO USE HALF MILK/HALF CREAM, FOR EXAMPLE.
IF YOU DON'T WANT YOUR ICE CREAM TO BE TOO RICH. BUT OH WELL, I DO LIKE IT CREAMY.
>>> BY THE WAY, DO NOT ADD ALCOHOL IF CHILDREN WILL BE EATING IT, BUT THAT GOES WITHOUT SAYING.

PREPARE: 6 EGG YOLKS, 200 G (1 CUP)
SUGAR, 150 ML (1 CUP) STRONG COFFEE,
3 TBSP. COFFEE LIQUEUR, 600 ML
(2 CUPS) CREAM, CHOCOLATE CHUNKS.

BEAT THE YOLKS AND SUGAR INTO
A WHITE FOAM.

ADD THE COFFEE AND A THIRD OF THE
CREAM.
STIR WELL INTO A SMOOTH SAUCE.

POUR THE SAUCE INTO A SAUCEPAN...

AND BRING TO A BOIL WHILE STIRRING,

UNTIL THE SAUCE THICKENS AND
STICKS TO THE SPOON, LIKE SO.

LEAVE THE CUSTARD TO COOL, I PUT IT
IN AN OPEN WINDOW.

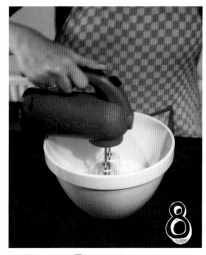

IN THE MEANTIME WHIP THE REST OF
THE CREAM.

FOLD IN THE COOLED CUSTARD AND THE
LIQUEUR (OPTIONAL!).

309

LINE A MOULD WITH PLASTIC WRAP.

POUR IN THE MIXTURE AND COVER.

FREEZE FOR AT LEAST 5 HOURS.

MEANWHILE MELT A LITTLE
CHOCOLATE OVER A BAIN-MARIE.

POUR INTO A PIPING BAG, CUT THE TIP
AND DECORATE IT ALONE.

...OR ALL TOGETHER.

BRRR...LET'S GET GOING

WARNING! IN THESE RECIPES THE EGGS ARE PROCESSED RAW, WHICH MEANS THAT YOU HAVE TO BE CAREFUL IF YOU PLAN ON SERVING YOUR ICE CREAM TO THE ELDERLY, THE SICK OR SMALL CHILDREN. THESE GROUPS TYPICALLY HAVE LOWER RESISTANCE AND COULD, IN THEORY, BECOME ILL.
SEMIFREDDO IS THE ITALIAN WORD FOR HALF-FROZEN.

PISTACHIO WAFERS WITH MARMALADE SEMIFREDDO

For approximately 12 people

3 oranges
75 g (2½ oz/⅓ cup) sugar
2 tsp vanilla sugar
100 g (4 oz) marmalade
500 ml (16 fl oz/2 cups) thick cream
250 ml (9 fl oz/1 cup) crème fraîche
5 egg yolks
pinch of salt
approx. 24 pistachio wafers, see recipe on page 363

Grate the skin of two oranges and squeeze all three oranges. Bring the juice with half of the sugar and vanilla sugar to a boil and cook for at least 10 minutes until reduced by one quarter. Stir in the marmalade and leave to cool. Bring the cream, the crème fraîche, orange zest and reserved sugar to a boil and lower the heat. Stir until the sugar has dissolved. Beat the egg yolks in a bowl. Pour in half of the hot cream and continue to stir. Pour the egg-cream mixture back into the pan with the remaining cream and stir until the mixture thickens. The cream has to be thick enough to stick to the back of a spoon. Add the cream to the orange syrup. Add the salt, stir and place in the freezer for at least 4 hours.

Place a scoop of semifreddo on a wafer. Top with another wafer, creating a 'sandwich'. Serve immediately or wrap them one by one in plastic wrap and keep in the freezer until used.

YOGHURT SEMIFREDDO WITH CRANBERRY CRUNCH

For 1 cake tin or 10–12 people
For the semifreddo
150 g (5 oz/⅔ cup) sugar
3 egg yolks
1 vanilla bean, seeds scraped
200 ml (6 fl oz/¾ cup) milk
200 ml (6 fl oz/¾ cup) thick cream
200 ml (6 fl oz/¾ cup) yoghurt

For the crunch
100 g (approx. 4 oz/½ cup) brown sugar
50 g (approx. 2 oz/⅓ cup) plain (all-purpose) flour
100 g (approx. 4 oz/1 stick) butter
100 g (approx. 4 oz/⅔ cup) dried cranberries (craisins) reserve some for the garnish)
50 g (approx. 2 oz/½ cup) oatmeal

First make the crunch. Heat the oven to 180°C (350°F/Gas 4).

Combine all ingredients in a food processor and blitz into a crumbly dough. Spread over a baking sheet lined with baking paper and press into a flat cake. Bake for 20–25 minutes until crisp and golden brown. Leave to fully cool.
Cover a cake tin with plastic wrap and allow the edges to hang over the tin. Beat the sugar with the egg yolks into a very stiff white foam. Bring the vanilla bean, together with the seeds and milk to a boil. Simmer for 10 minutes. Remove the vanilla bean and blend the milk with the egg yolks while stirring, return the mixture to the pan and continue to stir until it thickens. It has to be as thick as thin custard. Remove the pan from the heat. Leave the custard to slightly cool. Beat the cream until stiff. Carefully fold the cream and yoghurt into the custard and pour half of it into the cake tin. Crumble the cranberry crunch using a rolling pin. Sprinkle the crumbs on the semifreddo mixture in the mould and top with the rest of the semifreddo mixture. Reserve some of the crumbs for the garnish. Cover the semifreddo with the overhanging wrap. Place the mould in the freezer to harden overnight. Before serving, carefully lift the ice cream out of the mould. Slice. Arrange on small plates and sprinkle with the reserved cranberry crunch and a few dried cranberries.

THREE-COLOUR SEMIFREDDO WITH CHOCOLATE AND MINT

For 1 cake tin or 10–12 people

1 litre (4 cups) milk
650 ml (22 fl oz/2¾ cups) thick cream
1 vanilla bean, halved, seeds removed
8 egg yolks
180 g (approx. 6 oz/¾ cup) caster (superfine) sugar
100 g (4 oz) dark chocolate, in chunks
150 g (5 oz) milk chocolate, in chunks
150 g (5 oz) white chocolate, in chunks
few sprigs fresh mint, very finely chopped
⅓ cup chopped pistachio nuts for garnish

Heat the milk, half of the cream and the vanilla (seeds and empty bean) until very hot (do not boil) and allow to infuse for approx. 10 minutes. Beat the egg yolks with the sugar until white and foamy. While stirring, add one spoonful of the hot milk-cream mixture to the egg mixture and then pour the remaining egg mixture, while stirring, into the hot milk. Continue to stir until the custard thickens and sticks to the back of a tablespoon. Take the pan from the heat and remove the vanilla bean. Do not allow the custard to boil. In the meantime, melt each chocolate over a bain-marie, one by one, in three bowls. Leave them and the custard to slightly cool. Whip the remaining cream until stiff. Divide into three portions. Also divide the custard into three portions. Stir the 3 chocolates through the three custards. Stir the chopped mint through the white chocolate mixture. Fold the portions of whipped cream through each chocolate mixture. Line a cake tin with plastic wrap. Add the milk chocolate mixture. Cover and immediately place in the freezer. Place the other two bowls in the refrigerator. After an hour or two, when the milk chocolate ice cream has slightly frozen, add the white chocolate mixture. After a further two hours, pour in the last layer and completely cover the semifreddo in order for it to fully freeze. Serve in slices and sprinkled with chopped pistachios.

SAFFRON SEMIFREDDO WITH CITRUS COMPOTE

For this semifreddo you don't have to make custard. I thought that I would give you another variation. The ice cream will be quite light with this recipe.
For 1 cake tin or 10–12 people

few strands of saffron
4 eggs, separated
70 g (2 oz/⅓ cup) sugar
500 ml (16 fl oz/2 cups) thick cream

For the grapefruit compote
1 kg (2 lb) grapefruit
200 ml (6 fl oz/¾ cup) water
150 g (5 oz/⅔ cup) sugar
1 tbsp lemon juice
½ vanilla bean
3 tbsp liqueur, Verveine (lemon verbena), for example

Place saffron threads in a tablespoon of warm water and allow to soak briefly. Line a cake tin leaving excess plastic wrap hanging over the edges, as it will have to cover the ice cream later. In the meantime beat the egg yolk with the sugar into a creamy mixture. Add the saffron and stir. Beat the cream until nearly stiff. Whisk the egg whites until stiff in another bowl with a pinch of salt. Fold the egg yolk into the whipped cream and then, carefully add the cream mixture to the egg whites. Gently pour the mixture into the mould and fold the plastic wrap over it. Place in the freezer.
Prepare the compote.
Place a grapefruit on a chopping board. Using a sharp knife, cut away, from top to bottom, the peel and the white underneath. Move to the next section until the entire grapefruit is peeled. Over a bowl, remove the pulp from the sections, the juice will be collected in the bowl. Repeat for all of the grape-fruit. In a saucepan heat the water, sugar and lemon juice. With a sharp knife, remove the seeds from the vanilla bean and add to the mixture. Also add the empty bean, which you will later remove. Bring the mixture to a boil. Lower the heat and continue to cook until you have a syrup, (about 7 minutes). Add the grapefruit sections and the liqueur and leave the compote to cool until used. Prior to serving, remove the ice cream from the mould. Slice and serve with the compote.

311

EARL GREY TEA AND MINT SORBET

Serves four people as a dessert, but at least eight people as sorbet to cleanse your palate during a large dinner party as they do in posh circles...

750 ml (25 fl oz/3 cups) water
4 tea bags Earl Grey tea
small bunch fresh mint
225 g (approx 7½ oz/1 cup) sugar
juice of 1 lemon

You'll also need a bottle of champagne if serving during a dinner party.

Bring 600 ml (20 fl oz/2½ cups) of the water to a boil, transfer to large bowl, add the tea bags and allow to infuse for 7 minutes. Remove the tea bags and squeeze them thoroughly above the bowl. Wash the mint and add the sprigs (stalks and leaves intact) to the tea. Bring the remaining water and sugar to a boil in a saucepan and stir until the sugar has dissolved. Add the syrup and the lemon juice to the tea and leave the mixture to fully cool. Once it is lukewarm, place in the refrigerator to fully chill. Remove the mint sprigs. Churn into a sorbet in an ice-cream maker or place the mixture in the freezer and fluff it up every hour with a fork. The sorbet will be ready after approximately 4 hours, depending on your freezer.

For a palate cleanser, fill half a glass with champagne and drop a small scoop of sorbet into the glass. Serve immediately and provide a small spoon.

pineapple granita
with passion fruit

1 PINEAPPLE
2 TBSP (APPROX. 1/8 CUP) CASTER SUGAR
JUICE OF 1/2 LEMON
75 ML (2 1/2 FL OZ / 1/3 CUP) WATER
4 PASSIONFRUIT

PEEL THE PINEAPPLE AND REMOVE THE "EYES".
CUT THE FRUIT INTO FOUR SECTIONS AND REMOVE
THE CORE. CUT THE FRUIT INTO CHUNKS AND
PUREE INTO A PULP IN THE FOOD PROCESSOR.

HEAT THE SUGAR, LEMON JUICE AND WATER
INTO A SYRUP IN A SAUCEPAN. ADD THE PINE-
APPLE PULP → STIR WELL!

LET IT COOL DOWN AND PLACE IN THE FREEZER.
BEAT UP EVERY HOUR USING A FORK. AFTER
ABOUT 4-5 HOURS YOU WILL HAVE MADE
GRANITA! SERVE IN AN ATTRACTIVE
TALL GLASS COVERED WITH PASSION FRUIT.

GRANITA IS SIMILAR TO SORBET, BUT SINCE
LESS SUGAR IS USED → THE ICE CRYSTALS
ARE LARGER.

RASPBERRY SORBET

500 g (16 oz/4 cups) raspberries (these days easily available in your supermarket's frozen food section!)
150 g (5 oz/⅔ cup) caster (superfine) sugar
100 ml (approx. 3 fl oz/½ cup) water

Purée the raspberries in a blender. If you do not like small seeds, press the pulp through a strainer.
Heat the sugar and water in a saucepan, stir until the sugar has dissolved. Pour the syrup onto the raspberry pulp and leave to fully cool.
Churn the sorbet in an ice-cream maker for approximately 30 minutes or freeze the mixture in the freezer.
If using the freezer, fluff up the sorbet every hour and it will be ready in approximately 4 hours.

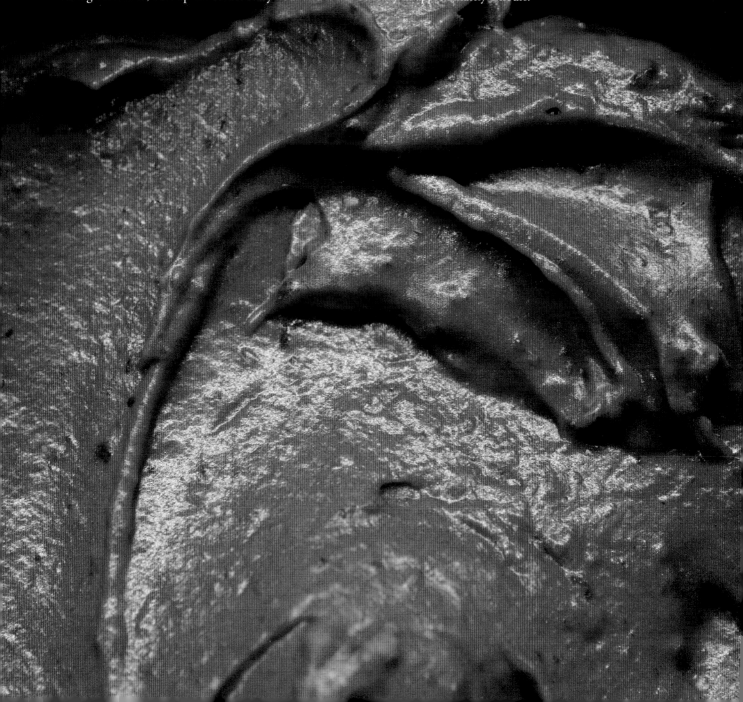

GREEN TEA ICE CREAM

2 tbsp green tea powder (or use 2 green tea bags)

2–3 tbsp boiling water

300 ml (10 fl oz/1¼ cups) milk

1 vanilla bean, cut open with the seeds scraped out

2 egg yolks

75 g (2½ oz/⅓ cup) caster (superfine) sugar

300 ml (10 fl oz/1¼ cups) thick cream

Leave the tea to soak in the water for 10 minutes.

Heat the milk until very hot but do not boil. Leave it to infuse with the vanilla bean and the seeds for 10 minutes. Beat the egg yolks with the the caster sugar until white and foamy. Strain the milk mixture into it and stir well. Also add the steeped tea. Return the mixture to the pan and stir over low heat until thicker, like a crème anglaise or thin custard.

Leave to fully cool.

Beat the cream until stiff and fold into the cold custard.

Transfer the cream mixture to the ice-cream maker and churn for approximately 20 minutes.

If you do not have an ice-cream maker, you can do this: place the ice cream in the freezer and briefly fluff up every hour with a fork into nice firm ice cream. It will be ready in approximately 4 hours.

☆ The time for churning depends on the ice-cream maker, follow your appliance manufacturer's instructions.

APPLE SORBET WITH APPLE CRISPS

For the sorbet
500 ml (16 fl oz/2 cups) organic apple juice
3 Granny Smith apples, peeled and cubed
juice of ½ lemon
75 g (2½ oz/⅓ cup) sugar

For the crisps
1 apple, Royal Gala or Elstar, for example

Bring all sorbet ingredients to a boil in a saucepan. Cook for 10 minutes on low heat and then purée into a smooth sauce using a hand blender. Leave to fully cool.
Pour the sauce into an ice-cream maker and churn for approx. 30 minutes. If you don't have an ice-cream maker, you can place the container in the freezer. Fluff up every hour with a fork. The ice cream will be ready in approx. 4 hours.

For the crisps, heat a fan-forced/convection oven to 60°C (140°F). Cut the apple into slices crossways with a sharp knife. Arrange the slices on a sheet of baking paper on a baking sheet. Dry them in the oven for approx. 3 hours. Turn them halfway through.

Before serving, stack the ice cream, alternating with the crisps. Secure with a skewer, just to be on the safe side.

BLOOD ORANGE SORBET

For the sorbet

juice of 1.5 kg (3 lb) blood oranges, or approx. 500 ml (16 fl oz/2 cups) juice

zest of 2 blood oranges

125 ml (approx. 4 fl oz/⅔ cup) water

250 g (8 oz/1 cup) sugar

For the compote

1 kg (2 lb) blood oranges, pink grapefruit and oranges

200 ml (6 fl oz/¾ cup) water

250 g (8 oz/1 cup) sugar

juice of ½ lemon

½ vanilla bean

1 tbsp liqueur, cranberry or bay, for example, see recipe on page 99

For the sorbet, heat the juice and the zest, the water and the sugar, until very hot, while stirring, until the sugar has dissolved. Do not boil or it will get bitter!

Remove the syrup from the heat and pour into a container that fits into the freezer. Leave the syrup to cool on the countertop and then place in the freezer. After 30 minutes, scrape along the edges with a spoon in order to release the ice crystals and stir well. Repeat this every hour until the right consistency is achieved, which will take 4 to 5 hours, depending on your freezer.

You can also churn the sorbet in an ice-cream maker, if you own one. In this case, you will make the sorbet in approx. 30 minutes.

In the meantime prepare the compote. Put an orange on the chopping board. Using a sharp knife, peel away the orange and white peel, from top to bottom. Proceed until the entire orange is peeled.

Cut away the pulp between the sections over a bowl, the released juice will therefore be collected in the bowl. Repeat for all oranges and grapefruit.

In a saucepan, heat the water, sugar and lemon juice and the collected juice. Using a sharp knife, scrape the vanilla from the bean and add it to the mixture. Also add the empty bean, and remove it later. Bring the mixture to a boil. Then lower the heat and simmer until you have a syrup. This will take approx. 7 minutes. Add the orange sections and liqueur and leave the compote to cool until used.

To serve, place a scoop of ice cream in a tall glass and add the compote.

YOGHURT ICE CREAM WITH VANILLA, WALNUTS AND DATES

For the ice cream
125 g (4 oz/½ cup) caster (superfine) sugar
1 tbsp cornflour (cornstarch)
pinch of salt
2 eggs
500 ml (16 fl oz/2 cups) milk
2 vanilla beans, cut open with the seeds scraped out
350 ml (approx 12 fl oz/1½ cups) whole (full fat) yoghurt

To garnish
a handful of walnuts and dates
maple syrup or pancake syrup

Beat the sugar, cornflour, salt and eggs in a large bowl into a smooth mixture. Heat the milk and the vanilla seeds and beans and leave to steep for 10 minutes. Strain the hot milk over the egg mixture, while stirring. Return everything to the pan and heat, while stirring, until it thickens into a nice custard. Leave the custard to cool and stir in the yoghurt. Place in the refrigerator to fully cool. Pour into an ice-cream maker and churn into an airy light ice cream.
Serve with halved, pitted dates and a few walnuts. Top with maple syrup.
If you don't own an ice-cream maker, have no fear, place the ice cream in the freezer and briefly fluff it up every hour with a fork. The ice cream will be ready in approx. 4 hours.

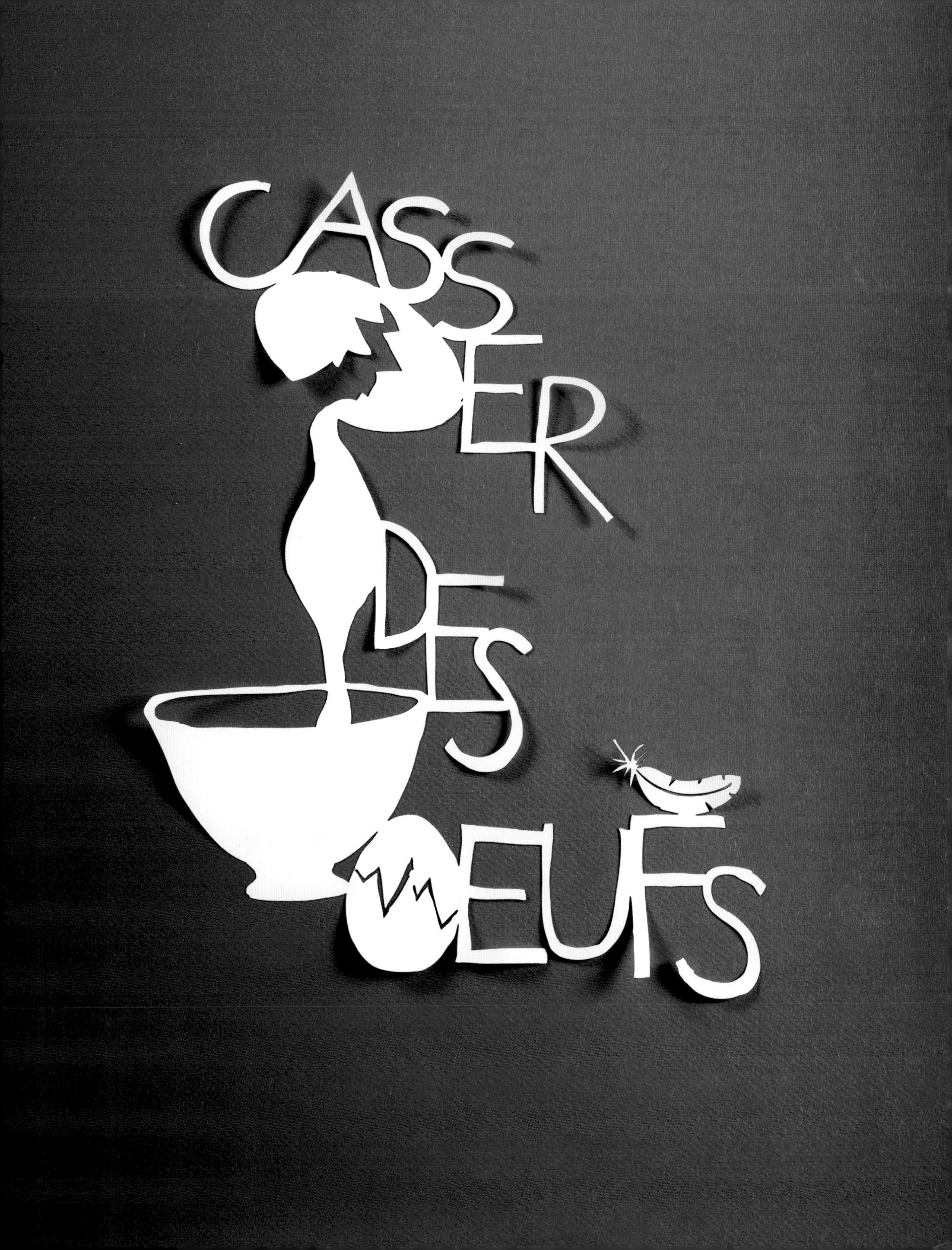
CASSER
DES
OEUFS

MAKING ZABAGLIONE

YOU WILL NEED A LITTLE PATIENCE TO MAKE ZABAGLIONE, BUT MAKE IT AND EVERYONE WILL LOVE YOU FOR IT.
SERVE AS IS, IN A SMALL BOWL, OR WITH LADYFINGERS FOR DUNKING. THE ART OF THIS DESSERT IS TO KNOW WHEN TO STOP
BEATING. IT HAS TO BE NICE AND THICK, BUT IF IT GETS TOO HOT, THE EGG WILL TURN INTO LUMPS IN YOUR DESSERT AND YOU WILL
HAVE TO START AGAIN. BUT IT WON'T COME TO THAT, SINCE YOU WILL JUST FOLLOW THE STEP-BY-STEP PLAN:

PREPARE YOUR INGREDIENTS: PER PERSON
USE: 1 EGG YOLK, 1 TBSP SUGAR AND
50 ML (2 FL OZ/4-5 TBSP) MARSALA.

PUT THE YOLK IN A BOWL, WHICH WILL
LATER FIT ON A PAN OF BOILING WATER.
ADD THE SUGAR.

PATIENTLY WHIP INTO AIRY WHITE FOAM.

POUR IN THE MARSALA, WHILE
STIRRING.

PLACE THE BOWL OVER A PAN OF
SOFTLY BOILING WATER, ENSURE THAT
THE WATER DOES NOT TOUCH THE
BOWL AND CONTINUE TO BEAT...

UNTIL AIRY AND THICK. IMMEDIATELY
POUR INTO GLASSES OR SMALL
BOWLS. >>>

LET'S GET GOING ...

EGGS SERVE ALL SORTS OF PURPOSES. IT ONLY GETS COMPLICATED WHEN YOU START HEATING THEM: IF THEY GET TOO HOT, ANY SAUCE OR CREAM THICKENED WITH EGG TURNS INTO SCRAMBLED EGGS. THE ART THEREFORE CONSISTS OF KEEPING THE MIXTURE NEAR THE BOILING POINT. ONCE YOU GET SOME PRACTICE, YOU WILL MAKE THE MOST DELICIOUS DESSERTS, JUST TAKE A LOOK:

VIN SANTO ZABAGLIONE WITH PINK GRAPEFRUIT

3 pink grapefruit
3 tbsp sugar
2 eggs
4 tbsp Vin Santo (Italian dessert wine or another sweet dessert wine)

Place a grapefruit on a chopping board. Using a sharp knife, peel the yellow skin and also the white pith from top to bottom. Proceed until the entire grapefruit is peeled. Over a bowl, remove the pulp between the sections, the juice will be collected in the bowl. Repeat for all grapefruit and stir a tablespoon of sugar through the juice with the grapefruit sections. Set aside. Beat the eggs, the remaining sugar and wine with a mixer into a foamy mass in approximately 5 minutes. Arrange the fruits in four attractive glasses, cover with the zabaglione and serve immediately!

CUSTARD

500 ml (16 fl oz/2 cups) milk
100 g (4 oz/approx. ½ cup) crème fraîche
1 vanilla bean, with the seeds removed from the bean and the bean itself, or
1 tsp vanilla extract
4 egg yolks
75 g (2½ oz/⅓ cup) sugar
1 tbsp cornflour (cornstarch)

Heat the milk with the crème fraîche, the vanilla seeds and the bean until hot (do not boil) and leave to simmer on low heat for 15 minutes. Then remove the vanilla bean. Beat the egg yolks with the sugar and cornflour into a foam, and while stirring, add the hot milk. Return the mixture to the pan. Heat slowly on low heat while stirring until the mixture thickens. Remove from the heat and leave to cool until used. The custard will further thicken. If you want to serve the custard warm, keep it over a bain-marie. Place a sheet of plastic wrap directly down on the surface of the custard to prevent a skin forming.

CRÈME ANGLAISE

This sauce is quite similar to custard, but no cornflour (cornstarch) is added here for thickening purposes. Crème anglaise is typically used as a sauce and custard is used as a dish. Once you have become handy, you can opt to use other flavourings instead of vanilla. See the recipe below.

500 ml (16 fl oz/2 cups) milk
2 vanilla bean, with the seeds removed from the bean and the bean itself
5 egg yolks
75 g (2½ oz/⅓ cup) sugar

Heat the milk with vanilla seeds and the beans until hot (do not boil) and leave to simmer on low heat for 15 minutes. Then remove the vanilla bean. Beat the egg yolks with the sugar into a foam, and while stirring, add the hot milk. Return the mixture to the pan. Heat slowly on low heat while stirring until the mixture thickens. Crème anglaise has to be as thick as a cream of asparagus soup. Remove from the heat and leave to cool until used. The sauce will slightly thicken. If you want to serve the sauce warm, keep it over a bain-marie. Place a sheet of plastic wrap directly down on the surface to prevent a skin from forming.

CHOCOLATE FONDANT CAKE

For one cake
(enough for at least 12 people)

150 g (5 oz/1¼ sticks) butter
1 package (250 g/8 oz) amaretti (light Italian almond biscuits, or another crisp biscuit)
100 g (4 oz) dark chocolate, in chunks
600 ml (20 fl oz/2½ cups) thick cream
2 tbsp sugar
75 ml (2½ fl oz/⅓ cup) Amaretto or Frangelico liqueur
cocoa for sprinkling

Line a baking tin, approximately 24 cm (9 inch) in diameter with plastic wrap allowing the excess to hang over the rim. Melt the butter. Crush the biscuits in a food processor or mortar. Mix the butter with the biscuit crumbs and press the mixture evenly on the bottom of the tin. Melt the chocolate in the microwave or over a bain-marie. Leave to slightly cool. Beat the cream and sugar until stiff. Carefully stir the melted chocolate into the whipped cream and add the liqueur. Fill the tin with the chocolate mixture and smooth out the top with a spatula. Cover the cake with the excess plastic wrap and place in the refrigerator to chill for at least 4 hours Before serving lift the cake out of the tin, remove the plastic wrap and sprinkle with cocoa powder. Serve small wedges with crème anglaise with lemongrass.

CRÈME ANGLAISE WITH LEMONGRASS

500 ml (16 fl oz/2 cups) milk
1 vanilla bean, seeds scraped
3 lemongrass stems, white part only, crushed
5 egg yolks
75 g (2½ oz/⅓ cup) sugar

See recipe for crème anglaise. Remove the lemongrass stems when you remove the vanilla beans from the hot milk.

CHAMPAGNE CREAM

This light cream can be used as a filling for many pastries, often combined with fresh fruit. Instead of champagne you could also use espresso and you will end up with a mocha cream, which is also delicious.

100 ml (approx. 3 fl oz/½ cup) thick cream
150 ml (5 fl oz/⅔ cup) champagne (more ordinary bubbles will also do)
75 g (2½ oz/⅓ cup) sugar
3 egg yolks and 1 whole egg
1 tbsp cornflour (cornstarch)
juice of ½ lemon

Beat the cream until stiff and set aside in the refrigerator. Beat the champagne, sugar, egg yolks, egg, cornflour and lemon juice with a mixer over a bain-marie into a firm white cream. Leave to briefly cool. Carefully fold in the whipped cream.

SPONGE CAKE

A basic recipe for many desserts. Great, for example, with whipped cream and jam between two layers and sprinkled with icing (confectioner's) sugar. It is a light cake, as it contains no butter, but you do have to practise. I personally have had a few failures in the past. Therefore strictly adhere to the recipe, REALLY do not open the oven, not even on the sly...

4 eggs
120 g (approx. 4 oz/½ cup) caster (superfine) sugar
pinch of salt
75 g (2½ oz/½ cup) plain (all-purpose) flour, sifted
25 g (1 oz/¼ cup) cornflour (cornstarch), sifted
butter and flour for the cake tin
(round: 22–24 cm/8–9 inch diameter)

Thoroughly grease the cake tin. Cut a circle the size of the bottom of the cake tin out of baking paper, cover the base with it and grease it. Dust the greased cake tine with flour and tap the excess flour off the tin. Preheat the oven to 170°C (340°F/Gas 3). Beat the eggs with the sugar and salt in a food processor (or take a very long time using a hand blender…) into a very foamy white mass. While stirring, fold the flour and cornflour into the batter. Try to keep as much air as possible in the batter but also spread the flour evenly through it. Pour the batter into the cake tin. Bake the cake in the oven for approximately 40 minutes. Do NOT open the oven during the first 30 minutes. Once the cake has cooled off, you can slice it, fill it and further finish it.

VANILLA FRITTERS WITH ZABAGLIONE

This recipe is for those who know Oof well and want to make him happy, for it is his favourite dessert.

For approximately 25 fritters
60 g (2 oz/½ stick) butter
250 ml (9 fl oz/1 cup) white wine or water
1 tbsp sugar
approx. 4 tsp vanilla sugar
zest of 1 lemon
pinch of salt
250 g (8 oz/1⅔ cups) plain (all-purpose) flour
4 eggs, separated
1 x zabaglione recipe, see page 326

And also:
generous oil for deep-frying
icing (confectioner's) sugar

Melt the butter with the wine in a saucepan, add the sugar, vanilla sugar, lemon zest and salt.
Remove the pan from the heat and stir in the flour with a wooden spoon. Return the pan briefly to the heat and stir into a smooth batter. Remove the pan from the heat again and, using a hand blender, fold in the egg yolks one by one.
Beat the egg whites with a pinch of salt in another bowl until stiff and carefully spoon the foam into the batter. Heat the oil in a deep pan.
Grease 2 coffee spoons with oil and scoop small balls from the batter, which you immediately slide into the hot oil. Fry the fritters for a few minutes until golden brown and cooked. Turn halfway through. Always fry small quantities.
Allow to drain on kitchen paper.
Serve the fritters on a large tray and dust with icing sugar or caster (superfine) sugar.
Serve with the zabaglione in a bowl as a dip.

RASPBERRY CLAFOUTIS

For 6 small glasses or 1 large dish

3 eggs

250 ml (9 fl oz/1 cup) milk

125 g (4 oz/½ cup) sugar

seeds from 1 small vanilla bean or 2 tsp vanilla sugar

pinch of salt

75 g (2½ oz/½ cup) plain (all-purpose) flour

75 g (2½ oz/approx. ½ stick) butter, plus extra for greasing purposes

50 ml (1½ fl oz/¼ cup) kirsch, rum or a delicious homemade liqueur, see page 98 and 99

250 g (8 oz/2 cups) raspberries

icing (confectioner's) sugar for dusting

Generously butter the glasses. Beat the eggs with the milk, sugar, vanilla, salt and flour into a smooth mixture.

Melt the remaining butter and fold it in. Add the liqueur.

Pour the batter into the glasses and top with the raspberries.

Bake in an oven preheated to 180°C (350°F/Gas 4) for approximately 15 minutes or until the clafoutis turns a lovely golden brown.

Leave to slightly cool and sprinkle with icing sugar.

 Serve warm with raspberry sorbet, see recipe on page 315.

TIP If you make the recipe for children and you do not want to use alcohol, replace liqueur with orange juice.

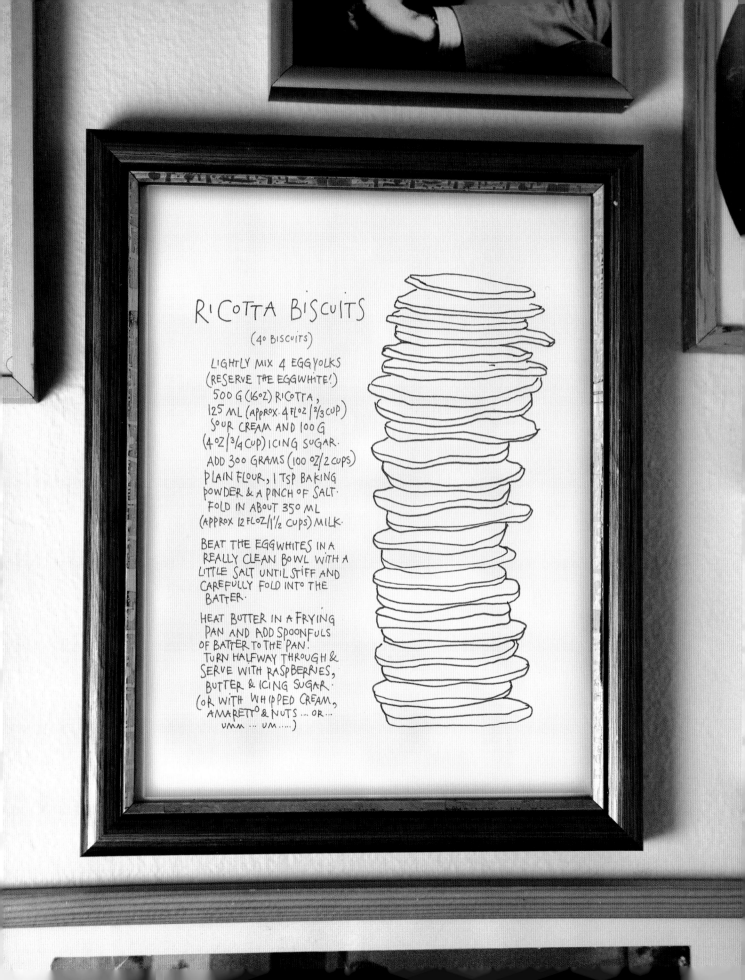

RICOTTA BISCUITS

(40 BISCUITS)

LIGHTLY MIX 4 EGG YOLKS
(RESERVE THE EGGWHITE!)
500 G (16 OZ) RICOTTA,
125 ML (APPROX. 4 FL OZ / 2/3 CUP)
SOUR CREAM AND 100 G
(4 OZ / 3/4 CUP) ICING SUGAR.
ADD 300 GRAMS (10 0 OZ / 2 CUPS)
PLAIN FLOUR, 1 TSP BAKING
POWDER & A PINCH OF SALT.
FOLD IN ABOUT 350 ML
(APPROX 12 FL OZ / 1 1/2 CUPS) MILK.

BEAT THE EGGWHITES IN A
REALLY CLEAN BOWL WITH A
LITTLE SALT UNTIL STIFF AND
CAREFULLY FOLD INTO THE
BATTER.

HEAT BUTTER IN A FRYING
PAN AND ADD SPOONFULS
OF BATTER TO THE PAN.
TURN HALFWAY THROUGH &
SERVE WITH RASPBERRIES,
BUTTER & ICING SUGAR.
(OR WITH WHIPPED CREAM,
AMARETTO & NUTS … OR …
UMM … UM ……)

Joris

PINK MINI TRIFLES

For 4 glasses

8 slices butter cake (here I used lady fingers—Italian sponge fingers)

150 ml (5 fl oz/⅔ cup) medium or cream sherry

1 x custard recipe, see page 328

250 g (8 oz/2 cups) red fruit, strawberries or raspberries or both

50 g (approx. 2 oz/¼ cup) sugar

Slice the cake. With a small glass, cut out rounds in the cake and sprinkle each round with a teaspoon of sherry. Make sure that you have twice as many cake rounds as glasses. Prepare the custard. Stir in half of the fruit. Leave to cool. Place a slice of cake in each glass. Cover with a spoonful of cream-fruit mixture and top with a second slice of cake. Cover with another spoonful of cream-fruit mixture. Seal all glasses with plastic wrap and place them in the refrigerator for at least 2 hours to set. In the food processor, purée the other half of the fruit with the sugar and strain. Collect the coulis (sauce) in a bowl and pour it into a decanter. Before serving add a dash of coulis to each trifle, covering the top of each glass with an even layer.

PEAR AND GINGER TIRAMISU WITH GRATED CHOCOLATE

For 4 glasses

1 pear

generous dash of ginger syrup

8 lady fingers (Italian sponge fingers)

dash Marsala wine

250 ml (9 fl oz/1 cup) strong coffee

3 eggs

100 g (approx. 4 oz/½ cup) sugar

250 g (8 oz/1 cup) mascarpone

2 pieces stem ginger

approx. 50 g (2 oz) chocolate (preferably dark) from the refrigerator

Peel the pear, quarter it and remove the cores. In a saucepan bring enough water to a boil to cover the pear and add a generous dash of ginger syrup. Keep close to boiling point and poach the pear for 20 minutes. Leave the pear to cool in cooking fluid and then slice. Very carefully cut the sponge fingers in half. Blend the Marsala with the coffee. Arrange four halved sponge fingers upright along the inside of four glasses. Pour a little coffee into each glass and gently swirl the glasses in order for all the sponge fingers to absorb the coffee. Separate the eggs. Beat the yolks with half of the sugar until the mixture turns light yellow. Beat in the mascarpone into a smooth mixture. Beat the egg whites until stiff. Add the remaining sugar and continue to beat into stiff peaks. Carefully fold the egg whites into the mascarpone mixture. Finely chop the ginger and add. Place the pears in the glasses between the sponge fingers. Top with a generous dollop of cream until the glasses are filled. Leave to chill in the refrigerator for at least 90 minutes. Serve sprinkled with the grated chocolate.

FRENCH TOAST WITH CINNAMON BREAD AND RASPBERRY SORBET

For the French toast

4 eggs

200 ml (6 fl oz/¾ cup) milk

2 tbsp raw caster (superfine) sugar

1 tbsp cinnamon

zest of 1 lemon

12 slices cinnamon bread

75 g (2½ oz/approx. ½ stick) butter

And also:

6 scoops raspberry sorbet, see recipe on page 315

icing (confectioner's) sugar to garnish

and little stars (optional)

Beat the eggs in a deep dish with the milk, sugar, cinnamon and lemon zest. Place the bread in the egg mix and allow it to briefly soak. Melt the butter in a frying pan. Place the bread in it and fry on both sides until golden brown. Serve two French toasts per person with a scoop of raspberry sorbet on a plate and sprinkle with icing sugar.

If desired, add little stars for that extra dramatic effect.

PAVLOVAS WITH FRUIT (FOR MY MOTHER)

Mum, this recipe makes 12 meringues, the size of large beer coasters, as for your birthday.
(You can also make 20 smaller ones, but, be careful, they will increase in size in the oven.)

For the meringues
6 egg whites
1 tbsp cornflour (cornstarch)
1 small tbsp white wine vinegar
2 tsp vanilla sugar
pinch of salt
375 g (13 oz/1¾ cups) caster (superfine) sugar
60 ml (2 fl oz/¼ cup) boiling water

In addition you will also need:
a lot of fresh fruit: 1 punnet strawberries, 2 bananas, 2 trays mixed forest fruit, fresh pineapple. In short, whatever's available
few sprigs of mint
dash of liqueur (whatever you have in the kitchen)
125 ml (approx. 4 fl oz/⅔ cup) thick cream
500 ml (16 fl oz/2 cups) sour cream
icing (confectioner's) sugar

Preheat the oven to 200°C (400°F/Gas 6). Line a baking sheet with baking paper and set aside.

Beat the egg whites in a large and very clean bowl. While stirring, pour in the sifted cornflour, the white wine vinegar, the vanilla sugar and salt. When the egg whites get foamy, slowly add the caster sugar, little by little, in order for it to be fully absorbed. Then add the boiling water, tablespoon by tablespoon, until the mixture is stiff and glossy.

Fill a piping bag with the egg whites and pipe small turrets, or using a tablespoon create small heaps on the baking sheet lined with baking paper.

Bake the meringues for 10 minutes in the hot oven, lower the temperature to 90°C (190°F) and bake for a further hour. Try not to open the oven, as they may collapse.

Turn off the oven and leave them to dry for at least 1 hour or preferably overnight in the warm oven.

All this can be done one day in advance.

Wash the fruit and cut it smaller if you find it necessary. Cut the mint into strips and blend in with the fruit. Also stir a dash of liqueur through the fruit salad. Whip the cream with a dash of liqueur and possibly some sugar to taste, but I don't believe it's necessary. Fold the whipped cream into the sour cream.

Place a meringue on each plate. Top with a generous dollop of cream. Cover with the fruit salad. Sprinkle with icing sugar and serve immediately.

TIP You can colour the meringues with food colourings. Always use just a tiny amount, since the colour is quite strong!

PANETTONE & CUSTARD PUDDING

You're probably familiar with the dessert 'bread & butter pudding'. An English dessert—but also good for breakfast, you know!—made with stale or leftover bread. It is rich but once you taste it you'll find it difficult to stop. In our restaurant we make a variation on this old recipe by using Italian panettone instead of regular bread, making it slightly lighter. A dessert for 4–6 people.

150 g (5 oz/¾ cup) pitted and steeped prunes
4 tbsp Amaretto (Italian sweet almond flavoured liqueur)
250 g (8 oz) panettone (Italian sweet brioche-like bread, easily available around Easter, otherwise use sponge cake)
75 g (2½ oz/approx. ½ stick) butter
400 ml (14 fl oz/1⅔ cups) milk
seeds from 1 vanilla bean or 2 tsp vanilla sugar
80 g (approx. 3 oz/⅓ cup) sugar
2 eggs
1 egg yolk
icing (confectioner's) sugar to garnish

You will also need: two oven dishes, one smaller and another larger.

Heat the oven to 180°C (350°F/Gas 4).
In an oven dish, cover the prunes with the Amaretto. Slice the panettone. Butter the slices and grill them under a hot grill until golden brown. Overlap the bread slices on top of the prunes in the dish.
Heat the milk with the vanilla and sugar in a saucepan until very hot (do not boil). Beat the eggs with the yolks and pour the hot milk into the eggs, while stirring. Pour the egg mixture onto the panettone in the oven dish. Place the dish in a larger dish or roasting tin in the oven and fill the larger dish with hot water until it reaches the rim of the smaller one.
Bake the panettone-custard pudding in an oven for 25 minutes until golden brown and before serving, sprinkle with icing sugar. Serve hot!

DOUGHNUTS WITH COCONUT-LEMON FILLING

For approx. 6 doughnuts.
½ x recipe for sponge cake batter on page 329

For the filling
4 egg yolks (reserve the egg white!)
100 g (approx. 4 oz/½ cup) sugar
40 g (1½ oz/⅓ cup) cornflour (cornstarch)
400 ml (14 fl oz/1⅔ cups) coconut milk (whole tin)
30 g (1 oz/5 tsp) butter
zest of ½ lemon

For the meringue
4 egg whites
pinch of salt
250 g (8 oz/1 cup) caster (superfine) sugar

First prepare the filling: in a bowl beat the egg yolks with the sugar and cornflour until foamy using a hand blender.
Heat the coconut milk in a frying pan. Stir a full tablespoon hot coconut milk through the egg batter and then add all of the coconut milk. Return the coconut mixture to the pan and bring to a boil, while stirring. The cream will thicken. Beat the chilled butter swiftly through the cream. Add the lemon zest and immediately remove the pan from the heat.
Pour the cream into a piping bag or clean mixing bowl and allow to fully cool.
Prepare the sponge cake batter, as described on page 329.
Grease a baking sheet and line the bottom with baking paper. Pour the batter onto the sheet and spread to approx. 1.5 cm (½ inch) thick. Bake the cake until done in approx. 15–20 minutes. Leave to cool.
Cut out circles with a glass. Plan 2 circles per person.
Beat the egg whites until stiff, add a dash of salt. Add the caster sugar, spoonful by spoonful, and beat into stiff white peaks.
Cover half of the cake rounds with two generous tablespoons of lemon filling. Top with a cake round.
Generously spread the beaten egg white on the doughnuts, on all sides. Use a spoon to slightly swirl the foam thus creating peaks in the mixture.
Line the baking sheet with baking paper.
Using a spatula, carefully arrange the doughnuts on the baking sheet and place in a fan-forced/convection oven with grill preheated to 175°C (340°F/Gas 4) for a further 5 minutes in order to colour them. Serve quite quickly.

BABA À LA LIQUEUR DE LAURIER

For 4 servings.

For the babas

1 sachet dried yeast (7 g/¼ oz/2¼ tsp)

1 tbsp sugar

50 ml (1½ fl oz/¼ cup) lukewarm milk

100 g (approx. 4 oz/⅔ cup) plain (all-purpose) flour

1 egg, loosely beaten

pinch of salt

3 tbsp butter, at room temperature

For the syrup

500 ml (16 fl oz/2 cups) water

150 g (5 oz/⅔ cup) sugar

1 generous glass bay liqueur, see recipe on page 99 (I use at least 150 ml [5 fl oz/⅔ cup], but less is okay)

And also

150 ml (5 fl oz/⅔ cup) thick cream

Grease 4 small round baking tins, preferably in the shape of a mug.

In a large bowl, leave the yeast and the sugar and lukewarm milk to stand for 5 minutes until it starts to foam.

Using a hand blender with dough hooks, beat in one-third of the flour into a smooth batter. Leave to rise, covered with plastic wrap, for 20 minutes in a warm place.

Lightly beat the egg with a pinch of salt in a bowl. Stir the remaining flour in two parts through the yeast mixture and finish with the beaten egg. Beat in the butter, spoonful by spoonful. Only add the new spoonful when the previous one is fully absorbed. Beat the batter for at least 5 minutes.

Distribute the batter between the greased tins. They should be approximately half full. Place on a baking sheet and allow to rise for a further 15 minutes or until the batter has risen to the edge of the tins.

Preheat the oven to 175°C (340°F/Gas 4).

Place the babas in the oven and bake for approximately 15 minutes until golden brown. Leave to cool for 5 minutes, lift them from the tins and leave to fully cool on a rack.

In the meantime, prepare the syrup: heat the water in a saucepan. Add the sugar and stir until it has dissolved. Leave the sugar syrup to cool. Stir in the liqueur.

Before serving, whip the cream. Place a baba in a soup plate. Cut lengthways, generously top with the liqueur syrup and serve with unsweetened whipped cream.

FOREST FRUITS AND CHAMPAGNE DELIGHT

Great, this recipe combines all sorts of recipes, which I have already described earlier.
You will have to go back and forth through the book, but you will benefit from it, just admit it!

½ x recipe for champagne cream, see page 329
½ x basic recipe for sponge cake, see page 329

3 tbsp blackberry or raspberry jam, see page 12 or 16
1–2 tbsp blackberry and thyme syrup, to taste
100 g (4 oz) marzipan, see recipe on page 356
pinch or drop of pink food colouring
500 g (16 oz/2 cups) mixed forest fruits
a lot of icing (confectioner's) sugar and you will need a toothpick

First prepare the champagne cream. Make the cake batter according to the recipe and pour into a square tin, if you have one, but a round one will obviously also do the job. Bake the cake and leave to cool. Lightly beat the jam with the syrup. Spread the jam on the cake and cover with the champagne cream. Colour the marzipan with the pink colouring and knead until evenly coloured. Roll into a rope. Dust a rolling pin with icing sugar and roll the marzipan out on a countertop, also dusted with icing sugar. Again dust with icing sugar when it starts getting sticky. Using a ravioli cutter (with a zigzag knife), or a sharp knife, cut a rectangular strip, which is twice as high as the cake and generously fits around it. Wrap the cake with the marzipan trim, secure with a toothpick and fill the top with fresh forest fruit. Dust with icing sugar.

PARISIAN APPLE TARTLETS

For 6 individual tartlet bases

300 g (10 oz/2 cups) plain (all-purpose) flour

150 g (5 oz/1¼ sticks) chilled butter

100 g (approx. 4 oz/½ cup) sugar

1 egg

1 tsp cinnamon

pinch of salt

For the filling

3 tart cooking apples with red skin

75 g (2½ oz/⅓ cup) caster (superfine) sugar

2 tbsp plain (all-purpose) flour

2 eggs

200 ml (6 fl oz/¾ cup) thick cream w

seeds from 1 vanilla bean

mix of 1 tbsp sugar & ½ tbsp cinnamon

150 ml (5 fl oz/⅔ cup) apricot jam

2–3 tbsp Calvados

6 tbsp crème fraîche

Combine the tartlet base ingredients swiftly into an even dough. This is easiest in a food processor.
Use a few drops of ice-cold water if necessary.
Leave the dough to rest in the refrigerator for 1 hour. Then roll out the dough on a countertop dusted with flour and use to cover 6 well-greased pie tins. Prick the bottoms with a fork.
Preheat the oven to 180°C (350°F/Gas 4).
Blind bake the pastry cases for 10 minutes (if you are making a large pie, say, 24 cm (9 inch) diameter, bake a little longer, i.e.: 15–20 minutes).
Quarter the apples, remove the cores, but not the attractive peel. Cut the sections into very thin slices. Stir the sugar through the flour. Stir in the eggs into a nice paste. Heat the cream, vanilla and bean, bring to the boil and then remove from the heat. Remove the bean and add the hot cream to the flour-egg paste, while stirring.
Pour that cream into the pre-baked pie crusts and cover with the overlapping apple slices.
Sprinkle with the cinnamon-sugar mix.
Bake the tartlets in the preheated oven for 15–20 minutes (a larger version will be done in approx. 25 minutes).
Leave to slightly cool.
Heat the apricot jam in a frying pan. Dilute with a tbsp of Calvados or water. Press the jam through a strainer over a bowl and spread the collected apricot jelly on the tartlets.
Serve the tartlets with a tablespoon of unsweetened good quality crème fraîche.

DU CHOCOLAT POUR TOUS !

MAKING CHOCOLATES

WHEN MAKING CHOCOLATES, YOU, FIRST AND FOREMOST, NEED SOME SKILL. MELTING CHOCOLATE IS JUST NOT THAT EASY AND YOU HAVE TO ACQUIRE SOME EXPERIENCE. STIRRING TOO MUCH IS BAD, SINCE THE CHOCOLATE WILL BECOME GRAINY. HEATING IT TOO MUCH IS ALSO BAD, SINCE IT WILL ALSO BECOME DRY AND GRAINY. UNDER ALL CIRCUMSTANCES, THE FOLLOWING APPLIES: IF AT FIRST YOU DON'T SUCCEED, TRY AND TRY AGAIN. AND BE PREPARED FOR SOME FAILURES. FOR YOUR FIRST CHOCOLATES, STOCK UP ON SOME EXTRA CHOCOLATE. THEN YOU CAN MAKE ANOTHER BATCH, NO WORRIES! THE BEST TEMPERATURE FOR CHOCOLATE IS 40C (104F), HENCE A LITTLE WARMER THAN BODY TEMPERATURE. JUST CHECK WITH YOUR FINGER.

FOR THE FILLING: (GANACHE).YOU NEED TWICE AS MUCH CHOCOLATE AS CREAM: 100 ML (1/2 CUP) CREAM AND 200 G (7 OZ) CHOCOLATE (70% COCOA).

HEAT THE CREAM IN A HEAVY-BASED SAUCEPAN. YOU CAN ADD FLAVOURING SUCH AS CINNAMON, LIQUEUR OR NOTHING!

MELT 2 TBSP BUTTER IN THE HOT CREAM.

FINELY CHOP THE CHOCOLATE AND ADD IT TO THE CREAM. TURN OFF THE HEAT AND LEAVE TO MELT.

STIR THE MIXTURE CAREFULLY INTO A GLOSSY SMOOTH MASS.

POUR THE GANACHE INTO A TRAY LINED WITH PLASTIC WRAP AND PLACE IN THE REFRIGERATOR FOR AT LEAST 2 HOURS.

TRANSFER TO BAKING PAPER.

CUT INTO EQUAL SQUARES.

MELT 200 G (7 OZ) CHOCOLATE OVER A BAIN-MARIE.

USING A CARVING FORK, QUICKLY DIP THE GANACHE IN THE CHOCOLATE...

AND LEAVE THE CHOCOLATES TO DRY ON BAKING PAPER.

CREATE A PIPING BAG WITH BAKING PAPER.

FILL IT WITH 100 G (4 OZ) MELTED WHITE OR MILK CHOCOLATE.

THIS IS HOW YOU DECORATE THE CHOCOLATES PROFESSIONALLY!

LEAVE TO DRY AND NEATLY TRIM. SERVE WITH COFFEE!

LET'S GO...

MAKING CHOCOLATES IS FUN, ISN'T IT? THERE ARE, OF COURSE, HUNDREDS OF VARIATIONS, BUT WITH A FEW BASIC RECIPES, I HOPE THAT YOU WILL START EXPERIMENTING. I LIKE TO LOOK IN THE DISPLAY WINDOWS OF PATISSERIES AND CHOCOLATIERS FOR INSPIRATION. BUT MAYBE YOU ARE A CREATIVE GENIUS!

ROSEMARY AND SEA SALT CHOCOLATES

You can also replace the rosemary in this recipe with chilli pepper, thyme or strong black or green tea.

For the filling
100 ml (3 fl oz/½ cup) thick cream
1 sprig rosemary
1 tbsp red wine vinegar
100 g (4 oz) dark chocolate
5 tsp butter
For the couverture
dark chocolate
5 tsp butter
1 tbsp salt flakes or coarse sea salt

Heat the cream, rosemary and salt until very hot. Leave to infuse for about 30 minutes, do not boil the cream and try not to stir it. Strain the cream, add the wine vinegar and the chocolate. Set aside in order for the chocolate to melt due to the heat of the hot cream. Carefully continue to stir for a few minutes. Beat in the butter using a whisk. Leave to slightly cool and transfer the filling to a piping bag. Pipe the filling in the shape of little balls on baking paper. Leave to set in the refrigerator. Melt the dark chocolate and butter over a bain-marie. Dip the fillings into the chocolate and swiftly return them to the baking paper. Sprinkle with a few salt flakes and leave to fully set.

MARZIPAN

Making marzipan is very easy. And once you have made a considerable quantity you will find that you can do all sorts of things with it. You can cover it with chocolate, for example. Instead of water you can also use liqueur or add colouring agents. It freezes easily, so make a lot of it!

250 g (8 oz/1½ cups) blanched almonds
250 g (8 oz/2 cups) icing (confectioner's) sugar
2–3 tbsp water or orange blossom water

Finely grind the almonds in a food processor. (Or use ground almond meal.) Sift the icing sugar over them and add a few drops of water or other liquid. Knead the marzipan by hand into a supple and smooth dough. Wrap the dough in plastic wrap and allow to rest in the refrigerator for a few hours.
You can easily roll out the marzipan if you keep the rolling pin and a countertop dusted with icing sugar.

FILLED DATES

It is great fun to make these Moroccan sweets with your home-made marzipan.

20 large dates (but regular ones are also fine)
100 g (4 oz) marzipan, made with orange blossom water
50 g (approx. 2 oz/⅓ cup) pistachios
1 tbsp extra orange blossom water
icing (confectioner's) sugar

Chop two-thirds of the pistachio nuts. Knead the marzipan with the chopped nuts and a little orange blossom water. Roll into 20 balls with your hands dusted with icing sugar. Carefully pit the dates and fill them with the marzipan balls. Press a whole pistachio nut on each date and serve them, preferably in one of those beautiful tiny paper cups, if you can lay your hands on them.

ALMOND CHOCOLATES

100 g (approx. 4 oz/1 stick) butter
125 g (4 oz) dark chocolate, (at least 70% cocoa)
125 g (4 oz/1¼ cups) almond meal
175 g (6 oz/1⅓ cups) icing (confectioner's) sugar
50 g (approx. 2 oz/2 tbsp) mascarpone
3 tbsp liqueur, to taste
approx. 25 whole blanched almonds
approx. 100 g (4 oz) milk chocolate

Melt the butter and the chocolate over a bain-marie. Carefully stir in the icing sugar, almonds, mascarpone and the liqueur. Remove from the heat and leave to set. Knead into oval balls and press them onto the countertop so that they stay put. Top with a whole almond. Melt the milk chocolate over a bain-marie and dip half the chocolates into it. Leave to dry on a rack or on baking paper.

CINNAMON STICKS

100 ml (3 fl oz/½ cup) thick cream
200 g (7 oz) dark chocolate, (at least 70% cocoa)
5 tsp butter at room temperature
1 tsp cinnamon + 2 tbsp extra
1 tsp ground ginger
2 tbsp caster (superfine) sugar

Heat the cream until very hot and turn off the heat. Grate the chocolate and add it to the warm cream with the butter, cinnamon and ground ginger. Let the chocolate melt and occasionally stir gently. Leave to set until nearly hard.
Beat using a mixer and transfer to a piping bag with a large round tip. Pipe sticks, 3 cm (1 inch) long, on baking paper. Leave to slightly set in the fridge. Stir the remaining cinnamon into the sugar and roll the sticks in this.

CRUNCHY CHOCOLATES

2 tbsp golden syrup, but honey also works well
5 tsp butter
100 g (approx. 4 oz/½ cup) caster (superfine) sugar
50 g (1¾ cups) puffed rice cereal
1 tbsp cocoa
100 g (4 oz) milk or dark chocolate

Heat the honey and the butter in a saucepan. Stir in the caster sugar, puffed rice and cocoa. Grease an oblong shallow baking tray. Add the mixture. Slightly press and even out with the back of a spoon or spatula. Leave to cool and transfer to a board. Heat the chocolate over a bain-marie. Pour over the cake on the board and even out using the spatula. Leave to set in the refrigerator and cut into cubes.

IRISH FUDGE

If you do not like alcohol, replace this with the same quantity of milk.

450 g (15 oz/2 cups) sugar
approx. 4 tsp vanilla sugar
100 g (approx. 4 oz/1 stick) butter
250 ml (9 fl oz/1 cup) thick cream
50 ml (1½ fl oz/¼ cup) Irish whiskey

Line a square brownie baking tray with baking paper. Combine all ingredients in a saucepan. Bring the mixture to a boil on low heat and simmer for 30 minutes. Test for consistency by putting a droplet into cold water. If you are able to knead it into a ball, it is ready! Leave the fudge to cool for a few minutes. Stir occasionally until it thickens into a slightly crumbly consistency. Pour into the baking tray, leave to fully cool and dry for 6 hours. Use the paper to lift it out and cut into cubes. Leave a little space between each one so that they to continue to dry.

357

COW PATS

Yea, funny name! But that's what I used to call them. They are actually peanut-raisin rock biscuits. You can replace the peanuts with cashew nuts or almonds.

350 g (12 oz) milk or dark chocolate
50 g (approx. 2 oz/½ stick) butter
125 g (4 oz/⅔ cup) raisins
125 g (4 oz/¾ cup) peanuts

Heat the chocolate and the butter over a bain-marie. Stir in the raisins and peanuts. Drop spoonfuls of the mixture on a large sheet of baking paper. Leave to dry and set in the refrigerator.
If you are in a decorative mood, you can melt a little white chocolate and with the help of a spoon run a thin trickle of white chocolate on the rocks. They will no longer look like cow pats, but perhaps that's for the best.

ROSEMARY SHORTBREAD

I didn't like shortbread as a child. I only started liking it later, especially if it is a little savoury, as the recipe here with rosemary. Make small biscuits, they taste better and are posher with coffee than those ridiculously large biscuits I received as a child.

150 g (5 oz/1¼ sticks) butter
50 g (approx. 2 oz/¼ cup) caster (superfine) sugar
1 tbsp honey
250 g (8 oz/1⅔ cups) self-raising flour
1 pinch salt
2 tbsp finely chopped rosemary
and extra rosemary sprigs to garnish

Preheat the oven to 170°C (340°F/Gas 3). Grease a springform or pie dish approx. 24 cm (9 inch) in diameter.
Beat the butter and the sugar and honey into a creamy mass. Stir in the flour, with the rosemary and salt. Do not beat too long, it just has to be well blended. Knead a few times on a countertop dusted with flour until it turns into a smooth dough ball.
Press the dough into the dish and even out. Cut the raw 'pie' into small wedges or fingers with the dull edge of a knife. Prick holes in the dough with a fork and garnish each wedge with a small sprig of rosemary.
Bake the shortbread in the oven for 15–20 minutes until light brown. Leave to cool in the dish for 10 minutes and then carefully remove it. You can now break it along the scored lines and serve.

ALMOND TUILES

In this recipe I say that you have to let them dry on a rolling pin, but if you carefully press them on a bottle cap, you will create small cups; which you can fill! With vanilla cream, for example, and red fruit.

For at least 20 tuiles
2 egg whites
a teeny pinch of salt
3 tbsp icing (confectioner's) sugar
2 tbsp plain (all-purpose) flour
3 tbsp softened butter
3 tbsp slivered almonds

Beat the egg whites, salt and the sugar until stiff. Stir in the flour and the melted butter. With the help of a spoon, drop dollops of batter on a baking tray lined with baking paper. Sprinkle with the almonds and bake the tuiles in an oven preheated to 180°C (350°F/Gas 4) for 5 minutes until golden brown. Always bake small quantities. While still very warm, remove the tuiles from the baking tray and place them on something round, such as a rolling pin or a small bottle. Leave them to 'dry', resulting in nicely curled biscuits.

ALMOND-CINNAMON BISCUITS

For a full biscuit tin
100 g (approx. 4 oz/½ cup) caster (superfine) sugar + extra
200 g (7 oz/1¾ sticks) butter
300 g (10 oz/2 cups) plain (all-purpose) flour
1 egg
zest of 1 lemon
1 tbsp cinnamon or mixed spices
100 g (4 oz/⅔ cup) slivered almonds
pinch of salt

To garnish
candied cherries, whole almonds, whole walnuts, etc.

Combine all ingredients in a food processor and grind. Roll into ropes with a diameter of approx. 2 cm (1 inch) and roll them through the extra sugar. Wrap them in plastic wrap and place them in the refrigerator for 1 hour to firm.
Preheat the oven to 180°C (350°F/Gas 4). Cut the rolls into slices, and garnish with a nut or cherry or whatever you have. Bake in the oven for 12 minutes until light brown. Leave to cool before serving.

COCO ROCHERS

Sophie, our French pastry chef, taught me how to make these fantastic French biscuits. You can make them as large as you wish. I love them small, almost like chocolates. This recipe is for approx. 20 biscuits.

125 g (4 oz/1⅓ cups) desiccated (shredded) coconut
125 g (4 oz/½ cup) sugar
2 egg whites

And also:
90 g (3 oz) white chocolate, in chunks
90 g (3 oz) dark chocolate, in chunks
1 tbsp desiccated (shredded) coconut

Beat the coconut, the sugar and the egg whites swiftly into a thick batter. Roll into balls the size of a golf ball and with thumb and index finger press a top, thus creating a 'hill'.
Preheat the oven to 170°C (340°F/Gas 3). Place the hills on a sheet of baking paper on a baking tray and bake for approx. 12 minutes until light brown. Leave to fully cool. Melt the chocolate over a bain-marie and dip the tops of the biscuits into the chocolate. Sprinkle with coconut and leave to set until the coffee is ready.

CHOCOLATE BISCUITS

For at least 30 biscuits
150 g (5 oz/1 cup) plain (all-purpose) flour
75 g (2½ oz/approx. ½ stick) butter, chilled
75 g (2½ oz/⅓ cup) sugar
2 tbsp cocoa powder
2 tbsp shaved dark chocolate

Knead all ingredients together into a smooth dough. Add a few drops of cold water, if it is too dry. Allow the dough to rest for at least an hour. Roll out on a flour-dusted countertop. Cut out small rectangles or use a cutter. Place them on a baking tray lined with baking paper. Preheat the oven to 180°C (350°F/Gas 4). Bake until done in approx. 10 minutes. Leave them to cool before serving, allowing the chocolate to set.

PISTACHIO WAFERS

For 15–20 wafers
150 g (5 oz) dark chocolate
100 g (4 oz/⅔ cup) pistachio nuts, skins removed
50 g (approx. 2 oz/¼ cup) raisins

Slowly melt the chocolate over a bain-marie. Stir as little as possible. Pour spoonfuls of melted chocolate onto baking paper and press them into round wafers with the back of the spoon. Press the pistachio nuts and raisins into the middle of the wafers and leave to fully harden. Peel them from the paper and serve!

HAZELNUT & LEMON CANTUCCINI

For approx. 24 slices
250 g (8 oz/1⅔ cups) self-raising flour
pinch of salt
2 eggs, beaten
125 g (4 oz/½ cup) sugar
2 tsp vanilla sugar
zest of 2 lemons
50 ml (1½ fl oz/¼ cup) sunflower oil
approx. 50 ml (1½ fl oz/¼ cup) milk
100 g (4 oz/¾ cup) hazelnuts, coarsely chopped

Preheat the oven to 175°C (340°F/Gas 4). Line a large baking tray with baking paper. Stir the salt into the flour. Beat two-thirds of the beaten eggs in a bowl using a hand blender (you will need the reserved one-third later to spread on the biscuits). While stirring, add the sugar and vanilla sugar as well as the lemon juice and oil. Sift the flour over a bowl and stir. Add the milk, add a little more if it appears necessary. Lastly, quickly knead in the chopped nuts. Cut the dough in half, and roll both halves into two equal 'ropes'. Slightly separate them on the baking tray and coat them with the reserved egg. Bake the biscuit ropes for 25–30 minutes or until golden brown. Leave to slightly cool on a rack and cut each into 12 equal slices with a sharp knife. Return to the baking tray and bake for a further 10 minutes on each side until golden brown. Leave to fully cool on a rack.

CANDIED CHOCOLATE ORANGE CURLS

For approx. 40 curls
3 oranges
600 g (21 oz/1¾ cups) sugar + extra
150 g (5 oz) milk or dark chocolate

Squeeze the oranges. Reserve the juice. Remove all of the white pulp and cut the peel into thin strips. Bring the peels, the juice and a glass of water to a boil, transfer to kitchen paper and leave to drain.
Bring the sugar and 600 ml (20 fl oz/2½ cups) water to a boil and simmer the peels in the sugar syrup for 1½ hours. Add more liquid if it boils dry. Remove the peels from the thickened syrup. Strain.
Sprinkle a little sugar on a plate and coat the peels one by one with the sugar. Leave to dry on baking paper.
Melt the chocolate over a bain-marie and dip half of the orange curls in it. Leave them to 'dry' again.
Keep in the refrigerator.

Orange Marmalade Drops

Preheat to 375°

Sift :
   2/3 cup sugar

Beat until soft :
   1/3 cup butter

Add sugar gradually. Blend these
ingredients till light & creamy. Beat
in :

   1 egg
   6 tablespoons orange marmalade

Sift :
   1 1/2 cups flour
   & resift with :
   1 1/4 tsp. baking powder

} if cookies too dry,
add more marmal.'
if too moist -
add flour & grated
lemon rind.

Stir sifted ingred. into butter mix
Drop batter from teaspoon, well apart
on greased sheet. Bake cookies for
8 minutes (or so).

Joanna's recipes

rose tea
Marshmallows

FOR THIS RECIPE YOU WILL REALLY NEED A FOOD PROCESSOR WITH A WHISK OR A HAND BLENDER AND LOTS OF PATIENCE

TO FILL A BAKING SHEET YOU WILL NEED :

• 3 LEAVES / OR 2¼ TSP GELATINE / POWDERED GELATINE
• 250 ML (8 FL·OZ / 1 CUP) ROSE PETAL TEA (...OR REGULAR TEA OF COURSE !)
• 500 GRAMS (16 OZ / 2¼ CUPS) GRANULATED SUGAR
• 150 GRAMS (5 OZ / JUST UNDER 1/2 CUP) GOLDEN SYRUP (THICK SUGAR SYRUP)
• PINCH OF SALT
• DROP OF PINK FOOD COLORING

1 SOAK THE GELATINE LEAVES IN COLD WATER (OR DISSOLVE THE POWDERED GELATINE IN A TBSP. OF WARM WATER)

2 BRING THE TEA, SUGAR SYRUP AND SALT TO A BOIL. SIMMER FOR ABOUT 7 MINS UNTIL IT FORMS A THICK SYRUP.

3 SQUEEZE THE GELATINE LEAVES, PLACE THEM IN THE FOOD PROCESSOR AND BLITZ ON MEDIUM SPEED OR ADD THE DISSOLVED GELATINE MIXTURE TO THE FOOD PROCESSOR.

4 POUR A THIN TRICKLE OF HOT SYRUP ONTO THE MIXTURE. IF IT TURNS WHITER, THE PROSESSORS' SPEED CAN BE INCREASED. → KEEP ON BLITZING INTO THIKC WHITE FOAM & UNTIL THE BOWL FEELS LUKEWARM. ⇨ THIS TAKES 15 MINUTES ! ADD THE COLORING .

5 GREASE A SHEET OF BAKING PAPER. PLACE ON A SERVING TRAY AND SPREAD THE MIXTURE ON IT: 2 CM OR ¾ INCH THICK. ←

6 LEAVE TO DRY FOR 8-12 HOURS. CUT INTO SQUARES OR CUT OUT SHAPES.

THIS IS HOW EASY IT IS ⇐

CHEWY WHOLEMEAL BISCUITS WITH CHOCOLATE

For approx. 40 biscuits

175 g (6 oz/1½ sticks) butter at room temperature

200 g (7 oz/1⅛ cups) caster (superfine) sugar

1 egg

100 g (approx. 4 oz/⅔ cup) wholemeal (whole-wheat) flour

2 tsp vanilla sugar

100 g (4 oz/¾ cup) toasted walnuts or pecan nuts, ground

½ tsp baking powder

pinch of salt

½ tsp cinnamon

250 g (8 oz/2 cups) oatmeal

approx. 200 g (7 oz) chocolate, grated or chopped into small chunks

Preheat the oven to 180°C (350°F/Gas 4).

Beat the butter and the sugar until creamy, stir in the egg. Combine all dry ingredients and half the grated chocolate and stir everything in the mixing bowl into a nice dough. Grease a baking tray or line it with baking paper. With clean hands, roll the dough into balls the size of a walnut and arrange on the baking tray, not too close to each other.

Bake in the oven until golden brown in 12–15 minutes.

Leave to fully cool.

Melt the remaining chocolate over a bain-marie. Leave to slightly cool and pour into a piping bag. Pipe thin trickles of chocolate onto the biscuits. If you don't own a piping bag, you can use a spoon. Leave to dry again and serve!

NUTTY WINTER BISCUITS

For approx. 45 biscuits

125 g (approx. 4 oz/1 stick) butter and a little extra for greasing purposes

250 g (8 oz/1⅓ cups) caster (superfine) sugar

3 tbsp peanut butter

2 eggs

2 tsp vanilla sugar

175 g (6 oz/1⅛ cups) plain (all-purpose) flour

75 g (2½ oz/approx. ⅓ cup) walnuts

75 g (2½ oz/approx. ⅓ cup) raisins

150 g (5 oz/1½ cups) oat flakes (organic store) or oatmeal

1 tsp baking powder

pinch of salt

1 tsp cinnamon

Beat the butter, sugar and peanut butter until creamy. Stir in the eggs, one by one, and then the vanilla sugar. Sift the flour over another bowl and blend with the oat flakes, baking powder, salt and cinnamon. Fold into the butter mixture. Finish with the nuts and raisins. Knead swiftly into a smooth dough and wrap in plastic wrap. Leave to rest in the refrigerator for one hour. Preheat the oven to 180°C (350°F/Gas 4). Line the baking tray with baking paper and coat with a little melted butter. Using two tablespoons, create oval balls from the dough, the size of a walnut, and place them on the baking tray, approx. 4 cm (2 inch) apart. Bake the biscuits for approx. 12 minutes, they will still feel soft, but that's how it has to be! Leave them to slightly cool on the baking tray and then using a spatula transfer them to a rack to further cool. Keep in an airtight sealed tin or box.

CHOCOLATE & CARAMEL TRUFFLES

125 g (4 oz) dark chocolate

75 g (2½ oz/⅓ cup) sugar

2 tbsp water

75 g (2½ oz/approx. ½ stick) butter

150 ml (5 fl oz/⅔ cup) thick cream

125 g (4 oz/1¼ cups) cocoa

and attractive chocolate or paper cups

Melt the chocolate in the microwave or over a bain-marie. Leave to briefly cool. Melt the sugar in the water in a heavy-based pan. Gently swirl the pan in order for the sugar to colour evenly. Remove from the heat when the caramel turns amber. Careful! CARAMEL IS BOILING HOT! Stir in the butter in pats until dissolved. Pour in the cream. This may splatter, so keep your distance. Stir into a smooth sauce on low heat. Add the caramel to the chocolate and leave the mixture to fully cool. Place in the refrigerator to further cool for at least 3 hours. Now you can create curls with a tablespoon from the hardened chocolate. Drop them into a bowl with cocoa powder and roll them with the help of two other spoons, so that all sides are covered with cocoa. Place the truffles immediately back in the refrigerator to firm again.

Serve in chocolate cups. Or paper cups.

LAPSANG TRUFFLES

75 ml (2½ fl oz/⅓ cup) crème fraîche

75 ml (2½ fl oz/⅓ cup) thick cream

50 g (approx. 2 oz/½ stick) butter

1 generous tbsp lapsang souchong tea leaves, (Chinese black tea with a smoky flavour)

200 g (7 oz) dark chocolate, chopped

approx. 150 g (5 oz) dark chocolate sprinkles

Bring the crème fraîche, cream and butter to a boil in a heavy-based saucepan. Stir in the tea.

Melt the chocolate over a bain-marie. Pour the cream through a fine strainer over the chocolate and stir carefully until the chocolate has an even colour. Leave to cool in the refrigerator.

Go do something else in the meantime…

When the chocolate has become 'hard', roll into balls with the help of two tablespoons. Roll them through the sprinkles.

Always keep in the refrigerator until ready to serve.

NUT-CARAMEL BAR WITH DRIED FIGS

For approximately 12 bars

200 g (7 oz/1⅓ cups) blanched almonds

200 g (7 oz/1⅓ cups) walnuts or pecan nuts

200 g (7 oz/1⅓ cups) sunflower seeds, pumpkin seeds (pepitas), or pine nuts or a mixture of the above

200 g (7 oz) dried figs, finely chopped

juice and zest of ½ orange

sunflower oil for greasing purposes

250 g (8 oz/1⅓ cups) caster (superfine) sugar

3 tbsp maple syrup

50 g (approx. 2 oz/½ stick) butter

pinch of salt

Preheat the oven to 175°C (340°F/Gas 4). Arrange the nuts over a sheet of baking paper on a baking tray and bake for approx. 15 minutes until golden brown and crisp, turn halfway through. Transfer the nuts to a bowl and stir in the figs and orange zest. Line a shallow rectangular baking tray with baking paper. Brush the baking paper with a thin layer of oil. Heat the sugar, syrup and orange juice in a heavy-based saucepan until the sugar has dissolved. Stir gently with a wooden spoon, but beware of splatters, since it will get very hot. Lastly, stir in the butter. The sauce will become thicker. Fold in the nuts and stir well. Pour the mixture into the greased baking tray and spread evenly.

After approx. 15 minutes, score the slab into bars with the back of a knife when it is nearly cold.

Leave to fully cool.

Break the slab along the score lines.

You can keep the bars for some time in a sealed box separated by sheets of baking paper.

MAKING MUSTARD

YOU PROBABLY NEVER THOUGHT THAT MAKING MUSTARD WAS THIS EASY. I WILL GIVE YOU THE RECIPE FOR BASIC MUSTARD. ONCE YOU HAVE MADE IT, YOU WILL NO DOUBT COME UP WITH NEW INGREDIENTS: TARRAGON VINEGAR, TOASTED MUSTARD SEEDS FOR A NUTTY FLAVOUR, NUTMEG, CLOVES, CARAWAY SEEDS OR WITH GARLIC, CHILLI PEPPERS OR HONEY INSTEAD OF SUGAR. BE CAREFUL WITH THE SUGAR: IT CAN CHANGE THE TASTE DRAMATICALLY. SOME PEOPLE LIKE A LOT OF SUGAR, OTHERS DO NOT LIKE IT AT ALL.

FOR 1 JAR YOU WILL NEED: 100 G (4 OZ) MUSTARD SEEDS, 200 ML (3/4 CUP) WHITE WINE VINEGAR, 1 TSP TURMERIC, 50 G (1/4 CUP) SUGAR, SALT, PEPPER.

FOR A SMOOTHER EFFECT, YOU CAN SOAK THE MUSTARD SEEDS OVERNIGHT IN THE VINEGAR, BUT THIS IS NOT ABSOLUTELY NECESSARY.

PLACE THE MUSTARD SEEDS AND THE VINEGAR IN A FOOD PROCESSOR.

ADD THE SPICES AND THE SUGAR.

BLITZ FOR APPROX. 6 MINUTES UNTIL IT'S A NEARLY SMOOTH MUSTARD. YOU CAN TAKE LONGER FOR A SMOOTHER MUSTARD IF YOU SO DESIRE.

TRANSFER THE MUSTARD TO A JAR, CLOSE THE LID AND PLACE IN REFRIGERATOR UNTIL USED. IT WILL GET BETTER WITH TIME.

LET'S GET GOING ...

MAKE ALL THESE SAUCES A DAY IN ADVANCE, SO THAT THEY ARE READY IN THE REFRIGERATOR AFTER A NIGHT ON THE TOWN.

KETCHUP

For approx. 4 jars

2.5 kg (5½ lb) tomatoes
1 red capsicum (bell pepper)
2 medium onions, finely chopped
1 garlic clove, crushed
100 ml (3 fl oz/½ cup) vinegar
75 g (2½ oz/⅓ cup) sugar
pinch of salt
2 tsp grated ginger
2 tsp ground paprika
2 tsp nutmeg
1 pinch cayenne pepper
1 tbsp coriander seeds
1 clove
freshly ground pepper

Wash the tomatoes and cut into chunks. Wash the capsicum and cut the pulp into chunks, remove the seeds. Combine the tomato, capsicum, onion and garlic and a little water in a pan and leave to simmer for approx. 1 hour. Stir occasionally to prevent burning. If necessary add a little water. Purée the sauce until smooth, away from the heat, using a hand blender. Return to the heat and add the vinegar, sugar and all spices. Leave the sauce to simmer for a further 1½ hours or until sufficiently thickened. Taste and add salt and pepper, as needed. Pour the hot sauce into sterile jars. (See instructions under jam making on page 12.) Seal the jars with a suitable lid and turn upside down until cooled. The ketchup has a shelf life of 1 year. Once opened, the jar must be kept in the refrigerator.

MUSTARD MAYONNAISE

1 egg yolk
1 tbsp lemon juice or vinegar
2 tbsp coarse or fine mustard (to taste)
200 ml (6 fl oz/¾ cup) sunflower oil or as much as needed
freshly ground pepper and salt

Ensure that all ingredients are at room temperature. Beat the egg yolk lightly in a bowl with the pepper, salt, lemon juice and mustard. While stirring with a mixer, blend the sunflower oil with the egg mixture, first drop by drop and then in a thin trickle, into a thick creamy mayonnaise. Great with chips or crisps of course!
OH! Be careful, this mayonnaise must be refrigerated and consumed within a few days since it contains raw egg.

OOF'S BARBECUE SAUCE

Oof makes a divine, very American, barbecue sauce, which I spoon up straight from the pan on bread.

500 ml (16 fl oz/2 cups) ketchup
½ can dark beer
100 ml (3 fl oz/½ cup) red wine vinegar
50 g (approx. 2 oz/¼ cup) raw caster (superfine) sugar
2 tbsp Worcestershire sauce
salt, to taste
1 garlic clove, finely chopped
pinch cayenne pepper
100 g (approx. 4 oz/1 stick) butter
1–2 tbsp jalapeño peppers, chopped

Cook all ingredients in a saucepan on low heat into a thick sauce. Leave to cool or serve warm, either way.

TOOMEH: LEBANESE GARLIC SAUCE

1 potato, peeled and boiled.
2–4 cloves garlic (or more!)
2 tbsp mayonnaise see recipe above
2 tbsp thick yoghurt
1 tbsp lemon juice, or more, to taste
salt and freshly ground pepper

Mash the potato. Crush garlic with a pinch of salt into a paste. Add to potato and stir well with pepper. Stir in mayonnaise, yoghurt and lemon juice.

ARAB LAMB BURGER

600 g (21 oz) minced (ground) lamb, from leg of lamb: preferably home-ground in the food processor

60 g (2 oz/⅓ cup) burghul (bulgur), steeped in 180 ml (approx. 6 fl oz/¾ cup) boiling water

1 onion, finely chopped

2 garlic cloves, finely chopped

1 tsp cinnamon

½ tsp allspice

1 tsp ground paprika

4 tbsp fresh coriander (cilantro), finely chopped

zest of ½ lemon

2 generous tbsp pine nuts, briefly toasted in a dry frying pan

salt and freshly ground pepper

and also...

4 flatbreads with chickpeas and sage from the grill, see page 273 (or just 4 good pitas)

toomeh, Lebanese garlic sauce, see page 380 or another sauce on that page

green salad and carrot salad, see page 274

Knead all ingredients into a firm ball. Separate into four or six equal parts and roll each part into a ball. Press flat into a patty. Heat a griddle until burning hot. Fry a few minutes until golden brown, turn halfway through and set aside until used.

When ready to use, grill the burgers on both sides until done. Carefully turn the burgers. I like it if the inside is still a little pink.

Cut the flatbread halfway to create a 'pouch'. Fill them with the burgers and a little green and carrot salad.

Serve with toomeh.

Toomeh, page 380, Flatbread with chickpeas, page 273, Carrot salad with cumin, page 274 and Arab lamb burger

OMELETTE WITH SAUSAGE, CUMIN, POTATOES AND SPINACH

250 g (8 oz) sausages: go for tasty Italian or French sausages

a little olive oil for frying

300 g (10 oz) spinach, washed

1 small onion, diced

1 large waxy potato, washed but not peeled, thinly sliced

6 eggs

100 ml (3 fl oz/½ cup) thick cream

1 tbsp cumin seeds, briefly toasted in a dry pan

1 ball buffalo mozzarella

salt and freshly ground pepper

Remove the skin from the sausages and crumble the meat into the hot olive oil in a non-stick frying pan.

Fry the meat while stirring until done and drain on kitchen paper. Cook the spinach in the pan on high heat. Fold the cooked spinach at the bottom of the pan over the uncooked leaves at the top. Transfer to a colander in the sink to drain. Heat a dash of oil in the pan. Add the onion and potato slices. Cook half covered with a lid for approx. 10 minutes on medium heat. Turn occasionally. Remove the lid and turn up the heat, allowing the potatoes to become crispy on the edges. Preheat the grill to 175°C (340°F/Gas 4).

Beat the eggs with the cream, cumin seeds, salt and pepper and pour over the mixture in the pan. If the pan does not fit into the oven, you can also use a pie dish lined with greased baking paper, and place the fried onion and potatoes on the bottom. Carefully shake the pan or pie dish back and forth in order for the egg to spread evenly. Spread the spinach and sausage on the omelette. Cover with mozzarella chunks.

Put the omelette under the grill and bake until done for approx. 7 minutes.

Serve in wedges with plenty of thick toasted bread.

AFTER A NIGHT ON THE TOWN

CLUB SANDWICH WITH CHEESE, BACON, SMOKED BEETROOT & CELERY SALAD

389

For this recipe, I assume that you still have some smoked beetroot left over, otherwise you can find the recipe on page 243, or you can use precooked beetroot.

For the celery salad
½ small celeriac or ¼ large one
juice of 1 lemon
125 g (4 oz/½ cup) crème fraîche
1 tbsp mayonnaise, see page 380
freshly ground pepper and salt
2 smoked beetroots (see page 243) or 2 regular, boiled ones

And also:
16 bread slices, preferably wholemeal (whole-wheat)
mayonnaise as a spread
8 slices bacon or thinly sliced pork belly, see page 195
a pat of butter
8 slices tasty farmhouse cheese
a few nice lettuce leaves, or rocket (arugula) salad, or regular butter lettuce

First prepare the celery salad: peel the celeriac and grate on fine setting. This is easiest with the grater in the food processor. Trickle lemon juice over it in order to prevent discolouration and then stir the other ingredients through the grated celeriac. Season the salad with salt and pepper and keep in the refrigerator until used. Rub the peel away from the beetroots and slice.
Toast the bread slices in a toaster or under a grill.
Fry the bacon in a pat of butter in a non-stick pan until crispy.
Spread mayonnaise on all bread slices. Cover the bottom 4 slices with lettuce and cheese. Top with a generous tablespoon celery salad. Cover with the next bread slice, also topped with lettuce, bacon and beetroot. Cover with another bread slice with lettuce, cheese and celery salad and add the last bread slice. Secure sandwich with two toothpicks and cut diagonally in half.

Charles

Bloody Mary

STICK A CELERY STALK IN IT!

A FEW DROPS OF LEMON JUICE

3 PARTS TOMATO JUICE

1 PART VODKA

TABASCO

THE ORIGINAL & GENUINE
LEA & PERRINS
SOS WORCESTERSHIRE

FLAVOR YOUR DRINK WITH TABASCO & WORCESTERSHIRE SAUCE!

STICKY CINNAMON SCROLLS

Right! A little bit of a hangover also requires something sweet of course. These are ready in a little over 30 minutes, really no time at all. And usually everything will be in the pantry, so you don't have to leave the house. An ideal breakfast.

For approximately 8 scrolls.

350 g (12 oz/2⅓ cups) self-raising flour (or plain/all purpose flour and 2–3 tsp baking powder)
75 g (2½ oz/approx. ½ stick) butter, chilled
150–175 ml (⅔–¾ cup) buttermilk (or regular milk)
pinch of salt
1 egg, lightly beaten

And also:
large chunk spreadable butter
sugar
cinnamon
raisins
nuts: walnuts, pecan nuts, peanuts, whatever you have in the cupboard, coarsely chopped

Preheat the oven to 180°C (350°F/Gas 4).
In a bowl, knead the flour with a little salt and the butter until the dough looks like coarse sand. Slowly add the buttermilk into a supple dough.
Roll the dough ball out into a very thin slab (say 0.5 cm/⅛ inch thick) on the countertop dusted with flour.
Liberally spread butter on the dough. Sprinkle with sugar, cinnamon, raisins and chopped nuts.
Roll the slab lengthways into a long rope.
Grease a baking tin. Cut the roll into equal small rolls and place them upright against each other in the tin. They don't have to fit tightly. Brush with the lightly beaten egg and bake the scrolls for approx. 25 minutes until golden brown and cooked on the inside.
Serve with chilled butter. Or also delicious with whipped cream or unsweetened crème fraîche.

BUTTERMILK PANCAKES WITH BACON

For 16–20 pancakes
125 g (4 oz/¾ cup) plain (all-purpose) flour
125 g (4 oz/¾ cup) wholemeal (buck-wheat) flour
1 tsp baking powder
2 tbsp sugar
500–700 ml (16–21 fl oz/2–3 cups) buttermilk
1 egg
2 tsp vanilla sugar
150 g (5 oz) bacon rashers
butter for frying

Combine all ingredients, except the bacon and butter, into a nice batter.
Melt the butter in a non-stick frying pan. Fry 2 slices of bacon on both sides until light brown. Pour a spoonful of batter onto each slice, fry on medium heat until holes form in the pancakes. Turn and allow the other side to colour.
Serve with homemade apple syrup jam.

APPLE SYRUP JAM

For 4–5 jars
2 kg (4½ lb) sweet-sour apples for cooking
250 g (8 oz/1⅓ cups) raw caster (superfine) sugar

Wash the apples and chop the whole apples. Bring these chunks to a boil in a layer of water. Simmer for approx. 30 minutes until the apples break open. Purée the mixture with a hand blender. Drain the apple sauce in a strainer over another pan while stirring occasionally. This will take at least 1 hour.
Bring the collected apple purée to a boil on high heat, and reduce to approximately one quarter. Stir occasionally.
Add the sugar while stirring. Continue to stir until it has fully dissolved and reduce further.
Pour the apple syrup jam into thoroughly cleaned jars, seal and set aside, upside down, for 5 minutes.
Leave to fully cool. The syrup will get thicker once it is cold.

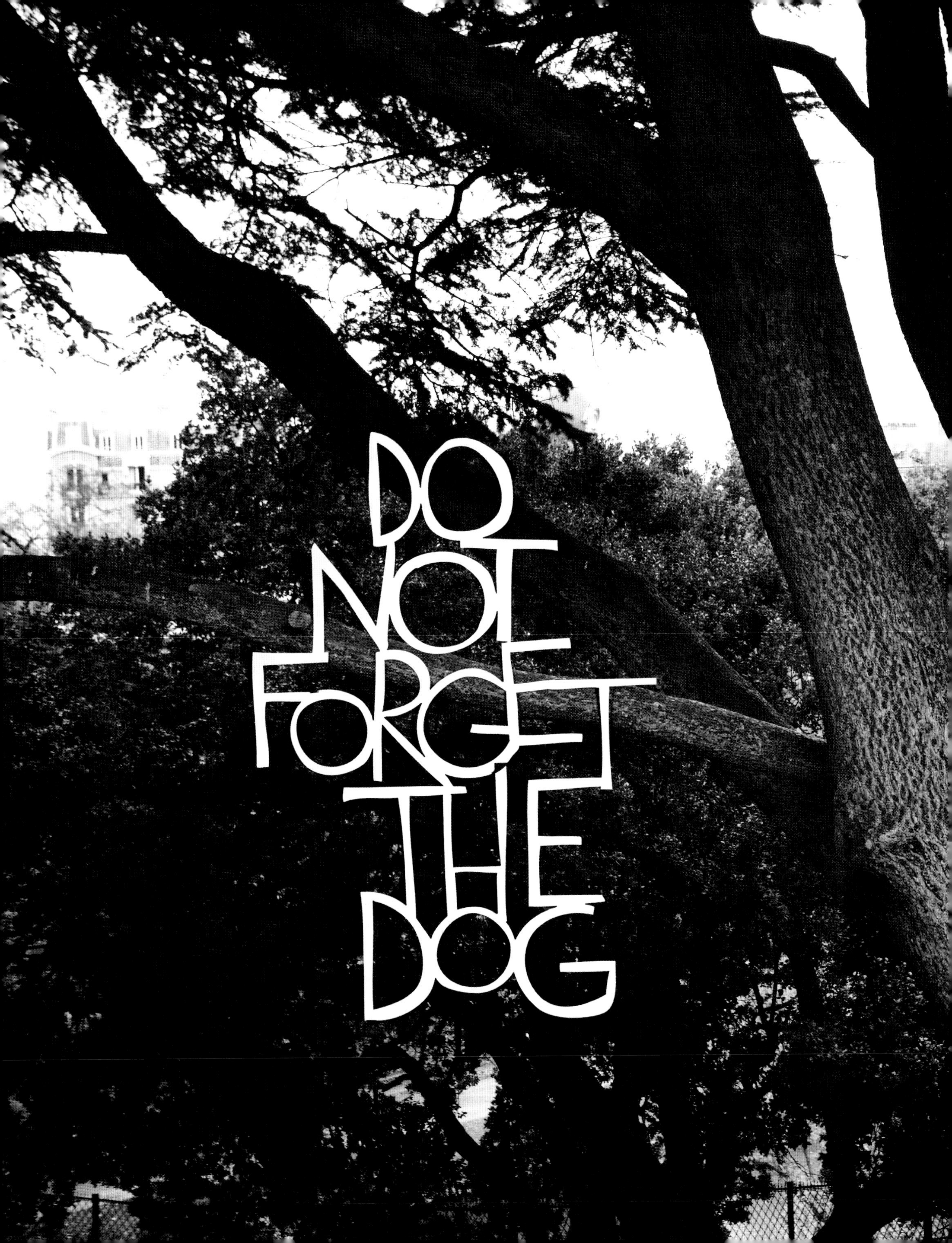
DO
NOT
FORGET
THE
DOG

CHICKEN BISCUITS

For 20–30 biscuits, depending on the size of your dog.
Make small biscuits for a small dog and larger ones for a great lump of a dog.

200 g (7 oz) boiled chicken (or leftovers from yesterday)
75 ml (2½ fl oz/⅓ cup) chicken stock (home-made, hence salt-free)
100 g (approx. 4 oz/⅔ cup) wholemeal (whole-wheat) flour
40 g (1½ oz/⅓ cup) cornflour (cornstarch)
1 tbsp butter at room temperature

Preheat the oven to 175°C (340°F/Gas 4). Grind the chicken with the stock and the butter in the food processor. Add the flour and cornflour. Knead the dough into a firm ball. Roll into a thin sheet on a flour-dusted countertop. Cut out shapes or cut into cubes. Bake until golden brown for 20 minutes. Leave to cool and keep in an airtight jar.

LIVER CHEWIES

50 g (approx. 2 oz/⅔ cup) wheat germ (organic store)
250 g (8 oz) chicken or beef livers
175 g (6 oz/1⅛ cups) wholemeal (whole-wheat) flour
3 eggs

Blend the ingredients in a food processor until smooth. Grease a brownie baking tray, square or rectangular, with a little oil and cut a sheet of baking paper the size of the bottom. Grease thoroughly. Press the mixture into the tray. Bake the biscuit for 20 minutes in an oven preheated to 175°C (340°F/Gas 4). Leave to cool and transfer to a board. Leave to fully cool then cut into small cubes using a large knife. Keep in the refrigerator or freezer.

DOGGY BISCUITS

150 ml (5 fl oz/⅔ cup) hot water or salt-free home-made stock (beef cubes often contain too much salt!)
2 tbsp olive oil
1 egg
1 garlic clove, crushed
400 g (14 oz/2⅔ cups) plain (all-purpose) flour

Combine all the ingredients into a firm dough in a bowl. Roll into a thin sheet approximately 0.5 cm (⅛ inch) thick on a flour-dusted countertop. Cut the dough into strips or cut out shapes using a biscuit cutter. Preheat the oven to 200°C (400°F/Gas 6) and bake the doggy biscuits for approx. 30 minutes until golden brown. Keep in a sealable jar.

Biscuits in the shape of dogs: doggy biscuits, biscuits that spell MARIE: chicken biscuits, the small diamond-shaped biscuits are the liver chewies.

Jessica

Joy

Valentijn

Horas

LES
ME-
NUS

SUNDAY BRUNCH

FOR APPROX. 6 SERVINGS

VEAL STOCK (SOUP)
GARNISH WITH A LOT OF CHOPPED CHERVIL, SEE RECIPE ON PAGE 128
*
EGGS BENEDICT
KEEP THE HOLLANDAISE SAUCE WARM IN A VACUUM FLASK OR OVER A BAIN-MARIE,
SEE RECIPE ON PAGE 39.
OR
SALMON AND PRAWN TERRINE
WITH BROAD BEANS AND PORTOBELLO MUSHROOMS, SEE PAGE 185
WITH IRISH BROWN SODA BREAD TOAST, SEE RECIPE ON PAGE 29
OR
OEUF COCOTTES
WITH FILLING OF YOUR CHOICE, SEE PAGE 36
*
FOREST FRUITS AND CHAMPAGNE DELIGHT, SEE RECIPE ON PAGE 349

BIRTHDAY BREAKFAST

FOR 2

STICKY CINNAMON SCROLLS,
MAKE HALF OF THE RECIPE ON PAGE 392
*
FRENCH TOAST WITH CINNAMON BREAD
SEE PAGE 338
MAKE TWO, SERVE WITH RASPBERRY SORBET, OR RASPBERRY JAM, SEE RECIPES ON PAGE 315 AND 16
*
PAVLOVAS WITH FRUIT
AND LIGHT A CANDLE, OF COURSE!
SEE RECIPE ON PAGE 341.

LUNCHES

EXQUISITE 3-COURSE LUNCH
EASILY PREPARED IN ADVANCE

FOAMY GARDEN PEA SOUP WITH BASIL AND AVOCADO CREAM (SERVE COLD!)
SEE RECIPE ON PAGE 150
*

POTTED PRAWNS
SEE RECIPE ON PAGE 198
*

PARISIAN APPLE TARTLETS
SEE RECIPE ON PAGE 350. TURN ON THE OVEN WHEN YOU SERVE THE MAIN COURSE
THE TARTLETS CAN BE HEATED WHILE YOU MAKE COFFEE

LUNCH BUFFET
FOR APPROX. 10 SERVINGS

TABOULEH WITH POMEGRANATE
DOUBLE THE RECIPE ON PAGE 48
*

LONG LEEK PIE
PREPARE THE RECIPE ON PAGE 289 TWICE OR PREPARE ONE LARGE ONE ON A BAKING SHEET
*

PICKLED MACKEREL
DOUBLE THE RECIPE ON PAGE 205
*

GREEN ASPARAGUS WITH PARSLEY GREMOLATA
DOUBLE THE RECIPE ON PAGE 286
*

ZUCCHINI PANCAKES WITH BASIL CREAM
TRIPLE THE RECIPE ON PAGE 54
*

TERRINE DE CAMPAGNE
SEE RECIPE ON PAGE 180
*

FRESH BEAN SALAD WITH RADISH AND CAESAR DRESSING
SEE RECIPE ON PAGE 278

HIGH TEA

FOR A FUN GROUP OF PEOPLE, SERVING 12-20

✳

CHOCOLATE-GINGER FUDGE CAKE WITH PECAN NUTS AND CINNAMON CREAM
SEE RECIPE ON PAGE 87

✳

PEAR-HAZELNUT CAKE
SEE RECIPE ON PAGE 83

✳

IRISH TEA BRACK
SEE RECIPE ON PAGE 84

✳

GINGERBREAD MUFFINS
SEE RECIPE ON PAGE 81.

✳

ROSEMARY SHORTBREAD
SEE RECIPE ON PAGE 359

✳

PAVLOVAS WITH FRUIT
SEE RECIPE ON PAGE 341.

✳

SCONES
SEE RECIPE ON PAGE 30.

✳

WITH JAM: APRICOT-ALMOND JAM
SEE RECIPE ON PAGE 16

✳

TASTY MINI MUFFINS
SEE RECIPE ON PAGE 25

✳

SAVOURY PIES
BAKE SMALL ONES, IF YOU HAVE SMALL BAKING TINS OR OTHERWISE TWO LARGE ONES CUT INTO SMALL CHUNKS
ALL RECIPES ON PAGE 60

✳

ZUCCHINI PANCAKES WITH BASIL CREAM
SEE RECIPE ON PAGE 54

✳

SERVE WITH TEA:
ELDERBERRY BLOSSOM TEA, FOR EXAMPLE, OR FRESH ICED TEA
RECIPES ON PAGE 77 AND 77
BUT ALSO CHILL SOME WHITE WINE OR CHAMPAGNE

COLD EVENING BUFFET

FOR GROUPS OF 20-30, CAN EASILY BE PREPARED IN ADVANCE

*

MARINATED SALMON IN FENNEL SEED AND PERNOD
RECIPE ON PAGE 188

*

WHOLE BEEF LOIN IN HERB CRUST WITH ROSEMARY SALMORIGLIO
MAKE 2 AND CUT AS THINLY AS POSSIBLE, SEE RECIPE ON PAGE 256

*

FRITTATA WITH MINT, SPINACH AND PECORINO,
MAKE THE RECIPE 2-3 TIMES, IN AS LARGE A DISH AS POSSIBLE AND CUT INTO SMALL CUBES
SEE RECIPE ON PAGE 46

*

HAM PIE
MAKE TWO, SEE RECIPE ON PAGE 187

*

APPLE-DATE CHUTNEY SERVED WITH PASTIES
SEE RECIPE ON PAGE 159

*

SALAD WITH LENTILS, APPLE AND CORIANDER
TRIPLE THE RECIPE ON PAGE 69

*

LUKEWARM SALAD OF FINE POTATOES, GREEN BEANS AND GIANT BEANS
TRIPLE THE RECIPE ON PAGE 270

*

GREEN ASPARAGUS WITH PARSLEY GREMOLATA
TRIPLE THE RECIPE ON PAGE 286

*

HOME-MADE FOCACCIA
BAKE AT LEAST TWO AND CUT INTO SMALL CHUNKS, SEE RECIPE ON PAGE 22
SERVE WITH A HIGH-QUALITY OLIVE OIL

DRINKS WITH SNACKS

FOR A GROUP OF 12-20

*

POMEGRANATE PROSECCO
AND DELICIOUS WELCOME DRINK, RECIPE ON PAGE 102

*

SMOKED PRAWNS WITH LEMON & ROSEMARY SALT
RECIPE ON PAGE 232

*

CROSTINI AND HERRING SALAD WITH BEETROOT AND VODKA
RECIPES ON PAGE 170 AND 192

*

LAVASH CRACKERS WITH BROAD BEAN MINT DIP
RECIPES ON PAGE 170 AND 113

*

POLENTA MUFFINS FILLED WITH SALMON IN CHAMPAGNE AND PUMPKIN PICKLES
RECIPE ON PAGE 120

*

DOLMAS FILLED WITH WILD RICE
RECIPE ON PAGE 175

*

LAMB BALLS WITH SESAME AND CORIANDER SALSA
RECIPE ON PAGE 122

*

CROSTINI WITH CHICKEN LIVER PÂTÉ
RECIPES ON PAGE 170 AND 184
SERVE WITH:
PICKLED CUCUMBER
RECIPE ON PAGE 158

*

DRUNKEN AVOCADO SOUP SHOTS
DOUBLE THE RECIPE ON PAGE 119

*

SEASONED LABNEH BALLS IN OLIVE OIL
MAKE THE RECIPE ON PAGE 298
SERVE WITH HOME-MADE FOCACCIA, SEE PAGE 22

SET UP A DRINKS BUFFET:
ALSO PROVIDE YOUR OWN HOME-MADE DRINKS, ENABLING PEOPLE TO MIX THEIR OWN DRINKS
SUCH AS, NUT WINE, VERMOUTH, GINGER ALE (RECIPES PAGE 98 & 99).
AND A LARGE PITCHER OF LEMONADE (PAGE 100) OR RHUBARB ICED TEA (PAGE 78) FOR DESIGNATED DRIVERS OR CHILDREN.
FILL A CRATE WITH ICE CUBES AND ALL YOUR DRINKS: BEER, WHITE WINE, ETC.
THIS PROVIDES YOU WITH BOTH ICE CUBES AND COOLED DRINKS.

ON THE BARBECUE

*

BOTH CHICKEN KEBABS
IN THE RECIPES ON PAGE 253

*

LOBSTER WITH LIME, SPRING ONION AND GINGER BUTTER
RECIPE ON PAGE 250

*

BEEF LOIN IN HERB CRUST WITH ROSEMARY SALMORIGLIO
CUT THE MEAT INTO THIN SLICES AND THREAD THEM ON METAL SKEWERS
THEY ONLY HAVE TO BE BARBECUED FOR A COUPLE OF MINUTES ON EACH SIDE
RECIPE ON PAGE 256

*

ARAB LAMB BURGERS
RECIPE ON PAGE 384

*

SPARERIBS
RECIPE ON PAGE 231

*

SMOKED PORK CHOPS
FIRST PICKLED, THEN SMOKED AND THEN GRILLED ON THE BARBECUE
RECIPE ON PAGE 235

FLATBREAD WITH CHICKPEAS AND SAGE
MAKE DOUBLE THE RECIPE ON PAGE 273

*

ALL SAUCES
ON PAGE 380

*

TABOULEH WITH QUINOA, CORN, SPRING ONION AND GOAT'S CHEESE
DOUBLE THE RECIPE ON PAGE 59

*

ZUCCHINI PROVENCAL STYLE
PREPARE AS MANY ZUCCHINIS AS THERE ARE GUESTS, RECIPE ON PAGE 282

*

CARROT SALAD WITH CUMIN
TRIPLE THE RECIPE ON PAGE 274

410

DINNER FOR 12

*

SMOKED TOMATO SOUP WITH LABNEH
DOUBLE THE TOMATO SOUP RECIPE ON PAGE 230
SERVE WITH A SPOONFUL OF SPREADABLE LABNEH ON PAGE 296
SERVE WITH COUNTRY BREAD WITH HAZELNUTS AND ROASTED CUMIN
RECIPE ON PAGE 22

*

ROTOLO WITH LOBSTER, WILD SPINACH & ROSEMARY BEURRE BLANC
SERVE EVERYONE ONE SLICE OF THE RECIPE ON PAGE 224

*

LEG OF LAMB WITH NETTLES AND GOAT'S CHEESE PESTO
PREPARE 2 LEGS OF LAMB FOR 12 PEOPLE, DOUBLE THE RECIPE ON PAGE 258

*

GREEN BEANS WITH WALNUTS
DOUBLE THE RECIPE ON PAGE 286

*

RÖSTI BISCUITS WITH ROSEMARY
MAKE DOUBLE THE RECIPE ON PAGE 277

*

CHEESE BOARD
RECIPE ON PAGE 295

*

SAFFRON SEMIFREDDO WITH CITRUS COMPOTE
RECIPE ON PAGE 311

*

COFFEE AND TEA WITH COCO ROCHERS,
ALMOND TUILES AND PISTACHIO WAFERS
RECIPES ON PAGE 362 AND 363

DINNER FOR TWO

*

MILLE-FEUILLES OF SMOKED AND RAW BEETROOT WITH COMTÉ
WATERCRESS AND NUT DRESSING
HALVE THE RECIPE ON PAGE 243

*

WARM CUCUMBER SOUP WITH DEEP-FRIED PARSLEY
HALVE THE RECIPE ON PAGE 137

*

TROUT WITH PARSLEY AND FENNEL SEED BUTTER
DOES NOT HAVE TO BE ON THE BARBECUE, CAN ALSO BE COOKED IN THE OVEN, HALVE THE RECIPE ON PAGE 254

*

GRILLED FENNEL SALAD
HALVE THE RECIPE ON PAGE 270

*

SPINACH AND GOAT'S CHEESE BUTTER BUNS WITH PISTACHIO NUTS
MAKE THE ENTIRE RECIPE ON PAGE 25 AND PLACE THE REST IN THE FREEZER

*

RASPBERRY SORBET
RECIPE ON PAGE 315

*

COFFEE AND FILLED DATES
SEE RECIPE ON PAGE 356

MÉNAGE À TROIS

*

SALMON TARTARE
PLAN ON 125 G OF SALMON PER PERSON, RECIPE ON PAGE 191

*

ONE-PERSON CHICKEN WITH SAGE AND MUSHROOMS
PREPARE ALL FOUR, IT WILL BE EATEN, OTHERWISE LEFTOVERS THE FOLLOWING DAY, RECIPE ON PAGE 263

*

GREEN ASPARAGUS WITH GREMOLATA
HALVE THE RECIPE ON PAGE 286

*

RÖSTI POTATOES WITH ROSEMARY
MAKE THE ENTIRE RECIPE ON PAGE 277 AND PLACE THE REST IN THE FREEZER

*

VANILLA FRITTERS WITH ZABAGLIONE
RECIPE ON PAGE 330

*

COFFEE AND A LOT OF CHOCOLATES
RECIPES ON PAGE 362 AND 363

*

WHAT TO COOK
FOR A FUNERAL

THIS MAY SOUND STRANGE
BUT I KNOW FROM EXPERIENCE HOW IMPORTANT FOOD IS AFTER A FUNERAL OR IN THE WEEK SURROUNDING A DEATH

THE SURVIVING FAMILY OFTEN DO NOT FEEL LIKE COOKING OR EATING OR HAVE NO TIME, BUT, IN THE MEANTIME THE HOUSE
IS FULL OF INTERESTED PARTIES
AS A GOOD NEIGHBOUR OR FRIEND, IT IS YOUR TURN TO BRING A MEAL

THE FOLLOWING ARE A NUMBER OF RECOMMENDATIONS

*

SWEET POTATO SOUP WITH BUTTERED CASHEWS
TRIPLE THE RECIPE ON PAGE 143

*

ITALIAN BREAD SOUP
TRIPLE THE RECIPE ON PAGE 144

*

CHUNKY CHOWDER
TRIPLE THE RECIPE ON PAGE 134

*

GNOCCHI ALLA ROMANA
TRIPLE THE RECIPE ON PAGE 211
SERVE WITH TOMATO SAUCE
TRIPLE THE RECIPE ON PAGE 212

*

AUTUMN PASTY
MAKE THE ENTIRE RECIPE ON PAGE 184
SERVE WITH CRANBERRY, WALNUT AND PEAR CHUTNEY
RECIPE ON PAGE 158

*

LENTIL SALAD
RECIPE ON PAGE 166
WITH SLICES OF FRIED SAUSAGE

*

BOILED HAM
RECIPE ON PAGE 201
WITH A LITTLE MUSTARD, SALAD AND RYE BREAD

*

BAKE CAKES FOR VISITORS:

BANANA RUM CAKE
RECIPE ON PAGE 84

*

ORANGE POLENTA CAKE
RECIPE ON PAGE 93

*

MAKE A LARGE POT OF SAGE & LEMON TEA, WHICH CALMS THE NERVES
RECIPE ON PAGE 76

TABLE OF CONTENTS

419

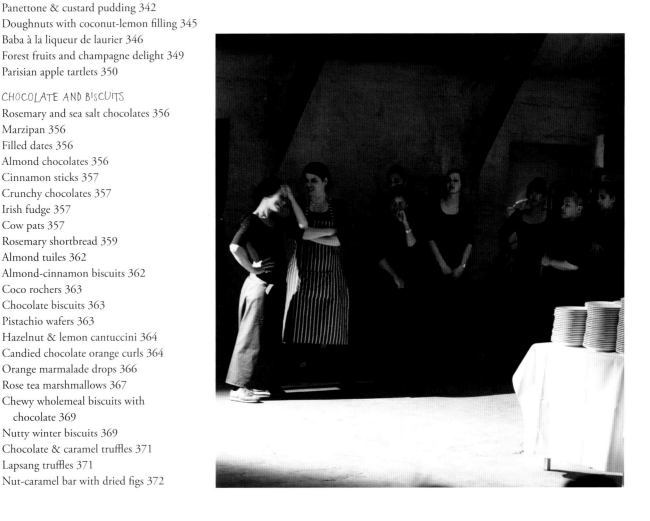

INDEX OF DISHES

INDEX OF INGREDIENTS

423

424

425

428

429

Joris

DANK JE WEL, MERCI, THANK YOU:
OOF, JORIS, DENISE, MARIETTE, VICTOR, SOPHIE, TON, EMILIE, LIESKE, JAAP, SOPHIE, CLAARTJE, JESSICA,
MEREL, VALENTIJN, HORAS, KELLY, LAURA, ALEX, HASSANE, JOY, MONA, MAS, JESSY, MICHELLE, CHARLES,
GEORGE, JAQUELINE, MAURICE, CHRISTOPHE, NORBERT, VALERIE, MATHIS, MAGALI, NICOLAS, MAXANCE &
DE VERDERE HELE FAMILIE COLOMBET, FLORIS, FINETTE, LOLA, JULIA, PAT, JOANNA, MONIQUE, EMMANUEL,
CAROLA, CARRIE, PIETER, XAVIER, LAURENS, RENSKE, MARTIJN, NICK, ERIK, ROELAND, DAVID, PIA, ROMAIN,
ANNETTE, LAURENS, MARTIN, INGE, BARTINA, ANNE, HENNIE > TANJA
& MARIE

Kelly, Sophie & Yvette

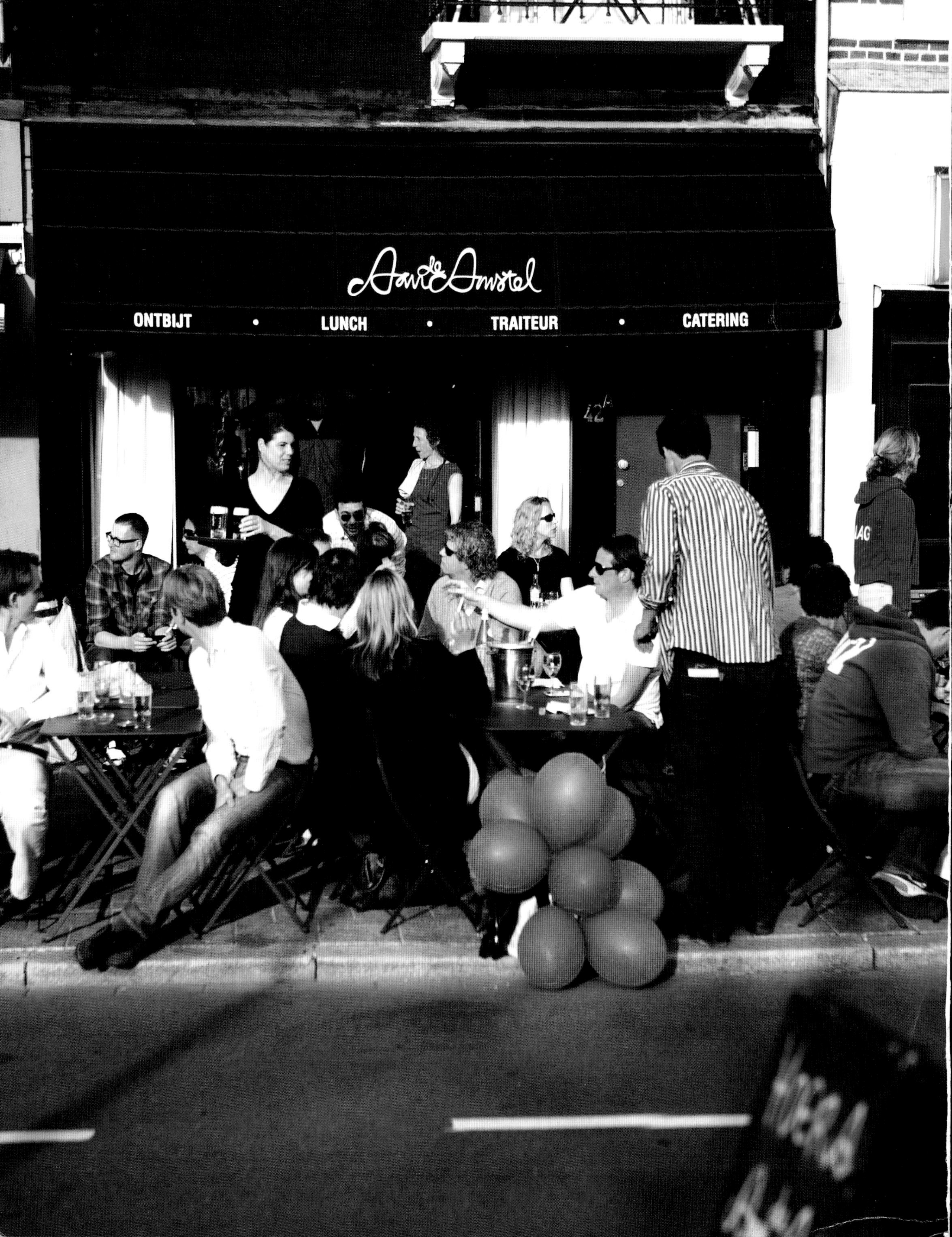
ONTBIJT • LUNCH • TRAITEUR • CATERING
42